Visualising Physical Geography

This practical guide breaks down the complex and broad field of physical geography, demonstrating how diagrams can be used by teachers to effectively explain the key concepts behind many natural processes and landforms. Featuring over 200 diagrams that cover the key topics taught in Key Stage 3 and 4 Geography, the book shows teachers how they can convey age-appropriate concepts without overwhelming or oversimplifying.

Supported by summaries of background knowledge, common misconceptions, questions to check understanding, and extension activities, the concepts and topics explored include:

- Rocks and weathering
- Plate tectonics
- Rivers
- Coasts
- Weather and climate
- Ecosystems
- Glaciation

Backed by research and evidence to support the use of diagrams in the classroom, this is an essential read for any geography teacher or subject lead who wants to support their students in learning key concepts in physical geography.

Luke Tayler is Head of Geography at St Christopher's School, Bahrain.

'For decades, evidence has been accumulating for the multimedia principle – the idea that people learn better from words and graphics than from words alone. *Visualising Physical Geography* by Luke Tayler examines why and how to apply the multimedia principle to teaching of physical geography. The book provides examples of how to incorporate graphics to explain a wide variety of topics in physical geography.'

Richard E. Mayer, *Distinguished Professor of Psychological and Brain Sciences at the University of California, Santa Barbara, and author of 'Multimedia Learning: Third Edition.'*

'Geography is a very visual discipline and diagrams are a key way of simplifying the complexities of environmental systems and conveying them to students. In this book Luke Tayler convincingly makes the case for diagrams in pedagogy and provides some excellent examples and ideas for ways to use them in the classroom. A great resource for all geography teachers.'

Professor Martin Evans, *University of Manchester*

'Geography, the ill-informed often quip, is about colouring in. In this wonderful book, Luke Tayler, shows us why good drawing matters and how effective visual representation of natural process and landforms can enhance geographical education and learning. This is a volume chock full of suggestions, ideas, and resources – definitely a book every teacher will want at hand when planning or revising learning resources in physical geography.'

Professor Alastair Owens, *President of The Geographical Association*

Visualising Physical Geography

The How and Why of Using Diagrams to Teach Geography 11-16

Luke Tayler

Routledge
Taylor & Francis Group

LONDON AND NEW YORK

Designed cover image: Luke Tayler

First published 2024
by Routledge
4 Park Square, Milton Park, Abingdon, Oxon OX14 4RN

and by Routledge
605 Third Avenue, New York, NY 10158

Routledge is an imprint of the Taylor & Francis Group, an informa business

© 2024 Luke Tayler

The right of Luke Tayler to be identified as author of this work has been asserted in accordance with sections 77 and 78 of the Copyright, Designs and Patents Act 1988.

All rights reserved. No part of this book may be reprinted or reproduced or utilised in any form or by any electronic, mechanical, or other means, now known or hereafter invented, including photocopying and recording, or in any information storage or retrieval system, without permission in writing from the publishers.

Trademark notice: Product or corporate names may be trademarks or registered trademarks, and are used only for identification and explanation without intent to infringe.

British Library Cataloguing-in-Publication Data
A catalogue record for this book is available from the British Library

ISBN: 978-1-032-30094-8 (hbk)
ISBN: 978-1-032-30105-1 (pbk)
ISBN: 978-1-003-30343-5 (ebk)

DOI: 10.4324/9781003303435

Typeset in Interstate
by Apex CoVantage, LLP

The diagrams from this book are available to download at: www.routledge.com/9781032301051

For Gaby, Leo, and Mara.

Contents

Acknowledgements		viii
About This Book		ix
Chapter 1	Why Use Diagrams?	1
Chapter 2	How Diagrams Support Learning	5
Chapter 3	How Diagrams Support Teaching	17
Chapter 4	The Diagrams	41
	4.1 Rocks and Weathering	42
	4.2 Plate Tectonics	70
	4.3 Rivers	102
	4.4 Coasts	143
	4.5 Weather and Climate	182
	4.6 Ecosystems	230
	4.7 Glaciation	257

Acknowledgements

I am very grateful to Annamarie Kino and Lauren Redhead at Routledge for taking this project on and for guiding me throughout. Thank you to the wonderful staff and students at St Christopher's School, Bahrain, for inspiring and developing my teaching.

A special thank-you to my wife, Gaby, who has offered nothing but encouragement and support from the outset. I would not have been able to write this book without you.

All errors, omissions, and opinions are my own.

About This Book

Trying to justify the importance of diagrams to the teaching of physical geography seems pointless. Frankly, it is hard to imagine a lesson without them. So much of what we teach is often either happening deep underground, on a scale too big or too small for students to fully comprehend, or about a topic too abstract to explain with words alone. So we, almost instinctively, turn to diagrams for support. Whether drawn onto a whiteboard, under a visualiser, or quickly onto a scrap of paper, putting pencil to paper and talking through what is happening allows teachers to guide students into the process or landform.

There are some diagrams teachers must have drawn countless times. How often have you drawn a subducting plate margin or a waterfall cross section? But there are also some diagrams that we are less familiar with and not that comfortable drawing from memory. Each geography teacher has topics they are more or less comfortable with, and their ability to draw the relevant diagrams is likely to follow suit. As a result, we might turn to an internet search engine and hope that something clear enough appears for "volcano caldera diagram." There will always be something that appears in the image search, but more often than not, the diagram is either too simple or too complicated, spoiled by a watermark, or the labels are not relevant. Too many geography lessons are blighted by irrelevant, blurry, or overcomplicated images pasted onto the teacher's slideshow!

The best way for a teacher to ensure that the diagrams used in class are relevant, clear, and easy to explain is if the teacher draws them by hand. Chapter 2 explores some of the research behind the use of live-drawn diagrams in a lesson, but put simply, if a teacher is drawing whilst explaining, then they have the ability to control both the pace of the explanation and the focus of the students.

The aim of this book is to provide teachers with a bank of ready-to-copy diagrams that can help both the planning and delivery of lessons. Although perhaps more useful for newer teachers and non-specialists, hopefully all teachers will find something useful to take from the book.

The book is divided into four sections:

- **Chapter 1** discusses why diagrams are so important in the teaching of physical geography.
- **Chapter 2** explores some of the research behind the use of diagrams in teaching.

x *About This Book*

- **Chapter 3** identifies some of the specific ways that diagrams can be used in the classroom.
- **Chapter 4** is then divided into the seven main topics of physical geography covered at Key Stages 3 and 4. Each topic contains all the relevant diagrams, along with the annotations and points to focus on during the explanation. There are also coordinates for some real-world examples, as well as some questions to support checking for student understanding.

All 200+ images are also available to download from www.routledge.com/9781032301051 as ready-to-use JPEG files. Teachers could add them to their lesson slides; print them as a guide to use whilst explaining a topic; or print one for each student to add to their notes.

Chapter 1   Why Use Diagrams?

Figure 1.1   Photograph of a coastline.

Newspaper Headline: Homes at risk as England's coast continues to crumble with rising sea levels (January 14, 2022).

Look at the photo from a newspaper article. It shows a person walking near a low, crumbling cliff by the sea.

As geography teachers, we see this image and *know* what it is about. We know this is coastal erosion, and the risks facing nearby homeowners.

DOI: 10.4324/9781003303435-1

2 Why Use Diagrams?

We can also extrapolate out further and consider a wider picture: there is no sign of any coastal management, so perhaps the land has been deemed not worth protecting. We note the loose sediment and consider the role of the local geology. We consider how wave action is responsible, and how the various erosional processes combine with sub-aerial processes. We note the month of the article and how winter weather may make the conditions worse. The headline references the climate crisis, and we quickly associate rising sea levels and changing weather patterns with the rate of cliff recession. We appreciate that local governments are probably having to weigh up the costs of coastal management compared to helping residents and businesses either adapt or relocate. We zoom out and can picture the UK made up of locally managed sediment cells and the ways these operate.

We do all this thinking quickly, and with relative ease. Try to rewind to when you first looked at the image. Play back your thought processes, and try to spot the moment you leap from one idea to another. It's almost effortless.

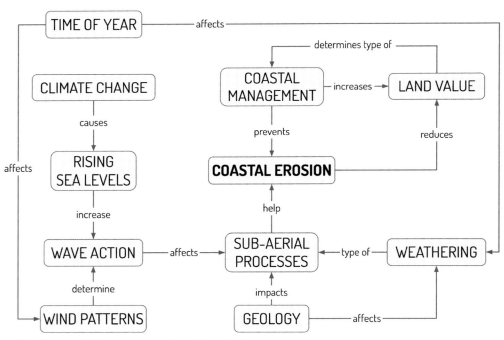

Figure 1.2 How we link our geographical knowledge.

We use our knowledge of those individual processes, concepts, and systems to put the photo and headline into a wider context. Figure1.2 shows how some of our ideas link together. It shows a range of typical geographical concepts and systems and how they are interconnected. It is our ability to see and use the links between them that makes us relative experts in this field, and it is this type of thinking that we want for our students. We teach geography because we want students to be able to look at the world around them and critically engage with it. We want them to ask questions, to consider, to examine, and to evaluate.

It is what makes geography such an important subject. Geography is about exploring how we interact with the environment, and a good geographer looks at a photo like the one earlier and asks those questions and more.

We, geography teachers, know how to ask those questions and consider the context of the photo because we are able to combine our specific *substantive* knowledge with our geographical *disciplinary* knowledge. In other words, we have a secure understanding of a whole range of geographical concepts and processes and are adept at linking them together. We *know* about weathering, coastal management, climate change, cost-benefit analyses, marine erosion, and geology. But crucially, we also have the ability to see the relationships between them. Which, of course, is what we want for our students. We want to put that same photo up on the whiteboard and for them to be able to make the same connections that we can.

Building Blocks

So what has this all got to do with diagrams? The amount of geographical knowledge required to look at the photo and make those synoptic links is quite considerable. Much of it is abstract and cannot be seen in the photo (e.g. rising sea levels and sub-aerial processes), so providing students with the geographical building blocks allows them to construct the "bigger picture" of what is happening.

The most effective way to provide students with these building blocks of knowledge is to carefully and deliberately teach them in a way that ensures the new information "sticks." Each block of knowledge, whilst a relatively simple part of the wider aim, may well be a new and potentially confusing bit of information. Without thoughtful delivery of this new information from the teacher, misunderstandings and misconceptions are likely.

To present the information to students in a careful and deliberate way, the teacher needs to be in complete control of the "information exchange," and the use of diagrams to explore a process or landform can help in two main ways. These, and others, are considered further in Chapter 2, but in summary, teaching through diagrams can help:

1. **Regulate the flow of information** from teacher to student. If a teacher actively engages with the class during the explanation, they can get immediate and fairly constant feedback from the students. This allows the teacher to pause a drawing or to revisit any parts of the explanation.
2. **Direct students' attention.** Drawing a diagram in real time (as opposed to just showing the completed version) allows the teacher to ensure the students are looking at the relevant part.

4   *Why Use Diagrams?*

These two important facets of an effective explanation are key components of *explicit instruction*, a system of teaching which follows the "I do, we do, you do" model, where the teacher initially shows the students something; the teacher and students then practise together, before finally the students practise on their own. Chapter 3 explores this further and looks at how diagrams can be used within a learning sequence, as well as providing other suggestions for how to use diagrams during a lesson.

Seeing the Unseeable

Many students, when asked, may well prefer human over physical geography. There may be a number of reasons for this, but a likely one is that many of the "human" topics, such as tourism, migration, and development, are *relatable* ideas that students will have had some personal interaction with in the past. For example, any student that has been on holiday can visualise a relevant scene when the class discussion is about the impacts of tourism. Similarly, stories of poverty and migration are regularly on our TVs, and so students, when asked to think about push-and-pull factors, will be able to relate the question to something concrete they have seen before. Physical geography, on the other hand, contains many concepts that are completely beyond a student's previous experience. It is very hard to visualise the condensation of water vapour in the air or the upwelling of molten mantle beneath a plate margin.

How, then, are we, the teachers, able to picture what is happening? We haven't personally witnessed water freezing within the joints of rocks or seen air rising above the rainforests, and yet we are able to teach them with relative conviction. Try it now. Try to visualise the water freezing in cracks within rocks. What are you picturing? Chances are, it is a diagrammatic version of events. You may well even be imagining the typical diagram we draw to show the process. Diagrams allow us, therefore, to see the unseeable. They provide the picture we use in our mind's eye to take an abstract concept and apply it to different situations.

Summary
- Experts can use "building blocks" of information to see the bigger picture.
- The best way to teach these building blocks is through explicit instruction.
- Diagrams can help deliver explicit instruction.
- Diagrams allow us to see the unseeable.

Chapter 2   How Diagrams Support Learning

Laura is staring blankly at the Powerpoint. She hasn't even started the first task yet. Everything she needs is on the slide. The tasks are there. Instructions on how to access the source material. A reminder about the learning objectives. Suggestions for stretch-and-challenge tasks. Relevant photos and icons to support the teacher's explanation. There are even some scaffolded sentence starters. And yet ...

People learn better from both words *and* pictures than from just words alone. This is the premise of the cognitive theory of multimedia learning (CTML). First suggested by Richard Mayer, one of education's pre-eminent researchers, it has shown that utilising *two* sensory channels (sight and sound) makes learning stuff easier than just using *one*. That may just sound like common sense, but Mayer and his colleagues have dedicated decades of research delving far deeper into how we learn and have developed a set of principles that can help how we both design *and* deliver our teaching.

Before getting into the practicalities of the principles, let's look at the overarching premise of multimedia learning. In this case, *multimedia* means presenting information in more than one format, usually the spoken word *and* pictures.

The cognitive theory of multimedia learning (CTML) is based on three assumptions:

1. There are two separate channels for processing information: the theory of dual coding.
2. We are limited in how much information we can take in at once: cognitive load theory.
3. Learning is an active process of selecting, organising, and integrating information: SOI model.

In recent years, these theories have become widely used within the teaching community, which is indicative of the narrowing of the gap between educational theory and teaching. Indeed, a 2021 survey by the Education Endowment Survey noted that 85% of teachers said that cognitive science strategies were central to their approach to teaching. I will not go into detail then about ideas that teachers are becoming increasingly familiar with, but given how important CTML is to the use of diagrams in the classroom, this section is a brief overview of the theory and how some of those principles can relate to our pedagogy.

DOI: 10.4324/9781003303435-2

Theory of Dual Coding

According to Alan Paivio, verbal and visual information are processed differently and through different channels. This means that it is possible to use both, together, to improve learning. Although the two channels, verbal and visual, are different, they can support each other.

Verbal information (listening to someone speak) is received and processed *sequentially* – that is, we can only hear and process one word at a time, one after the other – whereas visual information (looking at a diagram) can be received and processed *synchronously* – that is, we can take in some specific details *and* see the bigger picture at the same time.

So because the different incoming channels are processed in a different way, we can use them together to increase learning capacity.

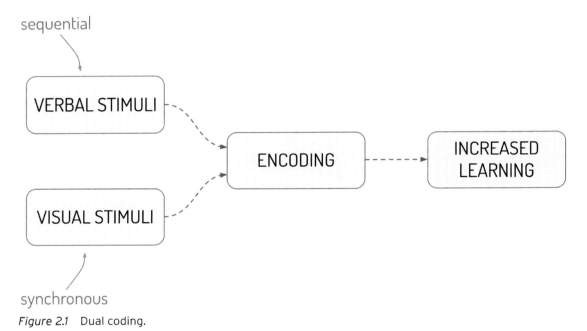

Figure 2.1 Dual coding.

Cognitive Load Theory

Our ability to learn something new is controlled by the interaction of the new information and what we already know. As we take in text, words, or pictures, our *working memory* scans, categorises, and processes it. The text, words, or picture will then only stay in our working memory for a few seconds before it is either forgotten or stored in our *long-term memory*. Whether it is stored or not depends on our ability to encode the new information into our pre-existing *schemas*, which are the mental structures that we use to organise our knowledge.

How Diagrams Support Learning 7

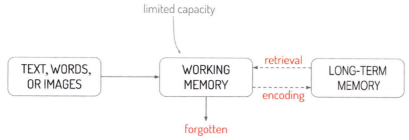

Figure 2.2 Cognitive load theory.

To improve learning, according to the theory, it is possible to help working memory by acknowledging that it has a limited capacity and therefore benefits from being presented with new information that is easier to process. You can start to see how dual coding, with its two ways of absorbing new information, can help ease the burden on working memory.

Select-Organise-Integrate Model

The third model on which CTML is based is Mayer's constructivist select-organise-integrate (SOI) model. It shows that there are three cognitive processes involved in learning.

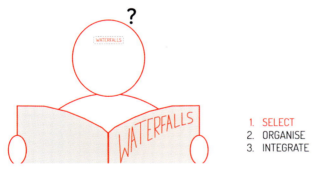

Firstly, we need to actively **select** the relevant information that we want to learn.

Figure 2.3 Select-organise-integrate (stage 1).

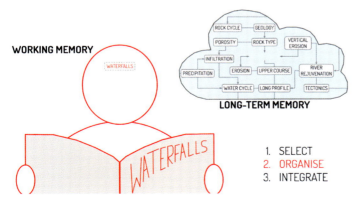

Then, we must **organise** this new information by comparing it with what we already know. By activating existing *schemas*, we can work out where in our long-term memory to store this new information.

Figure 2.4 Select-organise-integrate (stage 2).

8 *How Diagrams Support Learning*

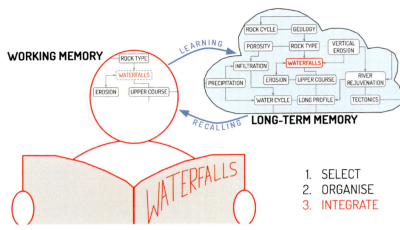

Finally, in order for the new information to stay learned, it needs to be **integrated** within our schemas. Without doing this part, the new information doesn't stick and becomes lost.

1. SELECT
2. ORGANISE
3. INTEGRATE

Figure 2.5 Select-organise-integrate (stage 3).

Cognitive Theory of Multimedia Learning

Mayer's theory, then, is that learning through multimedia is an active process, where the dual coding of new information can reduce the strain on working memory.

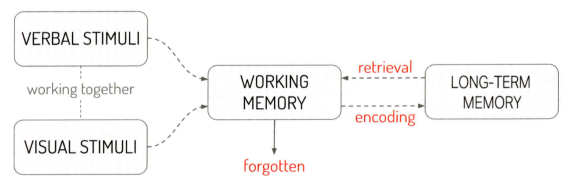

Figure 2.6 Cognitive theory of multimedia learning.

Through his extensive work, Mayer has developed 15 principles which help guide best practice for instructional design. These principles take the understanding of how the brain processes information and provide guidance on how best to utilise multimedia learning. Of the 15 shown in the following, I have selected 7 that I think are most relevant to the drawing of diagrams within a lesson.

Multimedia	**Coherence**	**Signalling**	Redundancy	**Spatial Contiguity**
Temporal contiguity	**Segmenting**	**Pre-training**	Modality	Personalisation
Voice	Image	Embodiment	Immersion	**Generative activity**

How Diagrams Support Learning 9

In the next section, these 7 principles are each taken in turn and linked to the use of diagrams in lessons.

The Multimedia Principle

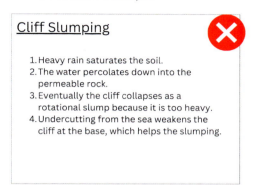 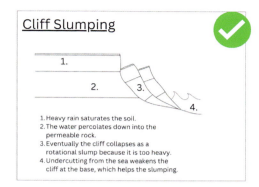

Figure 2.7   The multimedia principle.

People learn better from both words and pictures than from just words alone. This is the premise of the book, so hopefully, it doesn't need too much justifying! It is also fairly obvious to most teachers. That said, it is worth thinking carefully about *which* pictures/images are used. Dual coding is more than just using icons!

The Coherence Principle

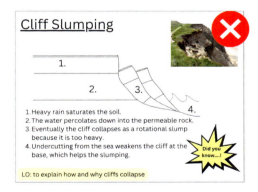 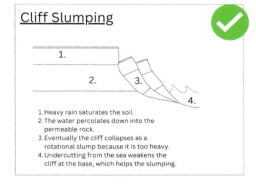

Figure 2.8   The coherence principle.

People learn better when extraneous words, pictures, and sounds are excluded rather than included. One of the (many) errors of which I was guilty earlier in my career was packing a Powerpoint slide full of *stuff*. The idea of a full slide was, apparently, to ensure that everyone was catered for: pictures for the so-called visual learners, extension tasks for

10 *How Diagrams Support Learning*

gifted and talented students, a reminder of the learning objectives, cool facts to make the lesson engaging ... Unfortunately, all it did was provide a lot of fluffy noise that distracted from the point of the lesson. As discussed on page 18, I am all for providing interesting hinterland-type context for a specific process, but once you get to the nitty-gritty of an explanation, it needs to be clear and focused.

The Signalling Principle

Figure 2.9   The signalling principle.

People learn better when they are shown clearly which part to focus on. Drawing diagrams live, as opposed to presenting a fully fledged, completed diagram, works well because students see the specific part you want them to focus on. When planning a lesson using a diagram, you should physically rehearse the diagram. Draw it out, say the words you will use in the lesson, and gesture to the diagram. Might seem silly, but I find it really helps if I'm not doing it for the first time in the actual lesson.

The Spatial Contiguity Principle

 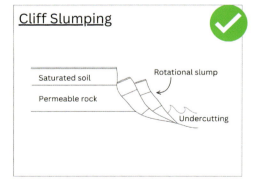

Figure 2.10   The spatial contiguity principle.

People learn better when corresponding words and pictures are presented near rather than far from each other on the page or screen. This is fairly self-explanatory but, like the signalling principle, works best if you have planned out the diagram. Use a cheat sheet (see page 23) so that your diagram is thoughtfully drawn out rather than you having to cram in annotations that don't properly fit. However, this does depend on the amount of text. Try to cram a detailed annotation onto the diagram and you run the risk of overloading the diagram altogether.

The Segmenting Principle

Script A: The Wrong Way	Script B: A Better Way
"The coastline is constantly moving, either through erosion or deposition. When the dominant force is erosion, a cliffed coastline will steadily retreat. Repeated wave action leads to erosional processes, such as hydraulic action and abrasion at the base of the cliff. This creates a wave-cut notch which undermines the cliff. Eventually, the cliff cannot support itself and collapses. The waves will continue to act on the fallen debris and transport them away. Over time, the cliff will retreat inland."	"Last lesson, we looked at the different types of erosion that affect the coast." Pause to check understanding of erosion. "If there is lots of erosion, then what do we think will happen to the coastline?" Pause to discuss what might happen. "If we look at a cliff" – pause to quickly check what a cliff is – "then where do we expect to see the erosion happening?" Pause to discuss, etc.

Script A is clearly an exaggerated example of how a teacher can get it wrong in the classroom. It is essentially a monologue on cliff collapse. There is so much information contained within the script that very few students will be able to take it all in. There is also no way that the teacher can know which, if any, of the students has understood any of it. Script B shows how a teacher can punctuate their explanation with lots of pauses to check for understanding.

Mayer found that people learn better when they have control over the pace at which chunks of information are released for a new topic. Whilst a learner having "control" over the pace of the information might seem counter to a direct-instruction-type lesson, in reality it is the teacher who is actually in control of the pace, but the teacher controls the pace in response to student understanding.

The pace of an explanation cannot be controlled by 30 individual students, but trying to ensure you aren't rushing through is important. Indeed, this is one of the reasons that sitting at a visualiser and facing the students is better than standing with your back to them at a large whiteboard. Glancing up from a desk to read the room is much easier than having to completely turn around.

The Pre-Training Principle

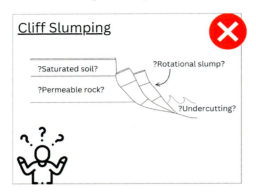 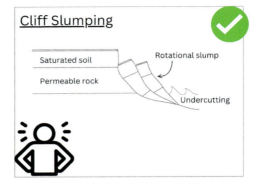

Figure 2.11 The generative learning principle.

People learn better when they already know the fundamentals of a topic. If you are teaching a lesson on types of rainfall, it is important that students' prior knowledge includes the relevant vocabulary. Having to stop an explanation to teach students what *condensation* means will disrupt their learning. This highlights the importance of a well-planned sequence of lessons. Each diagram later in the book comes with relevant prior knowledge students will need to access the explanation. It is a good idea to check the prior knowledge, perhaps as part of a Do Now, as this will also help activate the relevant schemas. If the student has *thought* about condensation already before you mention it in a diagram, then considering it during your explanation becomes an easier task for them.

The Generative Learning Principle

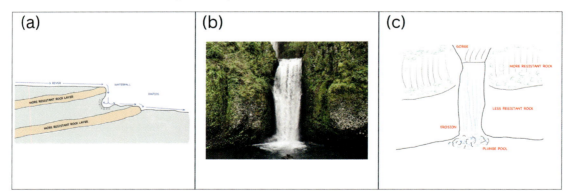

Figure 2.12 The generative learning principle.

People learn better when they are guided in carrying out generative learning activities during learning (e.g. drawing). Generative learning is one of the core tenets of teaching through diagrams. If students are asked to create something new for themselves, there is more *thinking* involved. Students will need to think about what they are being asked to create, what they already know about the topic, and then how they can connect their prior knowledge to the current task. Asking students to draw a different version of a landform or process will really test whether they know the topic. If they *do* know it, they will be able to identify what the key features are that need to be included and will be able to adapt their existing schema about that concept to fit the task.

The Figure 2.12 example shows how sketches can work in this way. Box A shows how, as a class, you have gone through the formation of a waterfall and drawn the fairly standard cross section together. The generative learning comes next. Students are presented with the photo (box B), and you can discuss how it is the same landform but from a different angle, and that in reality no two waterfalls are exactly the same. The students are then tasked with drawing a sketch of the waterfall from box B, but making sure they label on certain features (e.g. plunge pool). Students will be forced to consider what they have learned about waterfalls but won't just be able to replicate the same diagram in box A.

Diagrams Help "Show" Your Thinking

If a student were to ask you the difference between convergent and divergent plate margins, chances are, you might use your hands to show the relevant movements. Hand movements are used because they can quickly show what subduction looks like, rather than having to verbalise the same information (think dual coding!), and drawing helps in the same way but perhaps even more so. Consider subduction again. Two hands can show that downward movement, but that is about it. If you then wanted to show where fold mountains form or how a tsunami is generated, you quickly run out of hands! However, drawing a quick diagram allows you to show the same subduction *plus* all the other relevant features.

Perhaps even more useful is when students use diagrams to show *their* thinking. If a student wants to clarify how a tsunami is generated at a subduction zone, then hand them a whiteboard marker and ask them to draw out what they know already and see if you can tease out the correct answer as they draw it. Tell them, "Draw what you think happens." You can then "edit" their drawing to show any corrections or additions. Drawing in this way can be considered as "extending the mind."

14 *How Diagrams Support Learning*

The following sequence shows how I might want to explain the formation of a waterfall so that students can 'see' my thinking.

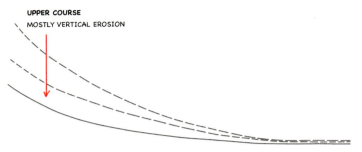

Figure 2.13   Explaining waterfalls (part 1).

Students are already familiar with the long profile of a river, so I draw that out. I also want to show how vertical erosion causes the profile to become gentler. I use dotted lines earlier to show the former positions of the land.

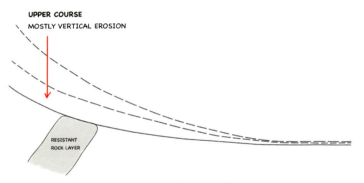

Figure 2.14   Explaining waterfalls (part 2).

Next, we start to consider what would happen if the land wasn't made of all the same rock type. What would happen if there was a big slab of resistant rock? If I had drawn that on first, students might be focusing on the rock rather than on the vertical erosion, which I wanted them to think about first.

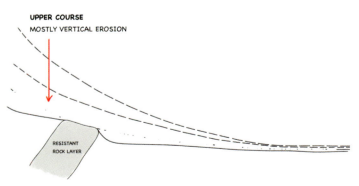

Figure 2.15   Explaining waterfalls (part 3).

Once we establish that the rock wouldn't be eroded, I can redraw the long profile to show how it would be affected. It doesn't matter that my diagram might start to look a little messy with some "rubbings-out," because we (the students and I) are going to draw an annotated neat version of this once the "I do" part has finished.

How Diagrams Support Learning 15

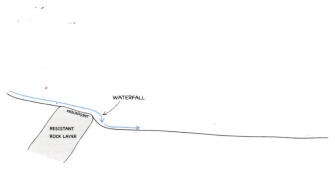

Figure 2.16 Explaining waterfalls (part 4).

Finally, I can rub out all the remaining long profile lines, leaving me with just the waterfall and the resistant rock layer. Had I not used a diagram to explain this and just shown the students this final image, it would have made the explanation part much trickier. The diagrams helped me show students my thinking.

Similarly, the hydrograph example in the following shows how, by drawing as you explain, it is possible to deviate away from the main diagram and quickly sketch additional drawings that help make a particular point to make. Having these as smaller, simple sketches just to the side means you can easily keep referring back to them. By the time the students are drawing with you, whilst you narrate and intersperse with questions, they have already seen the diagram being drawn and will have a much better idea both of what their drawing is going to look like and how the process happens or the landform is created.

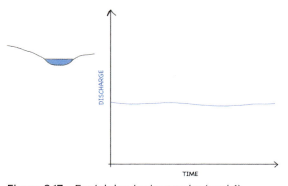

Figure 2.17 Explaining hydrographs (part 1).

Start with a simple graph, with time along the x-axis and discharge along the y-axis. Remind students about discharge with a simple sketch to the side. With the sketch, you can discuss that unless there is heavy rain or a drought, the discharge is likely to stay fairly steady. Draw a line (in the same blue as the river) to show a "normal" discharge.

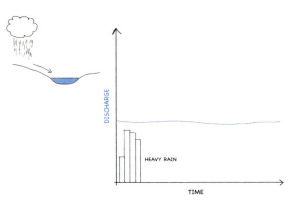

Figure 2.18 Explaining hydrographs (part 2).

Then draw on the heavy rain to the sketch. Discuss what will happen to the discharge. You can also draw on the rainfall as a bar chart onto the graph.

The great thing about teaching through drawing like this is that if the students still aren't sure what you mean, then …

16 *How Diagrams Support Learning*

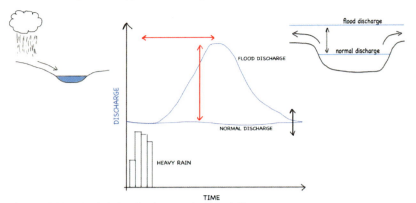

You can draw another sketch to show the difference between normal discharge and flood discharge. Once this is established, you can then draw on the "flood discharge" to the graph.

Figure 2.19 Explaining hydrographs (part 3).

With the hydrograph more or less complete, you can annotate other parts with arrows. Or ask questions of students about factors that might affect the discharge.

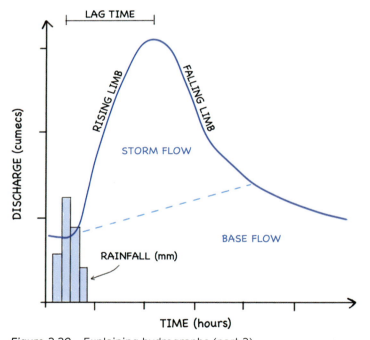

The final stage is to draw the diagram again, but as a neat version. Students draw it at the same time. This is the "we do" stage of the "I do, we do, you do" model. You explain the same features, using the same language as before, but this time the students will find it far easier to follow, and you don't have to spoil your neat hydrograph with messy explanatory annotations.

Figure 2.20 Explaining hydrographs (part 3).

Summary
- People learn better from words and pictures than from just words alone.
- There are a number of principles to follow when teaching with diagrams.
- Diagrams can help show students your thinking.

Chapter 3 How Diagrams Support Teaching

One of the fundamentals of teaching is being able to deliver effective explanations. To consider how diagrams can support our explanations, we need to know some of the principles behind an effective explanation.

This chapter is divided into three parts:

1. Some general points to consider when putting an effective explanation together.
2. How to actually include diagrams in your lesson.
3. Some tips on improving student penmanship.

What Makes an Effective Explanation?

Secure Subject Knowledge

We all know that feeling when you are teaching a topic that isn't one of your best. You teach the lesson, using resources that you just assume are accurate. You couldn't do a better job of putting the slides together because, frankly, you don't really know enough about it. Then all through the lesson, you're just hoping that a student doesn't ask you about that bit, because you will be exposed as not knowing!

For me, it was always glaciation. I didn't do it at school myself or at university, so I just don't have that same confidence that I do with, say, coasts or rivers. Perhaps I never will, but the best way to confront it is, of course, to catch up and learn about it. Even with topics that we do feel comfortable with, reading around the subject makes such a difference.

There is always more to learn too. Take plate tectonics as an example. Recently, I have made a concerted effort to develop my subject knowledge. Like many teachers, I used to teach that plates were simply driven by convection currents in the mantle. Teaching at KS3 and KS4, I was very happy covering plate tectonics just using the terms *crust*, *mantle*, and *convection currents*. I knew that other words like *lithosphere*, *asthenosphere*, and *slab pull* existed, but I couldn't really teach them because, frankly, I didn't really understand them myself. Plus, the textbooks and GCSE mark schemes were fine with the basic terms too, so what was the point in confusing things?

When we discuss *powerful knowledge* in education, we are usually referring to student knowledge. But for teachers, the confidence derived from a thorough and deep understanding of a topic allows teachers to anticipate misconceptions, skilfully steer discussions, and

DOI: 10.4324/9781003303435-3

answer questions clearly. Having this level of knowledge is also powerful, as it almost sets you free as a teacher, free to veer off from the path and explore aspects of the landform you hadn't planned on visiting. If a class appears interested, then it shouldn't take much for a teacher to want to teach more. A deeper subject knowledge allows teachers to deviate from the plan, and it shouldn't need mentioning that a teacher's enthusiasm for their subject is a wonderful way to engage a classroom.

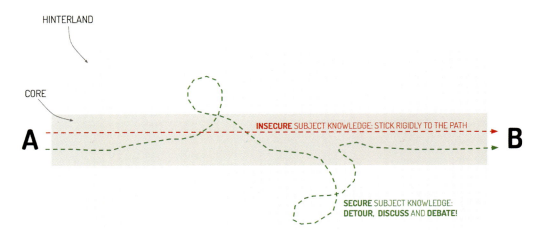

Figure 3.1 Core and hinterland.

Pitch Perfect Practical

What do they already know? What do I want them to leave the classroom knowing? Ask these two simple questions and use them to frame your planning. This highlights the importance of having a clear sequence of lessons and a well-thought-out curriculum. It can be easy to plan a lesson with the noble aim of nailing an important concept, but without the solid foundations of, for example, the relevant vocabulary, then it can quickly become a non-starter. If you need to postpone the *important concept* part so that you can secure the foundations or correct any misconceptions, then it is probably worth doing.

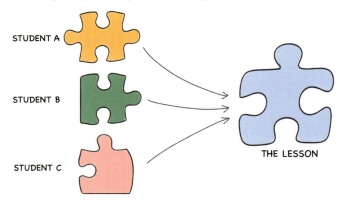

Figure 3.2 Students may have different prior knowledge.

Unfortunately, pressure to cover the content often means we try to cram in more than is sensible. This pressure is usually most intense with GCSE classes and, again, highlights the

How Diagrams Support Teaching 19

importance of a clear and realistic sequence of lessons. Assuming you have a clear understanding of what you want the students to have grasped from the lesson, then you can work back from there. Like all subjects, within physical geography, there are concepts and processes that can be taught with differing levels of detail and complexity depending on the age group.

It is also important to appreciate that different students will be starting the lesson with different levels of understanding about the topic. Despite your best efforts in previous lessons to ensure that everyone has reached the same level of understanding, there will be those that are ahead and those that have fallen behind.

Control the Flow

Once you are clear on what you want your students to leave the lesson knowing, then you can think about how to sequence the lesson and *chunk* the key ideas into manageable parts. This

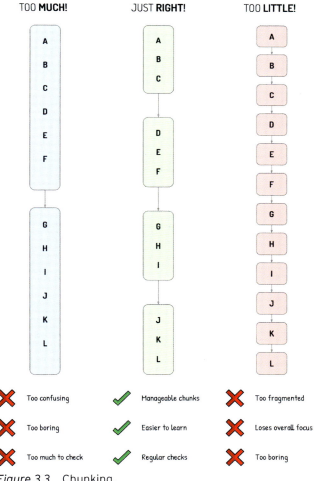

Figure 3.3 Chunking.

Figure 3.3 shows the importance of chunking material into the right-size portions.

may sound like oversimplification, and some lessons cannot be easily divided up in this way, but having the awareness that we, the teachers, control the rate at which new words or ideas are introduced into a lesson can be a useful tool to aid our delivery.

This is one of the advantages of using a visualiser over a Powerpoint presentation, as explained by the segmenting principle (see page 11). The section on diagrams helping to show your thinking on page 14 helps to show what this looks like in practice.

Abstract to Concrete

For students to grasp a new concept, especially something completely new, they will need to relate it to their own experiences. Imagine trying to explain the concepts of "left" and "right" to an alien on another planet via a radio. The aliens would need a reference point from which to build; otherwise, the concepts of left and right will remain impossible for them to comprehend. Granted, this is an extreme example, but trying to explain a new concept to students *without* a reference point is much harder. Not only does having a student-friendly reference point help them grasp some of the parameters of the new idea; it is also likely to be more interesting too. The reference points you use might be subtle and fleeting, but they will immediately help the student place *something* about the new concept. These personal reference points are likely to take the form of a metaphor or an analogy, helping take the student from something with which they are familiar to something unfamiliar. The following table lists some examples.

Geographical Concept	Metaphor/Analogy
Abrasion	Sandpaper
Rising molten mantle	Lava lamp
Cooled lava plugging a volcano	Toothpaste hardening in a tube

Diagrams can be considered as an extension to this way of thinking. Take the abrasion example.

Figure 3.4 Photograph of some sandpaper.

The teacher might ask students to think about sandpaper, something they are all likely to have used in design technology lessons before. The teacher might even have brought some to the lesson, and the class can discuss how sandpaper works to scrape away at a surface.

The teacher can reinforce the explanation of the sandpaper with a simple diagram.

Figure 3.5 Sketching the process of abrasion.

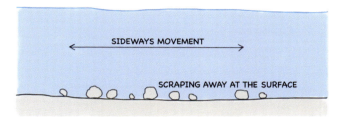

The final diagram showing abrasion now becomes much simpler for students to explain and draw.

Figure 3.6 The final neat version showing abrasion.

How to Put the Lesson Together

As discussed in Chapter 1, using diagrams in a way that this book advocates is very much an explicit style of teaching. The teacher has thoughtfully planned and deliberately sequenced the lesson and is in full control of its delivery. With that in mind, this section aims to explore how such a lesson might look. A note of caution, however: in no way is this prescriptive. The complexities of physical geography and the nuances of schemes of work mean that the topics to be taught rarely fit perfectly into 60-minute chunks (or however long your lesson times might be). Additionally, trying to time every section of a lesson does not work. There are plenty of times when you will, rightly, want to deviate mid-lesson and explore something based on a student question or the need to clarify an earlier point.

Figure 3.7 shows how some topics will require more time than others. This is one of the reasons that I would advocate the use of booklets in the classroom. They eliminate the idea that each new lesson should start on a new page of an exercise book with a new date and title.

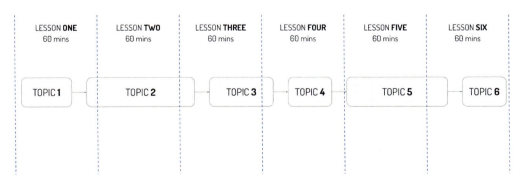

Figure 3.7 Different topics may not fit neatly into standard lesson timing.

That said, the flow diagram shown in Figure 3.8 does provide a useful framework to consider some of the ways that diagrams can be used within the lesson. This shows the different elements of how such a lesson might look. Each element is not equal, either in time spent preparing or time spent delivering. It is also not a fixed sequence. Elements might change or be removed if they don't suit a particular lesson. This chapter will take each of the elements of the flow chart and consider how they might relate to the use of diagrams.

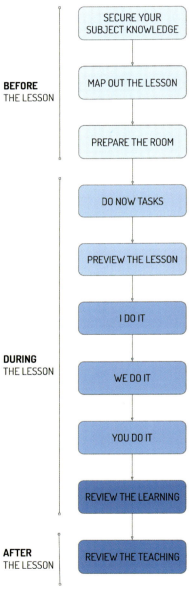

Figure 3.8 Typical sequence of a lesson.

Secure Your Subject Knowledge

Make sure that you know the *geography* involved in the lesson. Not just key words and processes that you are going to explain to the students but, ideally, more than they will need to know. If you are teaching a GCSE lesson, then read the A-level textbook on the same topic. Be ready for when students ask you why a certain process happens or how the landform was created in the first place. This is also the time to pre-empt any misconceptions that students might have. Put the time in and become a (relative) expert in the topic. Students feed off a teacher's passion, and a teacher who is unconfident on the subject matter will tend to rush through the lesson, hoping that students aren't going to ask them about the landform they aren't 100% sure they can explain.

Map Out the Lesson

What do you want students to have learned from this particular lesson? When they walk out of the door, what are the specific bits of knowledge or skills that you want them to feel confident about? Whatever they are, write them down as the learning outcomes, and then work backwards from there. The whole lesson should be focused on helping students achieve those outcomes. Having that focus will help your planning of the lesson as well as help provide a sense of purpose in the lesson. The temptation is to create a lesson that is resource-focused, rather than learning-focused. You might know of a snazzy task which would look great if someone was observing you, but trying to shoehorn it into a lesson makes it seem disjointed and clunky.

Cheat sheets can be a really useful way to ensure that you are ready and know your lines. Essentially, they are the script for your lesson. Admittedly, they do require a fair amount of

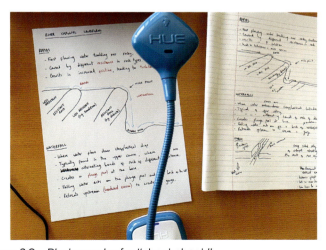

In Figure 3.9, on the left is the page I am showing students under the visualiser. The exercise book on the right is my cheat sheet for the lesson.

Figure 3.9 Photograph of a "cheat sheet."

planning time, but they are so helpful in a lesson when 30 pairs of eyes are watching you and your drawing. Figure 3.9 shows how a cheat sheet might be used.

There might be the temptation to try to hide the sheet away, in case it looks to students like you are "cheating," but I have found that, if anything, students are pleased to see that the lesson is well prepared and that you have put the time and care into the lesson! I usually just use lined paper for the cheat sheets and then keep them organised in a folder. Then the following year, they can just be reviewed and adapted accordingly.

Prepare the Room

Once you know what you are teaching and how the lesson is going to play out, then you can make sure that you have everything you will need. A teacher-led lesson really requires the teacher to be *on it*, and any scrabbling around, looking for the right paper or pens, will only serve to break the flow of the lesson and is a chance for students to lose focus. Figure 3.10 shows most of the equipment that I like to have on my desk. I have my pens, pencils, and colour pencils. From here I feel confident that I have everything at my fingertips.

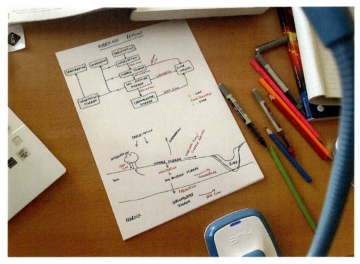

Figure 3.10 Photograph of some useful equipment for a lesson.

Textbook

Open at the relevant pages. Useful if you need a quick definition and don't want to have to make one up on the spot! Also, good to check you have covered the main points for each topic or diagram.

Cheat Sheet/Notes

Mapped-out lesson, ready to be copied or adapted. Allows the teacher to focus on delivering a clear explanation rather than having to think on their feet about what to say.

Pens and Pencils

Sharpened, checked, and ready to be used.

Visualiser

The best ones have an autofocus option and can be positioned so they don't get in your way whilst writing.

Paper

Several blank sides. Can be lined or plain. Plain paper is clearer for most diagrams, but lined paper can help students if they are also using lined paper in an exercise book.

Laptop

Any photos or videos to show students are lined up and ready. Useful websites are also ready to go.

Do Now Tasks

As students come into the room, ideally, they are quickly engaged in the lesson. That may be with something on the board to consider, or something on their desks. Ideally, you have established routines where students are expecting to be doing something as soon as they walk into the classroom. Do Nows serve a number of purposes. They can be used to help transition a student from "lunch mode" to "lesson mode" so that they stop thinking about any breaktime dramas and start thinking about geography. More importantly, these tasks can be used to activate any relevant prior knowledge. If you are about to teach the factors affecting different climates, then getting students to think about a previous lesson on air pressure can only help get them switched on. There are few different ways that diagrams might be used for Do Nows, and these are shown on page 30.

Preview the Lesson

If you want students engaged with your tasks and working with purpose in your lesson, they need to understand and value what the lesson is all about. This is like the introduction part of the lesson, where you let students know what the topic is, what they are going to get out of it, and why it is important. This might involve starting with a story, photos, video, or other "hook" into the topic. Make it relevant, make it interesting, link it to the students. This is easier with some topics than others. Figure 3.11 shows how thinking about this introduction as a funnel can help take the students on a "journey" from a more general, interesting idea to the focused point of the lesson.

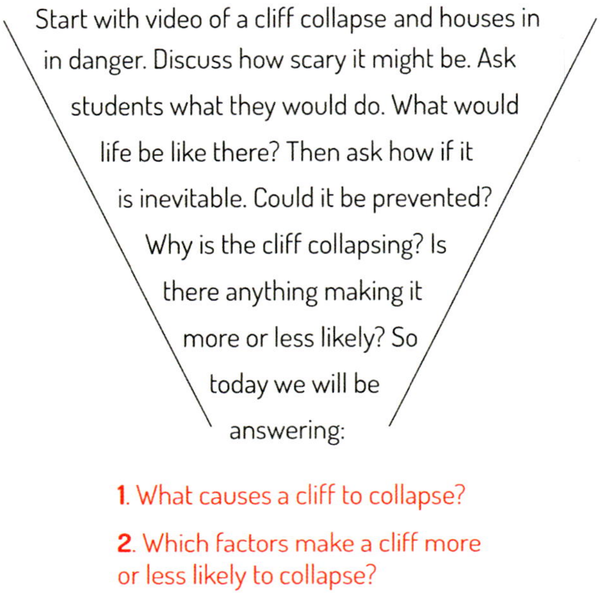

Start with video of a cliff collapse and houses in in danger. Discuss how scary it might be. Ask students what they would do. What would life be like there? Then ask how if it is inevitable. Could it be prevented? Why is the cliff collapsing? Is there anything making it more or less likely? So today we will be answering:
1. What causes a cliff to collapse?
2. Which factors make a cliff more or less likely to collapse?

Figure 3.11 Focusing the aims of a lesson.

Once you have established the learning outcomes or objectives for the lesson, then write these down. I usually write them either on paper, which I can keep referring back to via the visualiser, or on the whiteboard so that they remain in view throughout. Having them to hand makes it easy to remind students what the lesson is all about. Similarly, the photo or video used at the start of the lesson can become a useful reference point during your explanations. So when you are deep into a physical process, such as the role of impermeable rock in cliff collapse, you can keep referencing the houses on the cliff you looked at earlier.

HOW DO RAPIDS AND WATERFALLS FORM ?

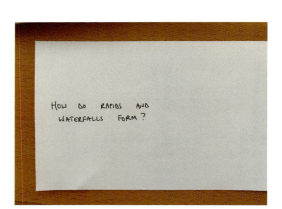

Figure 3.12 Introducing at the start of the lesson.

• Different rock types
• Different erosion rates
• Upper course
HOW DO RAPIDS AND WATERFALLS FORM ?
• Rapid → waterfall → Gorge
• Headward erosion
Also: River rejuvenation
- Tectonic uplift
- Falling sea levels

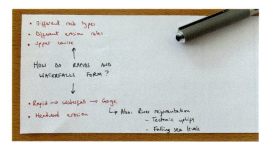

Figure 3.13 Summarising at the end.

I Do, We Do, You Do

The flow diagram shows just one sequence of I/W/Y, but of course, there may be more than one within the lesson. The first stage, or "I do," is where you, the teacher, clearly and carefully model and explain the process or landform. With a diagram, this is best done under the visualiser, and students are involved through questioning and perhaps noting down useful tips for when it is their turn. This is such an important part of the learning sequence. It is here that you are explaining the specifics of the topic. This is where the subject knowledge and the pre-lesson planning pay off. There are plenty of different ways you can approach this first part. For example, you might want students simply just watching and listening. You might want them to make notes. You might want to draw under the visualiser, or you might prefer drawing onto a whiteboard. Either way, this stage is the heart of the learning, as it involves the explanation of some new information.

The second stage of "we do" can also have several variations. One way could be to provide a scaffolded version of the diagram, where some of the lines have been added already. This makes the drawing easier for students and is a stepping stone to drawing the full version independently.

Another way could be to do a whole-class *deliberate diagram*, where each student draws the diagram step-by-step, as you carefully explain and instruct each line. Page 34 shows how this might look. It takes time but can be a very powerful way of ensuring students are clear about what exactly they need to draw.

Alternatively, you might want students to work in pairs and draw together. Having watched you already, they can work together and discuss as they each draw the same thing. This style of paired work does need structure and is best attempted when the students understand how working in pairs like this can work.

The third stage, "you do," should be fully independent work. Again, there are several ways this can be organised. Students might simply be tasked with drawing the diagram again. Just replicate what they have already done. This could then be followed by peer assessment, where you provide the class with some assessment criteria and they give each other feedback on their diagrams. The next section, *Review the Learning*, looks at how to provide effective feedback on diagrams. Another way to utilise the "you do" section could be to incorporate a relevant exam question for the diagram.

Figure 3.14 shows how a worksheet might be constructed for the "I do, we do, you do" sequence, and then Figure 3.15 has some possible variations for the worksheet.

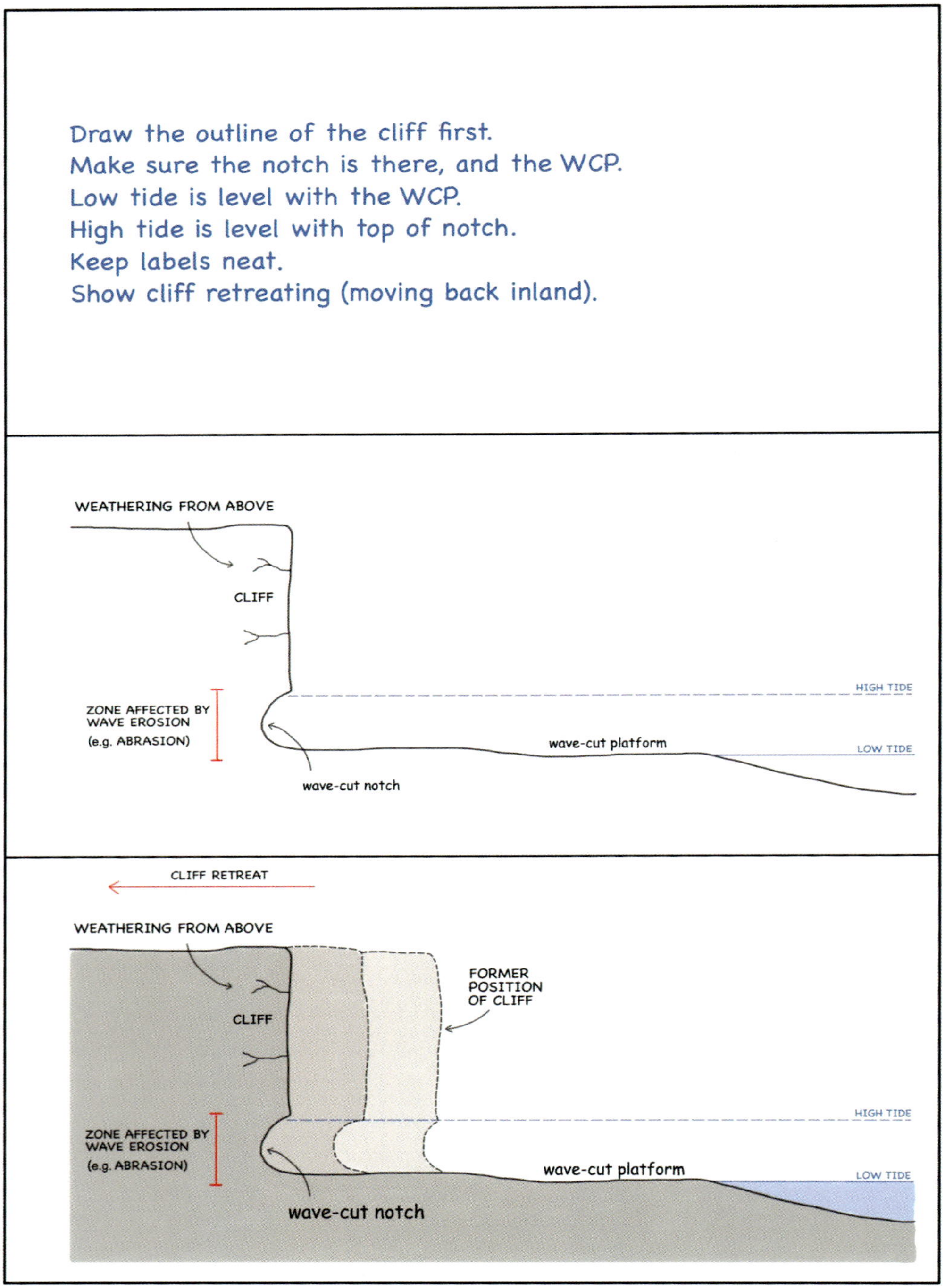

28 *How Diagrams Support Teaching*

Draw the outline of the cliff first.
Make sure the notch is there, and the WCP.
Low tide is level with the WCP.
High tide is level with top of notch.
Keep labels neat.
Show cliff retreating (moving back inland).

WEATHERING FROM ABOVE

CLIFF

HIGH TIDE

ZONE AFFECTED BY
WAVE EROSION
(e.g. ABRASION)

wave-cut platform

LOW TIDE

wave-cut notch

CLIFF RETREAT

WEATHERING FROM ABOVE

CLIFF

FORMER
POSITION
OF CLIFF

HIGH TIDE

ZONE AFFECTED BY
WAVE EROSION
(e.g. ABRASION)

wave-cut platform

LOW TIDE

wave-cut notch

Figure 3.14 "I do, we do, you do" example 1.

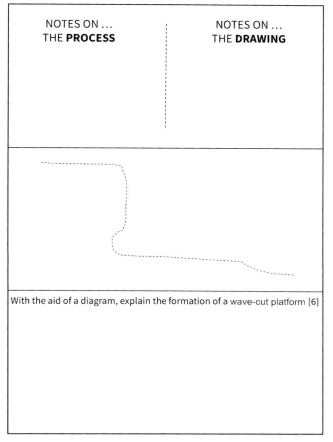

Figure 3.15 "I do, we do, you do" example 2.

Review the Learning

Providing timely and targeted feedback lets students know to what extent they have mastered a particular topic. Without feedback, students are likely to continue with misconceptions and continue making mistakes. With diagrams, there are two areas to focus on with feedback:

1. The geographical content. Are keywords used correctly? Are processes accurately explained? Are different parts correctly labelled?
2. The actual drawing. Is it neatly drawn? Is the shading evenly done? Are lines drawn too hard or too soft? Is the diagram too small?

Feedback on diagrams can be done immediately, either as a teacher circulates a classroom or when students are working in pairs with peer assessment. However, both of these methods might not be as thoughtful or useful as if the teacher were to spend more time on the feedback once the lesson has finished. Whilst that might mean the feedback is not so immediate, if it is done before the next lesson and used to help prepare for the next diagram, then it can be just as useful.

Feedback is only useful if students have the opportunity to act on it. If you tell a student that their diagram might be improved if they use more space on the page, then unless the student gets to try again soon, then that feedback may well be forgotten. This is why the "I do, we do, you do" method works so well: students have the opportunity to see a sequence of diagrams and can see the progression in their work.

Finally, effective feedback on student work should be targeted and provide the individual student with specific, personal targets for them to act on. The targets should not be too challenging. If a student just isn't very good at drawing diagrams, then keep the targets simple. Anything that is too difficult to achieve might put them off. Equally, targets that are unhelpfully simplistic won't challenge students enough to help them develop.

Review the Teaching

This is the easiest part to miss out. After a lesson, especially on a full teaching day, it is much simpler to just move on to the next class and not think about how it went. If you can, it is definitely worth putting in the time to review how the lesson went. This can often be done best by looking at the students' work. If the aim was to use diagrams to explain a specific landform, then it should be clear quite quickly whether they were able to do this from their work. If, whilst reviewing the work, there are the same errors made by a number of students, then perhaps this might be as a result of the teaching.

However, it is also important to consider that a neatly drawn and well-annotated diagram in a student's book does not necessarily mean that they have learned that landform. One of the best ways to review your teaching, therefore, is to test the students' next lesson. If they cannot explain how the landform forms, then, unfortunately, that might also be a reflection on the teaching.

It would be very surprising if a teacher were to reflect on the lesson and *not* find an area for improvement. The best teachers are reflective practitioners, and holding a mirror up to your teaching and classroom performance is a sign that you are prepared to be honest and will ultimately improve both your teaching and the students' learning.

Do Now Diagrams

When students come into your classroom, ideally you want them engaging immediately with the lesson. You can decide whether you want that to be something to pique their interest and get them asking questions about a photograph or video clip or whether you want them to

How Diagrams Support Teaching   31

be immediately trying to recall the key points from last lesson with a quick quiz. Either way, students should start *thinking* about whatever topic you have chosen.

Diagrams can be a great Do Now. They can work well as a way of engaging students with a topic, but in a way that is a little bit different to the normal starter activity. The following are some examples of how they might be used.

Deliberate Mistakes

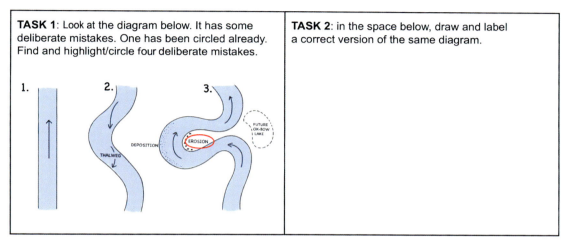

Figure 3.16 Spot the deliberate mistakes.

You deliberately draw a geographical feature with five deliberate mistakes. It is a relatively simple and self-explanatory activity, although it does require you to think about five noticeable errors, which isn't always that easy to do!

Draw a ...

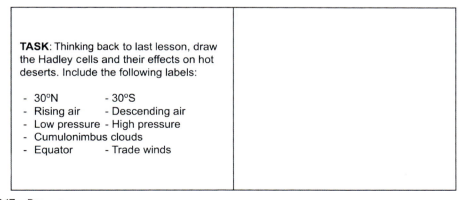

Figure 3.17 Draw a ...

32 How Diagrams Support Teaching

Very simple but a good way to assess how much students can recall from a previous lesson. You could also do this on a mini whiteboard, which would work as an effective way to gauge the whole class.

Label a ...

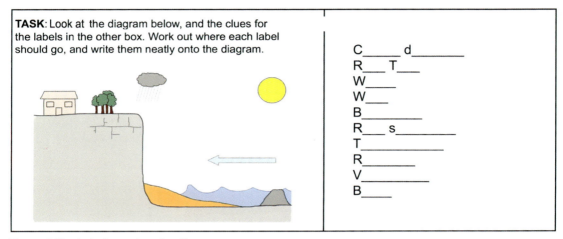

Figure 3.18 Label a ... (version 1).

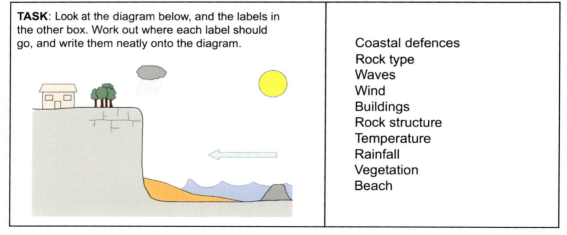

Figure 3.19 Label a ... (version 2).

Another simple activity, but it can be scaffolded easily enough by either just providing the instructions or providing hints to the labels, or all the labels themselves.

Finish a ...

TASK: Look at the Diagram Guide below. It will help you complete the diagram to show a volcanic hotspot. Thinking back to last lesson, complete the diagram, adding the labels from the other box too.

Lithosphere
Asthenosphere
Magma chamber
Rising mantle plume
Shield volcano
Extinct volcano
Eroded islands
Sea level
Direction on plate movement

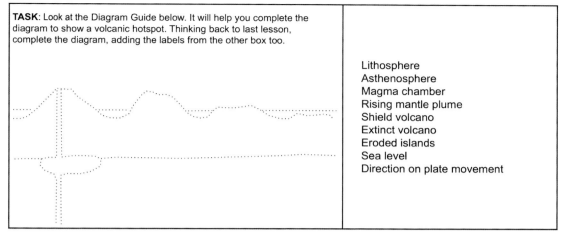

Figure 3.20 Finish a ...

This may look like a simple join-the-dots activity, but to a novice student, they might not see the seemingly obvious way that the lines need to be drawn. It will require some hard thinking from them to work out which line is which. As with the other Do Nows, this can be scaffolded with more or fewer labels.

Follow the Instructions

TASK: Below are detailed instructions of how to draw a river process that we studied last week. Follow the instructions carefully in the other box, and write down the name of the landform in the space provided.

1. Draw a horizontal line across the box, about 3 cm from the bottom.
2. Draw a wavy line, horizontally across the box, about 2 cm from the top.
3. About one third of the way along the first line from the left-hand side, draw a small circle sitting on the line.
4. Draw another circle, the same size, about 3 cm away from it at about a 45° angle.
5. Draw an arrow from the first to the second circle.
6. Draw a third circle, the same size, about two-thirds of the way from the left of the bottom line, so that it sits on the line at the same level as the first circle.
7. Draw an arrow from the second circle to the third.

Name of the process: ____________________

Figure 3.21 Follow the instructions.

This works best with simpler diagrams and can be a really fun starter task. It also probably works best if you do 4-5 on a worksheet for students to complete. The aim of the task is for students to be able to identify the landform(s) you have described.

Photo to Diagram

Figure 3.22 Sketch a photograph.

If the previous lesson was about a specific landform or process, drawing a diagram version of the sketch is a good way for students to apply their understanding. It is easy for students to just be able to draw the standard theoretical version of the landform, which can result in them not having an appreciation of what the landform might look like in reality.

Deliberate Diagrams

This involves the teacher slowly, carefully, and methodically drawing a diagram whilst the students copy your every move until they all have a clear and neat version. This always works well with students. It may not allow for any actual learning of the content, or for the students to be doing too much thinking for themselves, but it is not designed for that. Deliberate diagrams allow students, who may not be confident diagram drawers, to be guided through the process. It is more than just you drawing and them copying. It is more of a "How to Draw …" session, where the emphasis is on the specific elements of drawing. Students who are not confident drawers are often very proud of the finished diagram, even though they were simply copying. It will also look great in their notes, which, importantly, can help create a sense of confidence in their own drawing ability.

How Diagrams Support Teaching   35

Following is an example of how a teacher might lead a deliberate diagram.

Figure 3.23   Deliberate diagram (part 1).

"Okay, final check that everyone has everything they need. Plain paper? Sharp-enough pencil? Pen? Good. First, making sure you aren't gripping too tight on the pencil, draw a single line that runs across the page. It starts flat, then drops down for the cliff, flat for a bit, and then drops down as the seabed."

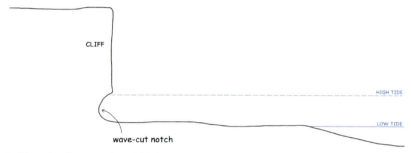

Figure 3.24   Deliberate diagram (part 2).

"Next, add the sea. We know there is a low tide and a high tide, and we saw from the video that the range decides how big the notch is. Draw the low tide line as a solid (blue pencil if you have it), and high tide as a dotted line. Anyone suggest why we use dotted lines for diagrams? Good. Now let's add some labels. Who can point to where we should label the cliff?"

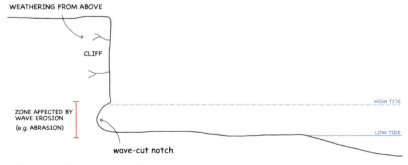

Figure 3.25   Deliberate diagram (part 3).

"Now let's pause for a minute and swap your diagram with your partner's. Compare it to my diagram, and let them know if there is anything missing. You can also pass on any positive feedback or advice."

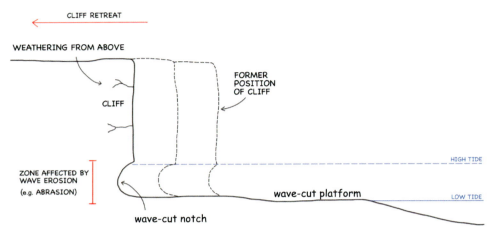

Figure 3.26 Deliberate diagram (part 4).

"Back to your diagram. Next, we need to show how the cliff has been retreating inland. Who can remind us what that means, 'retreating inland'? Again, use dotted lines to show something that isn't there now or has moved. We can also label the areas where erosion happens at the base. And where weathering weakens the cliff at the top."

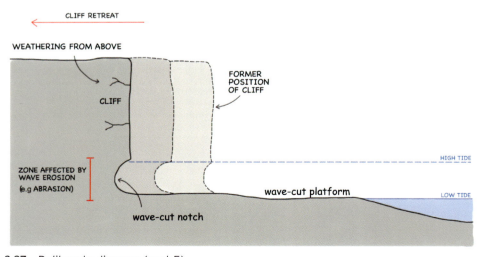

Figure 3.27 Deliberate diagram (part 5).

How Diagrams Support Teaching   37

"The final part to the diagram is to add some colour, and to check the rest of the labels. When you are shading in the cliff, remember how to hold your pencil at an angle so that you aren't pressing down too hard. Keep the shading smooth and even. Top tip for you: watch how I use my finger to help guide the shading, and keep it neat."

As mentioned, this is not necessarily going to be the activity or time when students are doing the actual *learning* about cliff retreat and wave-cut platforms. However, there are so many diagrams in geography, and so many students are not confident with their drawing skills, that it can be very useful to just have them think about what makes a good diagram.

Drawing Diagrams 101

"But I can't draw!" How often do you hear that in a classroom? Some students love drawing and will open their pencil case to reveal an absolute armoury of pencils and colours. Unfortunately, there are also those students who really do seem to dislike drawing. This is usually because they are not very good at it and, therefore, don't enjoy any drawing tasks.

This is an important point, and one that is not addressed very often in a geography classroom. We, as teachers, may take for granted the importance of drawing diagrams to show off different landforms and processes. We have also had plenty of practice. How many times have you drawn that classic waterfall diagram or a volcano cross section? So it is important that we don't just assume that all students can comfortably pick up a pencil and draw a simple diagram. So taking the time to teach the basics of diagram drawing is definitely worthwhile.

The following suggestions may seem almost too basic, but the techniques and exercises are useful. I would suggest spending 15 minutes with a class, using a visualiser to show how you hold your pencil, and then getting them to practise some of the basic drawing techniques, such as simple lines and shading. Page 34 discusses the deliberate diagram, and carefully, slowly, and deliberately drawing something together might be the natural follow-on from the exercises that follow.

The Posture

If you are sitting uncomfortably, perhaps hunched over or leaning across a desk, this tends to show through in your drawing. If you are having to hold your body in an unnatural position, you may end up gripping the pencil too tightly. Sit square to the desk or table. Relax your shoulders and shake out any tension. If your feet are flat on the floor, the rest of your body follows and you end up more stable, with your arms ready for drawing. Flat feet make all the difference!

TASK: Sit in front of your paper with a pencil, and shift your position and posture. Notice the difference between feet flat and feet on their side.

The Grip

Students have hopefully already been taught how to hold a pencil. Demonstrate how you hold it, and talk through how you grip it between your thumb, middle, and index fingers. Discuss how lightly or tightly you grip the pencil. A common error is for students to grip too tightly. This leads to thick and un-erasable pencil lines.

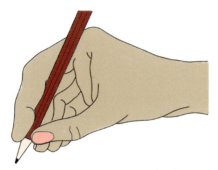

Figure 3.28   Importance of grip.

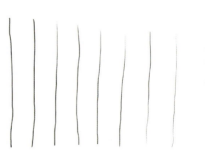

Figure 3.29   Vertical practice lines.

TASK: Draw a series of lines that start very light and finish very firm. Make the start of the line a 1, and the end a 10. Discuss what level of tightness is likely to work best for a diagram.

The Action

Draw with your whole arm, not just your wrist. This means keeping your wrist off the paper or table. Your hand and forearm should move together. If you rest your wrist or arm on the table, you lose some control and can end up with extra curves in your lines where your grounded hand restricts your drawing. Keep your little finger just skimming the surface of the paper. Maintaining a very slight contact with the paper will help you keep control of the thickness of the line. The pencil should be held at an angle, not vertical. If a pencil is just sharpened, then suggest that you scribble a few lines on a scrap paper to stop it being so scratchy. Equally, if you allow your lead to become too blunt, then the lines lose clarity. So monitor your pencil!

Putting It All Together

Use the visualiser to demonstrate your grip and your action. Then get students to copy some basic lines and shapes that you draw. Keep it really simple initially, but concentrate on the firmness of the grip. Ask students to imagine a scale of 1–10, where 1/10 is barely holding the pencil and 10/10 is almost squeezing the life out of it. Discuss which grip gives the best control of the pencil.

TASK: Draw a few simple shapes that require some hand movement. Try it where you and the students are all drawing the images that follow. Keep reminding the students about posture and arm position. Get them to deliberately slouch, grip too hard, or ground their hand on the paper, and see what happens to the lines.

Practise trying to draw horizontal, straight lines between two vertical ruler-drawn guides. It isn't easy!

Draw the lines in Figure 3.31 by pivoting from the elbow. These help students consider how different hand and arm actions can influence the line.

Figure 3.32 are more examples of various shapes that might be useful whilst drawing geographical diagrams. Being able to draw cubes or any 3D is a crucial skill, as they can help demonstrate a wide variety of landforms.

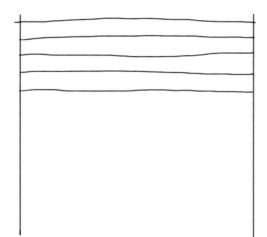

Figure 3.30 Horizontal practice lines.

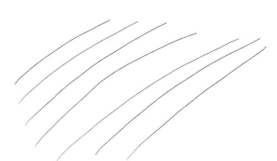

Figure 3.31 Angled practice lines.

40 *How Diagrams Support Teaching*

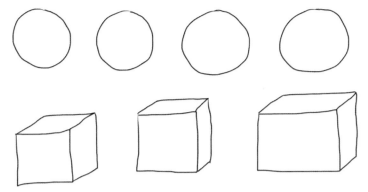

Figure 3.32 Practice shapes.

Summary

- Effective explanations in a lesson require a combination of ingredients:
    - Secure subject knowledge
    - Appreciation of the class's ability
    - Controlled flow of new information
    - A connection between any new ideas and what students can relate to
- There are specific ways that diagrams can be included.

Chapter 4 The Diagrams

DOI: 10.4324/9781003303435-4

4.1 Rocks and Weathering

4.1.1 Geological Timescale Difficulty to draw: ●●○
Difficulty to explain: ●●○

> **What Students Should Already Know**
> - Earth was formed 4.5 billion years ago.
> - Since then, dinosaurs have been and gone.
> - Alongside mammals, there are also reptiles, amphibians, birds, fish, and insects.

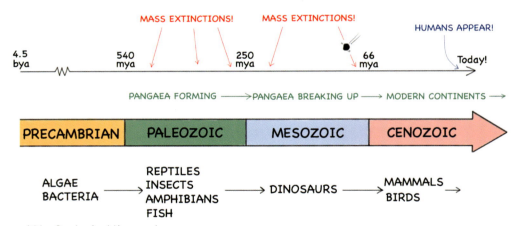

Figure 4.1.1 Geological timescale.

1. Earth was formed about 4.5 billion years ago. It took billions of years for even the first simple cells to first appear.
2. Since then, geological time is divided into four stages. Different species of animals, including dinosaurs and mammals, evolved over time.
3. Throughout time, the continents have kept changing shape. There have also been several mass extinction events, including the one where the dinosaurs were wiped out.

The Explanation

Trying to get your head around 4.5 billion years is far too difficult. Even the difference between a million and a billion is hard to grasp. One way to try to show the difference is to use a piece of graph paper. Ask students who wants to be a millionaire? Shade in one single tiny square on a piece of graph paper. Ask them to imagine that it represents a single millionaire. Then discuss how many squares would represent a billionaire. Usual answers include 10 or 100. Then shade in 1,000 squares (which is 25 little squares by 40 little squares). The difference now looks significant!

Lead this on to a discussion about the past. The usual reference points for students are perhaps 2,000 years, or even 10,000 years, if they've studied the Ice Age before. Ask them to consider 1,000 years in time. Use the same graph paper to show how, if one single square represents 1,000 years, the 1,000 shaded squares from before represent a million.

Draw the timeline part of the diagram from right to left. Start with today at the far right-hand side, then mark off the 66-, 250-, and 540-million-year marks. Explain that the beginning of the line should show 4.5 billion years, so to draw a continuous line would be hundreds of metres! This is why we use the jagged line to show a jump in time.

Then mark on the four major geological eras. These can be characterised by adding the different species of animals that evolved during that time. Then optional extras, such as the formation and disappearance of Pangaea, and different extinction events can also be added.

There are lots of discussions to be had around geological time here, and it is because of the huge timescales involved in the Earth's history that geologists think differently about what is considered to be "recent" compared to geographers.

Using the Earth clock in the following is another good way to help students appreciate these ideas.

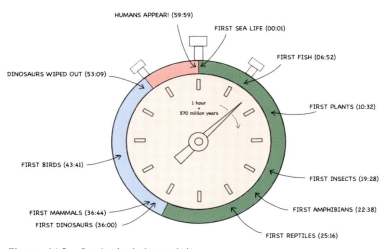

Figure 4.1.2 Geological stopwatch.

To show 570 million years in one hour, each minute equals 9.5 million years, and each second equals 158 thousand years.

So to add to the clock, take the event (millions of years ago), divided by 9.5, which gives the number of minutes ago that the event occurred, then you will need to minus that from 60 to show where on the clock it should fit.

Check for Understanding

- When did the Earth form?
- What are the four geological eras?
- When did the dinosaurs disappear?

4.1.2 The Rock Cycle

Difficulty to draw: ●○○
Difficulty to explain: ●●○

What Students Should Already Know

- The Earth, and its crust, is made of different rocks.
- The crust can be moved and changed by huge tectonic forces.
- Weathering and erosion cause rocks to break down into smaller parts.

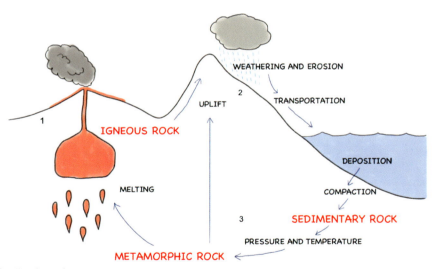

Figure 4.1.3 Rock cycle.

1. Lava that cools and hardens becomes igneous rock. Sometimes it cools and forms rock below the surface.
2. Over time, the surface rocks are broken down and end up carried to the sea, where millions of pieces of tiny rock are compacted together to form *sedimentary rock*.
3. Both sedimentary and *igneous rock* can be forced back down underground, where they are heated and squeezed to form *metamorphic rock*.

The Explanation

Given that the three groups of rocks are classified by how they are created, it is important to go through the rock cycle. Draw the outline of the mountains, the *magma*, and the sea. It is probably worth starting with igneous rock, as students are likely to appreciate the basic idea of lava cooling and becoming solid. Then move on to how weathering and erosion can break down rock to its mineral components, which become compacted into the layers that become sedimentary rocks. Whilst this diagram is useful in showing where the different types of rock are formed, Figure 4.1.4 shows the relevant processes in more detail.

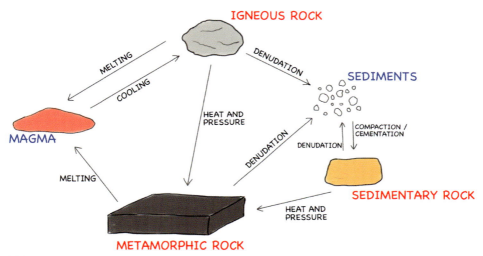

Figure 4.1.4   Rock cycle processes.

Figure 4.1.4 shows in more detail the processes required to change one rock to another. There are a number of potentially new keywords here. It is perhaps worth getting students to write out the definitions of these terms. Remind them that these words are all key processes that will help later in the course.

TIP: Show the Etymology

Sedimentary	*sediment-*	(Latin) *sedimentum*, "settling, sinking down"
	-ary	(Latin) "connected with"
Igneous		(Latin) *igneus*, "fiery"
Metamorphic	*meta-*	(Greek) "trans, change"
	-morph-	(Greek) "form"
	-ic	(Greek) "to do with"

Checking for Understanding
- What are the three types of rock?
- How might sedimentary rocks form?
- If rocks are subjected to enough heat and/or pressure, what will they become?

4.1.3 Igneous Rocks

Difficulty to draw: ●○○
Difficulty to explain: ●●○

What Students Should Already Know
- The rock cycle shows how rocks can be changed over time.
- Magma forms underground and can be erupted from volcanoes.

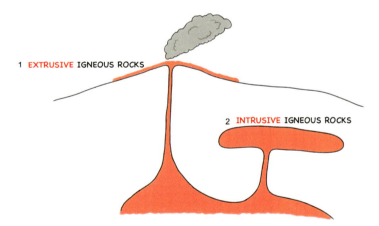

Figure 4.1.5 Intrusive vs extrusive.

1. Volcanoes often eject molten rock as *lava*. This cools rapidly once it reaches the surface and becomes *extrusive* igneous rock.
2. Magma that forms underground but does not reach the surface may also cool and harden. It forms intrusive igneous rock and may appear on the surface only after the overlying rock is worn away by *erosion* and *weathering*.

Rocks and Weathering 47

The Explanation

Teaching about rocks can, to be fair, seem pretty dull. And it probably will be if you launch straight into a comparison of the mineral compositions of sedimentary and igneous rocks. Instead, try to capture their imagination. Tell them a story. Show them why you love learning about rocks! Show them a picture of your favourite volcano, favourite old stone building, or favourite kitchen work surface. Whatever it is, lead them from something every day towards the importance of appreciating what those rocks are made of and how they came to exist.

Better yet, have some examples of rock. I have two pieces I use: lava from an Icelandic volcano, and sandstone from a trip to Arizona. I have had them for years, and they really help show students that I have so much love for rocks I'm prepared to carry them back from holidays.

Start this diagram with students considering what happens to lava when it erupts from a volcano and flows down the side. Hawaii is a good example of somewhere with lots of cooled lava visible on the surface.

Then ask students what might happen if the rising magma within a volcano just stopped rising and never made it to the surface. You have this huge chamber of molten rock that eventually is going to cool down and harden to form igneous rock but still hundreds of metres below the surface.

The crystals within igneous rocks are the clues to whether the rock cooled on the surface or underground. Rocks that cool on the surface do so very quickly, so the crystals that form when the rock goes from molten to solid don't have time to grow very much. Conversely, an igneous rock with larger crystals is likely to have cooled more slowly underground. A *pluton* is a large body of igneous rock that forms within the crust.

Figure 4.1.6 is a way of showing what we mean by different crystal sizes. As you are explaining the preceding paragraph, draw out two images that might be seen under a microscope. They are likely to end up messy, as you won't be able to draw neatly if mid-explanation, but do aim to get the relative sizes different to show the difference.

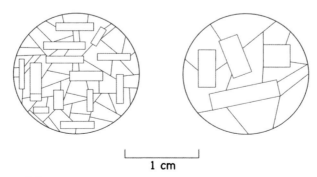

Figure 4.1.6 Igneous crystals.

48   *Rocks and Weathering*

The image on the left shows smaller crystals from an extrusive igneous rock that cooled quickly. The drawing of the crystals does not need to be perfect; it is the relative sizes that are more important.

Case Studies

44.5904, -104.7151 Devil's Monument, USA (exposed intrusive igneous rock)
19.3977, -155.2586 Kilauea, Hawaii, USA (recently erupted lava: extrusive igneous rock)

Checking for Understanding

- Where do extrusive rocks form?
- How are intrusive rocks eventually exposed?
- Why are the crystals in extrusive igneous rock usually small?

4.1.4 Sedimentary Rocks

Difficulty to draw: ● ● ●
Difficulty to explain: ● ● ●

What Students Should Already Know

- The rock cycle shows how rocks can be changed over time.
- Erosion and weathering are processes that break down rocks into small fragments.
- Fragments of rock can be transported by wind and rivers.

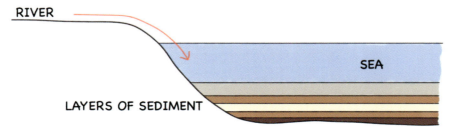

Figure 4.1.7   Sedimentation.

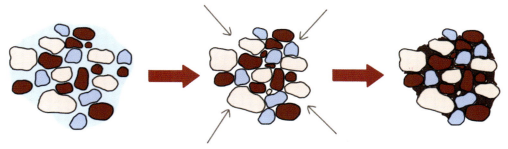

Figure 4.1.8 Sedimentary rock.

1. Fragments of old rock that have been eroded or weathered away collect in layers on the seabed.
2. As they build up, over thousands of years, they are compacted by the weight of new layers.
3. Any water is squeezed out, leaving behind minerals that act as a natural glue to stick the rock fragments together into a new sedimentary rock.

The Explanation

Sedimentary rocks are the result of the three processes of erosion/weathering, transport, and then deposition. These three processes should be explained first. If you have a piece of rock in the classroom, ideally with larger grains, this can help show students that rocks are made up of different grains that can be broken apart, albeit some more easily than others. Compare your rock sample to the rock cycle, and ask students to imagine it was on the surface, exposed to the wind and rain. Then ask them to just consider one of the grains that might be eroded. How and where might it go? Eventually, it might reach a stream before being steadily carried towards the sea.

There are different types of sedimentary rock, and although this might be unnecessary detail for your class, it is useful to have this information to hand to aid explanations.

Clastic Sedimentary Rock

Forms when bits of weathered rock (known as clasts) are compacted and cemented together over time (e.g. sandstone).

Organic Sedimentary Rock

Forms when organic matter accumulates in layers and is compacted over time (e.g. coal).

Chemical Sedimentary Rock

Results from chemical processes that crystallise minerals which have built up in layers on the sea floor.

50 *Rocks and Weathering*

> **Case Study**
>
> 30.3222, 35.4518 Petra, Jordan (observable layers of sedimentary sandstone)

> **Checking for Understanding**
> - What are sedimentary rocks made out of?
> - Why are there often layers found within sedimentary rocks?
> - What holds the grains together once the seawater has been squeezed out?

4.1.5 Metamorphic Rocks

Difficulty to draw: ●○○
Difficulty to explain: ●●○

> **What Students Should Already Know**
> - The rock cycle shows how rocks can be changed over time.
> - The crust overlies the mantle.
> - Magma is molten rock.

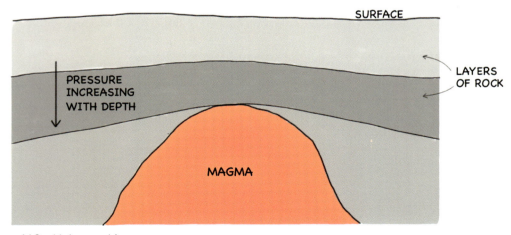

Figure 4.1.9 Metamorphism.

1. Temperature and pressure increase with depth.
2. Both sedimentary and igneous rocks are altered (or metamorphosed) as they are buried under new layers.
3. Rocks can also be altered if they come into contact with hot magma that is forced up into the crust.

The Explanation

The common misconception is that melting occurs to form metamorphic rocks. The rocks never actually melt (otherwise, they would be igneous rocks), but they do undergo a change to the mineral structure of the rocks. The concepts of increasing temperature and pressure should be simple enough to comprehend, and then it is about students appreciating that rocks are capable of changing. Referring to the rocks as being made up of different grains not only helps paint the picture of the rocks being alterable but also allows you to introduce the idea that it is the different make-up of minerals and grains that partly determines how the rock will change.

Figure 4.1.10 shows how some rocks become *foliated*, that is, the intense pressure results in the minerals becoming lined up into layers. Gneiss is a good example of a foliated metamorphic rock.

Rocks that are altered by contact metamorphism, where they have been intensely heated by near contact with an igneous intrusion, do not display the same layering.

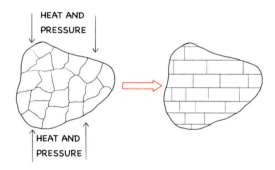

Figure 4.1.10 Metamorphic layering.

4.1.6 Freeze Thaw

Difficulty to draw: ●
Difficulty to explain: ●

What Students Should Already Know

Water freezes when the temperature drops below 0°C.

52 Rocks and Weathering

Figure 4.1.11 Freeze thaw.

1. Rainwater fills up cracks within the rock.
2. Overnight, the temperature drops below 0°C and the water freezes, which expands it by 9%.
3. The repeated process widens the cracks, which allows more water to enter and freeze. Eventually, blocks of rock are prised away and fall d\own the slope.

The Explanation

When you draw the two diagrams, to show the before and after of the frost action, make sure that the cracks on the second are larger. Water expands by 9% when it freezes into ice, and this relative size increase can be shown by asking students to look at a ruler. Get them to draw a 10 cm line in their notes, and then a 10.9 cm line next to it.

Another way to show this process is to freeze some water in a sealed ice cream tub overnight. As a homework before the lesson, it is a fun way to show the power of the expansion as the lid is forced off.

A common misconception is that this process will occur most often in polar regions, where it is coldest. In fact, it is the diurnal temperature changes that are most significant. Sketching out Figure 4.1.12 helps to highlight why.

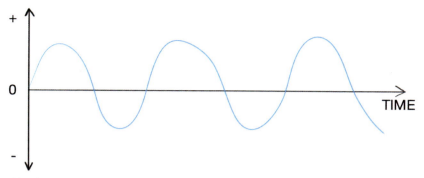

Figure 4.1.12 Fluctuating temperatures.

Figure 4.1.12 shows the importance of the regular changes in temperature. It is a simple but effective addition to a student's notes to complement their freeze thaw explanation.

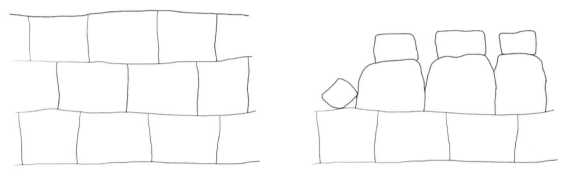

Figure 4.1.13 Presence of joints.

Another useful sketch is to show the importance of *jointing* within rocks. Those rocks that are well-jointed provide natural places for rainwater to collect.

Freeze Thaw Analogy

Water freezing within cracks in a rock can be an extremely powerful force, as water will expand by 9% when it turns into ice.

Ask if any students have had burst water pipes at home during the winter. When water freezes within the pipes, it expands and needs to expand into somewhere.

54 *Rocks and Weathering*

Case Study
58.3844, -4.9428 Scottish Highlands, UK (suitable climate for freeze thaw)

Checking for Understanding
- By how much does water expand when it is frozen?
- What happens when rainwater collects in the cracks of a rock?
- Why is a fluctuating temperature important for freeze thaw to happen?

4.1.7 Heating and Cooling   Difficulty to draw: ● ○ ○
Difficulty to explain: ● ● ○

What Students Should Already Know
- During the day, the sun heats up the Earth's surface.
- At night, the temperature drops and the surface becomes cooler.
- Different colour surfaces heat up and cool down at different rates.

Figure 4.1.14   Onion skin weathering.

1. During the heat of the day, different minerals within rocks will expand at different rates.
2. Overnight, they will contract at different rates. This causes internal stresses to the rock.
3. Repeated heating and cooling results in the outer layers of the rock breaking off.

The Explanation

Start the explanation by showing a rock under the heat of the sun. The key concept here is that minerals will react differently when they are heated. A good example to use is *granite*, which is mostly made up of the minerals quartz and feldspar. Use a photo that shows the different colours, as quartz expands more than feldspar when heated, which causes internal stresses to the make-up of the rock. Ask students to imagine a house made of two different types of brick. If one type of brick was to slightly but repeatedly expand and contract more than the other type, then the cement around them would become stressed, and eventually whole walls would become unstable.

Rocks are poor conductors of heat, so it is usually only the outer layers of the rocks that are affected by this type of weathering. This process, also known as thermal stress, results in the shattering of the rock surface.

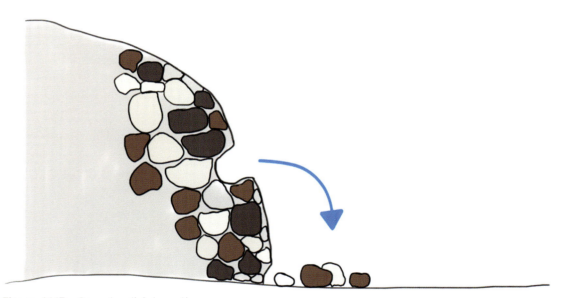

Figure 4.1.15 Granular disintegration.

Figure 4.1.15 can be used to show how the different reactions of minerals to heating and cooling can cause individual grains to break away from the rock. This is known as *granular disintegration* and is one way that rocks can react to weathering. Some rocks, which are well-jointed, experience *block disintegration*, and this can be shown using Figure 4.1.13 on page 53.

56 *Rocks and Weathering*

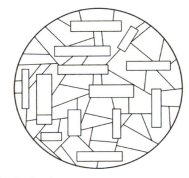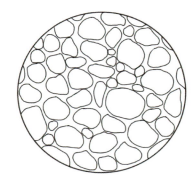

Figure 4.1.16   Grain size.

Explaining granular disintegration is also an opportunity for students to consider how the different shapes and alignments of minerals will affect how the rock is broken down by weathering. Figure 4.1.16 shows two rocks and what they might look like under a microscope. This is not particularly easy (or quick!) to draw during a lesson but can help explain an important concept to students.

Case Study
35.2980, -115.6195 Mojave Desert, USA (suitable climate for heating and cooling).

Checking for Understanding
- Do all minerals in a rock expand at the same rate when heated?
- What happens when different minerals expand and contract at different rates?
- How is granular disintegration different to block disintegration?

4.1.8 Carbonation
Difficulty to draw: ● ●
Difficulty to explain: ● ●

What Students Should Already Know
Carbon dioxide is one of the gases in the atmosphere.

Rocks and Weathering   57

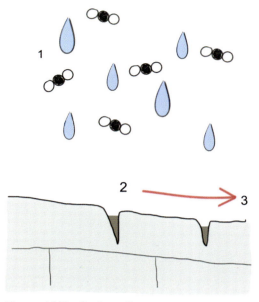

1. Rainwater absorbs *carbon dioxide* that is found in the atmosphere. This mixing creates a weak carbonic acid.
2. Rocks such as limestone contain a mineral called calcite, which reacts with the carbonic acid. A new substance forms, called calcium hydrogen carbonate.
3. The calcium hydrogen carbonate can be dissolved in water and so is easily washed away.

Figure 4.1.17   Carbonation.

The Explanation

The diagram for this one draws attention to the presence of carbon dioxide in the atmosphere. CO_2, as the abbreviation suggests, is made up of one part carbon (drawn as the black circle) and two parts oxygen (drawn as the white circles). Make sure students appreciate that these are not drawn to scale but are drawn in this way to show how they react with the rain. Page 228, which looks at the greenhouse effect, also uses CO_2 drawn in this way because it helps if students can have something to look at when discussing an invisible gas.

The other aspect of this diagram to note is the joints and *bedding planes* associated with limestone. Page 65 shows the typical karst scenery which results from this type of weathering.

Case Study

54.0728, -2.1586 Malham Cove, UK (limestone pavement, carved out by carbonation)

Checking for Understanding

- Which gas is responsible for carbonation?
- How is carbonic acid created?
- What does the carbonic acid react with to create the calcium hydrogen carbonate?

4.1.9 Salt Crystallisation

Difficulty to draw: ●○○
Difficulty to explain: ●●○

> **What Students Should Already Know**
> - Seawater contains salt.
> - Water will evaporate in warmer conditions.

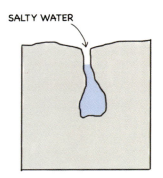
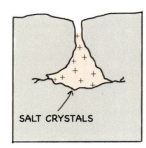
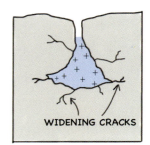

Figure 4.1.18 Salt weathering.

1. Salt spray from breaking waves lands on nearby rocks.
2. Whilst the water evaporates, the salt crystals are left behind.
3. Over time, the salt crystals accumulate and put pressure on the cracks from within.

The Explanation

Salt crystallisation is sometimes confused as a type of chemical weathering. However, given that there are no chemical reactions or changes to any mineral structures, it is a physical process. The salt crystals that are left behind grow and expand when temperatures rise.

It is a common process in coastal desert regions, where there is plentiful supply of both salt and heat. Different rocks will be affected more by salt crystallisation than others. Greater *permeability* and *porosity* lead to faster decomposition rates. Likewise, a larger grain size will see rocks breaking down more quickly. This can be shown using Figure 4.1.15 from page 55.

Studies have shown that this type of weathering is more effective at breaking down rocks than both freeze thaw and heating and cooling; 27°C has been shown to be the ideal temperature for salt crystallisation.

Case Study

- 24.4311, 14.6450 Namib Desert, Namibia (ideal conditions for salt crystallisation).

Checking for Understanding

- Why do salt crystals accumulate in the cracks of some rocks?
- How do they put pressure on the rocks?
- What is the ideal temperature for salt crystallisation to happen?

4.1.10 Biological Weathering

Difficulty to draw: ● ●
Difficulty to explain: ●

What Students Should Already Know

- When plants grow, their roots extend down to seek out moisture and nutrients.
- Beneath the soil are layers of rock, or bedrock.

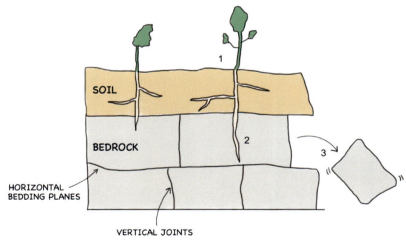

Figure 4.1.19 Biological weathering.

1. If the soil is shallow, then the roots from trees can extend into cracks within the bedrock below.
2. As the tree grows, the roots can wedge open the rock along natural joints.
3. On slopes, this can cause sections of the slope to break off and fall down the slope.

60 *Rocks and Weathering*

The Explanation

Students may have seen this along pavements, where tree roots have forced up the concrete – such is their power. Start the diagram with the two layers of bedrock and soil. Draw on the vertical joints and horizontal bedding planes. It may be worth reminding students that these occur in some types of rock but not others, and that some rocks have more than others. This effect can also occur when seeds from trees land in the cracks of rocks or cliff faces and then germinate and grow there.

Vegetation can also affect the rate of chemical weathering, because decomposing leaf litter will release organic acids that speed up some types of weathering. Similarly, the increased presence of CO_2 from plants creates more carbonic acid, which is used in carbonation. Interestingly, however, increased leaf litter can also slow down rates of physical weathering, because the layer of decomposing vegetation acts as a blanket and reduces the rate of freeze thaw.

Checking for Understanding

- How can tree roots help break up the rock below?
- How else can vegetation affect other types of weathering?

4.1.11 Factors Affecting Weathering

Difficulty to draw: ● ● ●
Difficulty to explain: ● ● ●

What Students Should Already Know

- There are a range of types of weathering.
- Each type of weathering only happens under certain conditions.
- Each type of weathering will affect some rocks more than others.

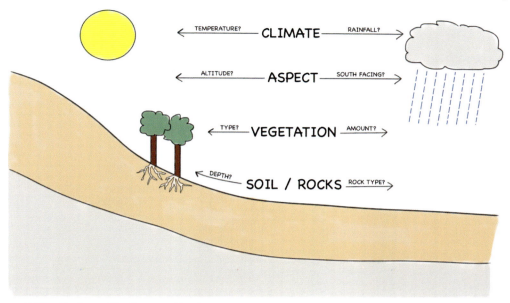

Figure 4.1.20   Factors affecting weathering.

1. The different types of weathering only occur where the conditions are right.
2. The most important factor is climate, as this determines whether certain types of weathering can happen.
3. *Aspect* refers to the direction that the place is facing. South-facing places receive more sunlight, whereas north-facing places are generally colder.

The Explanation

It is important to remind students that the types of weathering that occur don't just happen by chance; they are the result of the specific conditions of that place. If, suddenly, the climate of hot tropical rainforests were to change to a cold and frosty climate, then freeze thaw weathering would soon start, and the warm/wet chemical weathering would soon stop.

Climate determines which type of weathering will occur, and also the speed at which it operates. Figures 4.1.21 and 4.1.22 can help show how different parts of the world experience different types of weathering according to the temperature and amount of rainfall.

The other factors, such as rock type and aspect, are more local factors. Start the explanation with a review of the different types of weathering you have covered and collect suggestions for factors that might cause the weathering types to speed up or slow down. Of the factors listed on the diagram, aspect might require some additional explanation, so be prepared to explain how the sun's position in the sky changes throughout the day, and that some places are in the shade all day.

62 Rocks and Weathering

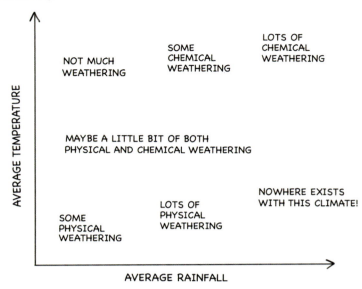

Figure 4.1.21 Simple Peltier diagram.

This simple graph can help students consider where in the world will be affected by different types of weathering. It is a simplified version of the Peltier diagram, which is commonly used at A level.

However, it is not perfect, as it really only considers freeze thaw for the physical weathering. If students can point out this graph's flaws, then that can make for a good discussion about why it is not ideal and where in the world might have places that "break the rules" of the graph.

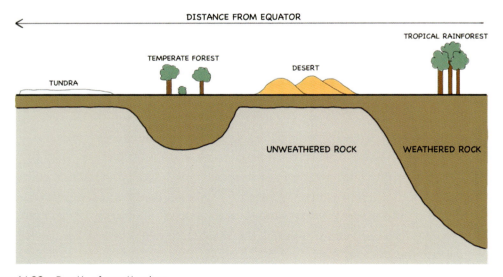

Figure 4.1.22 Depth of weathering.

Figure 4.1.22 shows how the amount of weathering increases or decreases according to latitude. It relies on students appreciating how increased rates of weathering will lead to more rock being weathered. This can be seen if you were to dig down under the soil and see how much of the bedrock has been weathered. As expected, there is little weathering below the surface at deserts and colder regions.

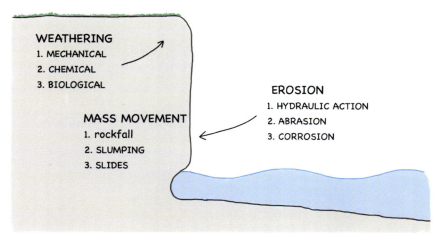

Figure 4.1.23   Weathering vs erosion vs mass movement.

Figure 4.1.23 could be used at any stage when teaching about weathering, as it helps to distinguish between weathering and erosion, as well as allowing for a discussion about mass movement. It is set by the coast but could easily be adapted to show a river or simply a hillside.

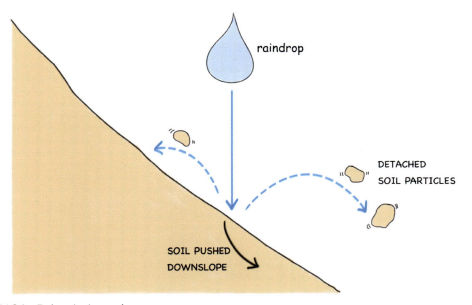

Figure 4.1.24   Rainsplash erosion.

64   *Rocks and Weathering*

The types of erosion associated with rivers and the coast are relatively well covered, but raindrops can also erode. This is a good way to remind students about the difference between erosion and weathering, in that erosion requires an additional agent, such as waves, wind, or raindrops. Weathering is the breakdown of the rocks *in situ*, meaning, there is nothing acting to remove the broken-down material.

Rock Resistance Analogy

A more resistant rock will erode relatively slowly compared to a less resistant rock. This may be down to how much water can get into the rock, or the size of the rock's minerals, or how well connected the minerals are together.

> *Show students two different types of biscuit, and ask them to consider which one will survive longest when dunked into your cup of tea. The idea that not all biscuits are the same transfers well to not all rocks are the same.*

Checking for Understanding
- What is the main factor in deciding which type of weathering happens?
- How does the amount of vegetation affect weathering?
- What is the aspect of a place?

4.1.12 Limestone Landscapes

Difficulty to draw: ● ● ●
Difficulty to explain: ● ● ●

What Students Should Already Know
- Carbonation is a type of chemical weathering.
- Limestone is a type of rock.
- High permeability and porosity of a rock mean it allows water to easily enter and pass through.

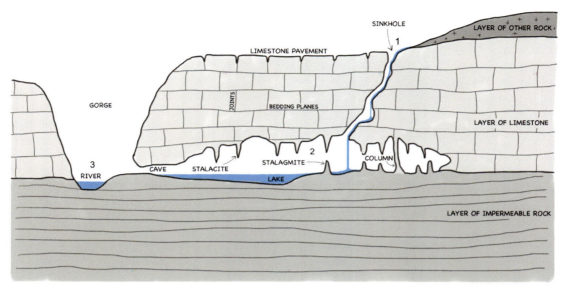

Figure 4.1.25 Karst landscape.

1. Limestone is a very permeable rock, as it has plenty of joints which allow water to soak into.
2. Limestone contains calcium carbonate, which is easily eroded by the process of carbonation.
3. Rainwater passes through joints and bedding planes, enlarging them and, over time, creating a network of tunnels, caves, and underground rivers.

The Explanation

The scale and complexity of a *karst landscape* make it relatively complicated to draw. It might be worth drawing this from a pre-prepared outline rather than onto a blank page.

Start with the layers of rock. In this instance, the limestone is on top of an impermeable layer of other rock. This keeps the water within the limestone; otherwise, it would not stay long enough to carve out the features. Make sure the limestone is well jointed, so that the water has a route to travel. Then discuss the journey that rainwater would take, from landing on the surface to slowly filtering down through the limestone. At this stage you could switch to using Figure 4.1.26 to show how *limestone pavement* forms, and the widening of the joints into grikes allows water to collect. A reminder of carbonation, using Figure 4.1.17 on page 57, would also help.

66 Rocks and Weathering

Underground, the formation of stalactites and stalagmites will also require additional explanation, and Figure 4.1.27 shows how the calcium carbonate collects on the roof and floor of the caves.

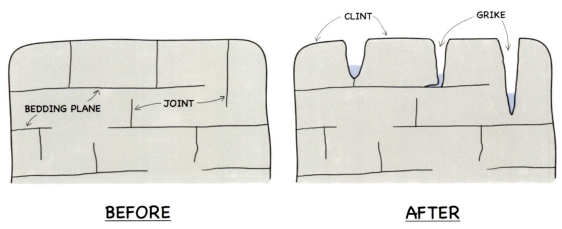

Figure 4.1.26 Limestone pavement.

Figure 4.1.26 shows the formation of *clints* and *grikes* (or grykes) as limestone is weathered by carbonation. Remembering which is which, clint or grike, can be difficult for students. A simple way is to think of them alphabetically: as you descend, clints are first, then grikes are farther down. It's always worked for me!

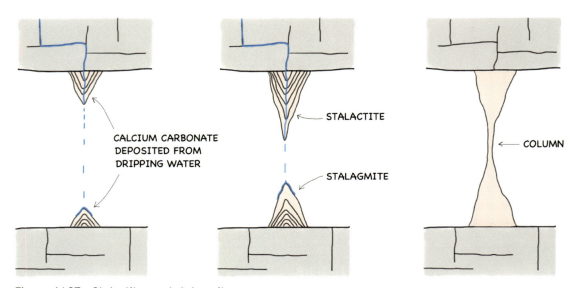

Figure 4.1.27 Stalactites and stalagmites.

Rocks and Weathering 67

Water slowly dripping in a cave will deposit calcium carbonate as it falls from the roof (which builds up as a *stalactite*) and deposit calcium carbonate where the drips land below (and build up as a stalagmite). Draw this by imagining a cross section of both, and show the layers of how they build up over time. The column forms when, inevitably, the two meet in the middle.

Case Study

24.9643, 110.4286 Yangshuo County, China (karst landscape).

Checking for Understanding

- Which type of weathering affects which type of rock to create a karst landscape?
- How do joints and bedding planes help?
- How do stalactites and stalagmites form?
- What are clints and grikes?

4.1.13 Tors

Difficulty to draw: ● ●
Difficulty to explain: ● ●

What Students Should Already Know

- Weathering is the breakdown of rocks.
- Granite is a type of rock.
- The presence of joints lets water into the rock, which helps speed up any weathering.

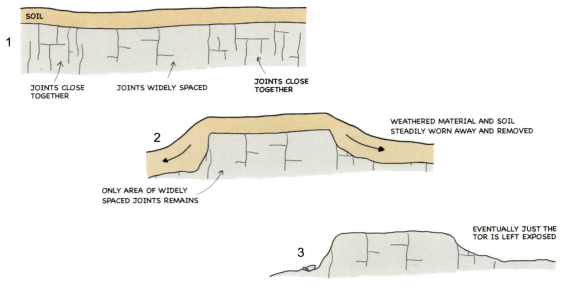

Figure 4.1.28   Tor formation.

1. Rocks, such as granite, will have some parts of it that have more joints than others.
2. The well-jointed areas are weathered more quickly, and the weathered material is removed by rain and wind.
3. Over time, the weathered material is all removed, leaving just the exposed *tor*.

The Explanation

There are a number of theories about exactly how tors are formed. The diagram used here shows one of the theories, and it is likely that different tors form according to their local conditions.

Start the diagram with a layer of granite, overlaid with some soil, or even another layer of other rock. The point is to show that the tor is the remnant left behind when overlying soil or other rock is removed. Tors form where sections of the rock have relatively few joints, so be sure to space them carefully on your diagram.

Figure 4.1.13 on page 53 shows the importance of the presence of joints in the weathering of rocks, and it can be used to support this explanation. The different theories all agree that it is the spacing of the joints that is important, but disagree on whether the weathering is predominantly physical or chemical.

Rocks and Weathering   69

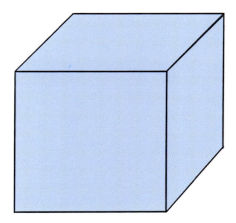 

Figure 4.1.29   Increasing surface area.

This is really hard to draw neatly, but even as a messy sketch it can be used to show how the presence of joints and bedding planes will increase the surface area of rock. More surface area means more weathering can happen, and so the overall rate of weathering will increase. The joints also allow more water to penetrate the rock, making it more permeable and more easily weathered.

In this case, if the single larger cube of rock has edges 4 m long, the total surface area is 96 m^2.

If joints were to divide it into smaller cubes each with 2 m edges, the total surface area becomes 192 m^2.

Case Study
- 0.1176, 34.5407 Kisumu, Kenya (granite tor)

Checking for Understanding
- Which type of weathering affects which type of rock to create tors?
- How do joints and bedding planes help?

4.2 Plate Tectonics

4.2.1 Structure of the Earth

Difficulty to draw: ●●●
Difficulty to explain: ●●●

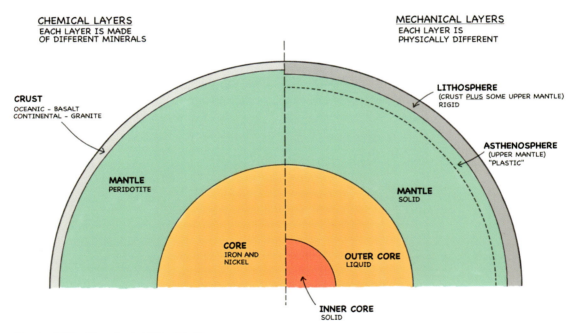

Figure 4.2.1 Structure of the Earth.

1. The Earth can be divided into three layers based on what those layers are made of.
2. The mantle is green because it is mostly made of rock called peridotite, which contains a green mineral called olivine.

Plate Tectonics   71

3. Geologists also divide the Earth up into layers depending on whether they are more solid or liquid.

The Explanation

Students should really use the terms *lithosphere* and *asthenosphere* rather than just *crust*. This is because it helps move away from the oversimplified idea that the crust "floats" on the mantle. When a tectonic plate moves, it is both the crust and part of the mantle that move. Therefore, it is worth spending time on this diagram, encouraging students to see that *crust* and *mantle* are not incorrect terms but that it is often more useful to use *lithosphere* and *asthenosphere*.

Use a compass to draw the layers to keep it neat. Many students may already be familiar with the crust/mantle/core sequence, so start with that on one side of the diagram. Depths and temperatures can also be added to the layers for further detail. It is worth noting that the diagram is not to scale.

Using a green for the mantle might raise some questions, but not using the classic "hot" yellow or orange also helps dispel the misconception that the mantle is molten.

Checking for Understanding

- What are the three chemical layers of the Earth?
- What are the five mechanical layers of the Earth?

4.2.2 Plate Tectonics

Difficulty to draw: ●●
Difficulty to explain: ●●

What Students Should Already Know

- The Earth is divided up into layers.
- The outermost layer is the lithosphere, which sits atop the asthenosphere.

72   *Plate Tectonics*

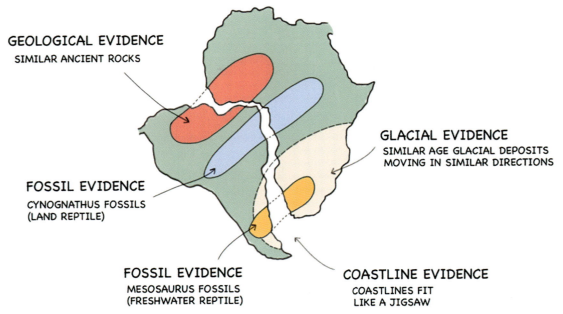

Figure 4.2.2   Evidence of plate tectonics in South America.

The Explanation

Presenting map evidence like this is definitely best done with a map of the two continents, especially as the "jigsaw" evidence relies on them fitting together. If students cut out the two continents, then physically placing them next to each other works well before adding the fossil and other evidence.

There are other places in the world where matching evidence can be found, but these two work well because of the range of types of evidence found between two continents.

4.2.3 Plate Movement

Difficulty to draw: ●●●
Difficulty to explain: ●●●

What Students Should Already Know

- The Earth is made of several layers.
- The outer layer, the lithosphere, is constantly moving and is divided into tectonic plates.
- Some tectonic plates are moving apart, and some subduct beneath others.

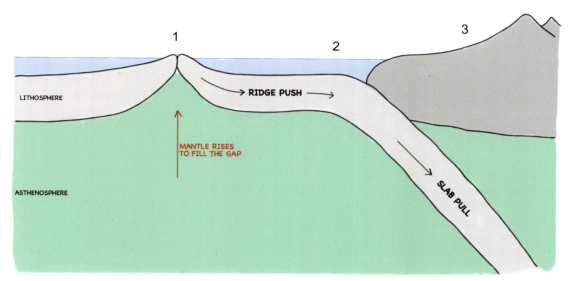

Figure 4.2.3 Plate movement.

1. As plates move apart, they thin, allowing mantle rock below to move upward. The rising rock decompresses and so melts to become magma.
2. The rising magma erupts to create new sea floor. Over time, this moves out and away as it is replaced by newer sea floor. This constant movement pushes the rest of the plate ahead of it.
3. As a tectonic plate subducts down into the mantle, it drags the rest of the plate behind it.

The Explanation

One of the most common misconceptions in geography is that the mantle is liquid and that tectonic plates float on top, moving along because of rising convection currents of molten magma. Unfortunately, the misconception is easier to explain than the reality!

It may be preferable to teach what happens at each type of plate boundary before explaining these processes, because this diagram shows how some plates move apart and some are subducted beneath others.

Fundamentally, the actual movements of slab pull and ridge push are not difficult to understand for students. It becomes trickier when explaining the concepts of decompressional melting and the formation of the ocean ridge. As discussed on page 18, there are often times when you need to judge the level of detail appropriate for your class. In this instance, keep the two processes simple and perhaps use analogies to help the explanation.

74   *Plate Tectonics*

Plate Movement Analogies

Ridge push happens when two plates are moving away from each other at a divergent plate margin. Newly created lithosphere pushes the older lithosphere ahead of it.

Imagine a tightly packed single-file queue of people waiting to get into the lunch hall. As another person joins the back of the queue, they push the rest of the queue ahead of them. The person at the front ends up getting pushed into the hall.

Slab pull happens when a subducting plate sinks deep into the mantle. The older, colder slab of lithosphere drags the rest of the lithosphere down with it.

Imagine the same queue of people from before. Now they are actually queuing up, waiting to jump out of a plane for a big group skydive. They are all attached together by a safety harness. The first two people jump out of the plane. Everyone else is dragged down with them!

Checking for Understanding
- How does ridge push move tectonic plates?
- How does slab pull move tectonic plates?

4.2.4 Convergent Margins

Difficulty to draw: ● ○ ○
Difficulty to explain: ● ● ○

What Students Should Already Know
- The outer layer, the lithosphere, is constantly moving and is divided into tectonic plates.
- Some of these plates are moving towards each other.

Plate Tectonics 75

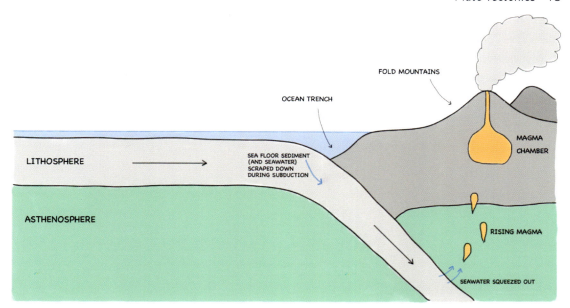

Figure 4.2.4   Convergent margin.

1. Denser oceanic lithosphere subducts beneath continental lithosphere. Seawater is carried down during subduction.
2. Seawater is finally squeezed out into the mantle, which helps melt the mantle into magma.
3. Magma rises through the mantle and collects in a magma chamber.
4. Fold mountains and volcanoes form as the lithosphere is squashed.

The Explanation

Start by drawing the oceanic and continental lithospheres moving towards each other. The oceanic lithosphere is denser (about 2.9 g/cm^3) than continental lithosphere (2.7 g/cm^3) so is forced down. Add the ocean and explain that seawater is carried within sediment from the seabed that is scraped down during subduction. Incidentally, the amount of water in magma is one factor in determining how explosive the volcano can be.

At depth, temperature and pressure increase, which squeezes out the seawater. In turn, the ejected seawater lowers the boiling point of the surrounding mantle rock, turning the "wet" bits into molten magma. The magma slowly rises up through the mantle, often collecting in a magma chamber. If pressure builds enough within the chamber, then the magma is forced up and out as a volcanic eruption. Some magma chambers may develop underground but simply cool and solidify.

Volcanoes are often found amongst fold mountains, which are created when the huge pressures force the lithosphere to buckle and fold. Evidence of the folding can often be seen in exposed rock faces as anticlines and synclines (see Figure 3.5).

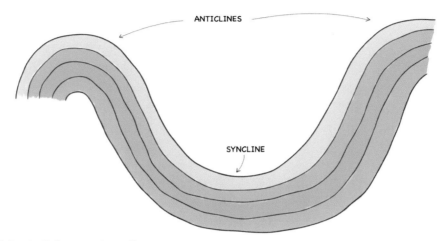

Figure 4.2.5 Anticlines and synclines.

Fold Mountains

Layers of sediment, originally laid down in horizontal bands, can be squashed together to buckle and fold. These produce telltale anticlines and synclines. Laying out a thick folded towel on a table and squashing it together produces a good analogous effect.

How Much Detail?

Plate tectonics is a very good example of a tension that exists whilst teaching many aspects of physical geography. The complex nature of the science makes deciding how much detail to include in a Key Stage 3 or 4 lesson very challenging. On the one hand, you don't want to overcomplicate an explanation with undergraduate-level geophysics, but equally, you don't want to teach incorrect information. Therefore, it can be a good idea to let students know that the mechanisms behind the processes they are learning about are actually very difficult to understand, and so you don't want to overcomplicate the lesson.

If you get the basics right at Key Stage 3, for example, then when you come to explain processes like decompressional melting at Key Stage 5, you build on their understanding rather than having to replace their previous knowledge.

Case Studies

27.5437, 53.0774 Fars Province, Iran (fold mountains)
− 20.7372, -71.3068 Atacama Trench, Chile (ocean trench)

Checking for Understanding

- Why does oceanic lithosphere subduct beneath continental lithosphere?
- What role does seawater play in the melting of the mantle?
- How do volcanoes form?

4.2.5 Divergent Margins

Difficulty to draw: ●
Difficulty to explain: ●●

What Students Should Already Know

- The outer layer, the lithosphere, is constantly moving and is divided into tectonic plates.
- Some of these plates are moving away from each other.

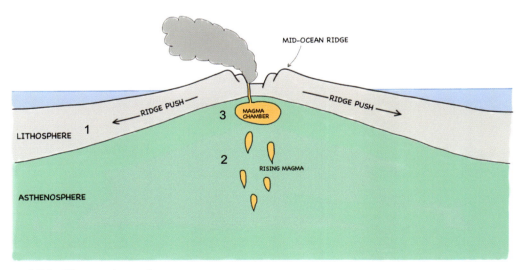

Figure 4.2.6 Divergent margin.

1. Two oceanic plates move away from each other.
2. The plates become stretched and thinner, which makes room for mantle rock to expand into. As the mantle rises, it pushes the lithosphere up to form a ridge.
3. The rising of the mantle leads to decompressional melting, and magma forms, which lead to shield volcanoes.

The Explanation

This is another formation that can be oversimplified and taught incorrectly. The standard explanation is that convection currents pull the plates apart and magma rises through the gap to form volcanoes, which occur in a long line as a mid-ocean ridge. The reality is more complex but can be chunked into a manageable sequence. It is the idea of decompressional melting that is probably the hardest part, and so you will need to judge whether it is suitable including it for your class.

When drawing the two tectonic plates, try to avoid drawing just a gap between them that is then filled by rising magma. Draw steps down into a central valley, where sections "drop" down as the plates diverge. Volcanoes tend to emerge through faults that are created as the plates are stretched and pulled apart so do not need to necessarily be central.

The "ridge push" labels on the diverging plates could be replaced with "oceanic plates" to make the diagram simpler, as the concept of ridge push may not yet have been taught.

You may also want to show how rift valleys form. Two diagrams to show a before and after should suffice. If the lithosphere is stretched from both sides, lines of weakness will develop.

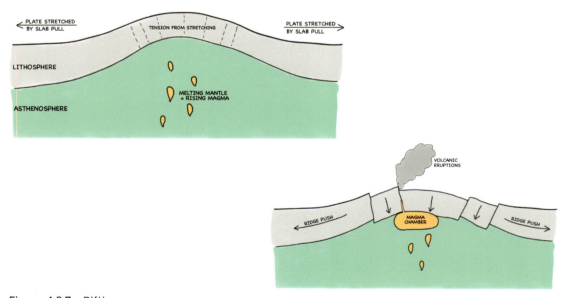

Figure 4.2.7 Rifting

Plate Tectonics 79

With continued stretching, blocks of lithosphere will drop down to create a large rift valley. There is also the potential for volcanoes to form as magma that collects below can rise through the gaps.

Case Studies

64.0701, -18.2375 Lakagígar Volcanoes, Iceland (mid-ocean ridge)
- 20.7372, -71.3068 Atacama Trench, Chile (ocean trench)
9.4256, 40.1828 Awash River Valley, Ethiopia (rift valley)

Checking for Understanding

- What type of lithosphere creates a mid-ocean ridge? Oceanic or continental?
- Why does magma rise at a divergent boundary?
- How does rifting occur?

4.2.6 Conservative Margins

Difficulty to draw: ● ●
Difficulty to explain: ●

What Students Should Already Know

- The outer layer, the lithosphere, is constantly moving and is divided into tectonic plates.
- Some of these plates are sliding past each other.

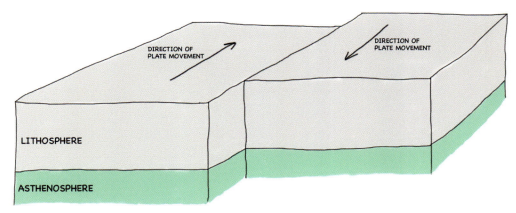

Figure 4.2.8 Transform fault.

1. Two tectonic plates are pushed past each other, or one moves faster than the other in the same direction.
2. There is no subduction, because they are the same density, although the grinding can produce some land deformation.
3. Earthquakes occur because of the friction, but there are no volcanoes.

The Explanation

Although the diagram contains fewer components than the other plate margins, this is often harder to draw because it is a 3D block diagram. Start by drawing the flat tops of the two blocks. Ideally, they are the same size but different positions. This shape, a parallelogram, might need some practice, but being able to draw 3D blocks is a useful skill for several other geographical diagrams, so it is worth mastering!

If the vertical lines are all the same length, then the bottom lines will be easy to complete. Divide the blocks between lithosphere and asthenosphere (or crust and mantle, if that is easier to explain) to help remind students of the processes that lead to the plates moving.

The common earthquake formation diagram is similar to this, as it helps show how friction can build up before being released. You can easily add an earthquake to this diagram.

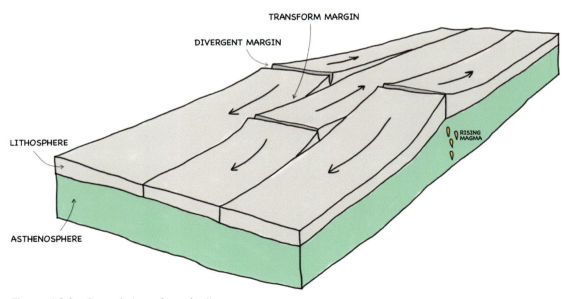

Figure 4.2.9 Oceanic transform faults.

Plate Tectonics 81

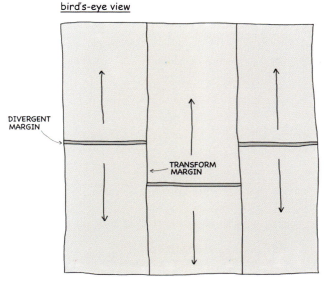

Figure 4.2.10 Oceanic transform faults 2.

Having discussed three types of plate margin, it is perhaps worth explaining that tectonic plates actually have many faults or cracks as they grind around. For example, transform faults are found at divergent margins, where the spreading between two plates is uneven, leading to the mid-ocean ridge being a series of staggered ridges with transform faults between them. Be warned that the 3D diagram is very difficult to draw neatly as part of an explanation!

Case Studies

35.1033, -119.6343 San Andreas Fault, USA (conservative margin)
-7.1574, -12.3940 South Atlantic Ocean (transform faults)

Checking for Understanding
- How are the plates moving at a conservative plate margin?
- Why is there no subduction?
- Why are earthquakes common?
- Why do transform faults happen at divergent plate margins?

4.2.7 Hotspots

Difficulty to draw: ● ●
Difficulty to explain: ● ●

What Students Should Already Know

- The outer layer, the lithosphere, is constantly moving and is divided into tectonic plates.
- All the plates are moving.
- Molten mantle becomes magma, and this rises towards the surface.

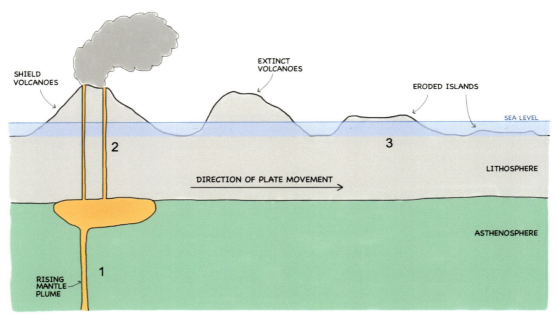

Figure 4.2.11 Hotspot.

1. At hotspot locations, a plume of hot mantle rock rises to the lithosphere.
2. It passes through the lithosphere and forms shield volcanoes.
3. Although the plume is stationary, the lithosphere keeps moving above it. Once past the plume, volcanic islands start to erode and shrink.

The Explanation

There is still much that is not fully understood about hotspots, so it is worth accepting that there may be some questions that you simply cannot answer in class! For example, the causes and nature of mantle plumes are still a subject of debate.

The diagram should start with the layers of lithosphere and asthenosphere, with a plume that rises and expands as the magma collects at the lithosphere. Note that the magma

Plate Tectonics 83

chamber is stretched in the direction of plate movement. Volcanic islands above the mantle plume should be large enough so that the older islands can progressively decrease in size.

Hotspot Analogy

Hotspots are rising plumes of heat from one particular location. As the lithosphere moves over it, the heat punctures through the lithosphere, creating a line of volcanic islands.

Ask a student to tightly hold a horizontal piece of paper. That represents the lithosphere. Hold a pencil vertically below, pointing up. That is the rising plume of heat. Keeping the pencil still, slowly have the paper move over the pencil. Jab the pencil up to create a "volcano" through the paper. Then have the paper move again and again as you keep jabbing through the paper to create an island arc.

Case Study

20.3677, -156.0818 Hawaiian Islands, USA (chain of hotspot islands)

Checking for Understanding

- What is a mantle plume?
- How does a hotspot island form?
- Why do the islands shrink over time?

4.2.8 Volcano Features

Difficulty to draw: ●
Difficulty to explain: ● ●

What Students Should Already Know

- Magma can build up under the surface of the Earth.
- It can reach the surface in the form of a volcano.

84   Plate Tectonics

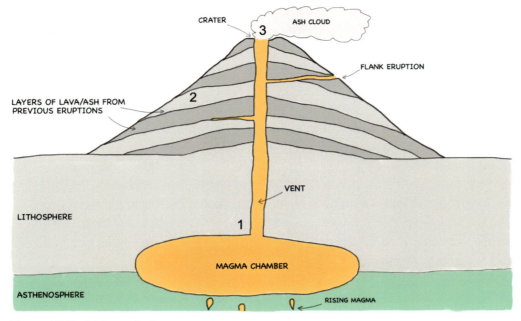

Figure 4.2.12   Volcano features.

1. Magma reaches the surface through the main vent.
2. Layers of ash and lava from previous eruptions build up to form the volcano.
3. A crater forms where the lava and ash come out.

The Explanation

Draw the lithosphere and asthenosphere first. Remind students about how magma is more buoyant and so will rise and collect in a magma chamber. When pressure builds enough, the magma will be forced to rise. This is often through faults created when the rock is cracked by tectonic plate movement.

Add a small eruption of lava. Explain that this cools the vent plugs with solidified lava until the next eruption. Draw this as either more lava or perhaps an ash explosion. Continue to build the layers until you have a larger volcano. Then you can show how the magma might be forced along other weaknesses within the volcano if the pressure builds again but the main vent has become blocked.

Checking for Understanding
- What does lava travel along to reach the top of the volcano?
- Why are volcanoes often made of different layers?
- How does a flank eruption sometimes happen?

4.2.9 Types of Volcanoes

Difficulty to draw: ●●○
Difficulty to explain: ●●○

> **What Students Should Already Know**
> Magma can build up beneath the surface and erupt as a volcano.

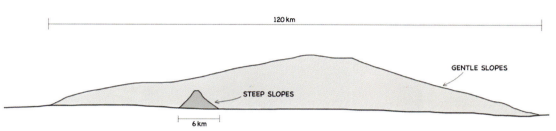

Figure 4.2.13 Comparing shield and stratovolcanoes.

1. A volcano that produces very hot, runny lava will have long, gently sloping sides. These are shield volcanoes and are usually found at divergent margins and hotspots.
2. Volcanoes that produce cooler, stickier (viscous) lava are more explosive and lead to smaller but steeper-sided volcanoes. These are stratovolcanoes and are found at convergent margins.

The Explanation

The two volcano outlines are very simple, but drawn together, they help dispel the common mistake that stratovolcanoes are larger. Adding the relative widths helps students see the differences. The gentle-sloping sides of the shield volcano can be explained by the hotter, runny lava being able to travel much farther until it eventually cools.

The reasons for the different shapes are largely due to how explosive the eruption is. Explosivity is largely determined by the amount of gas trapped within the lava. Thick, "sticky" lava traps gas bubbles which can build up and explode out of the volcano. Runny lava allows gas bubbles to escape, so the eruption is more effusive. This idea should be easy enough to show students using Figures 4.2.16 and 4.2.17.

What is more complicated is the reasons that lava is sticky or runny in the first place. This is down to the silica content. More silica leads to stickier lava. Less silica results in runnier lava. This is shown in Figure 4.2.18.

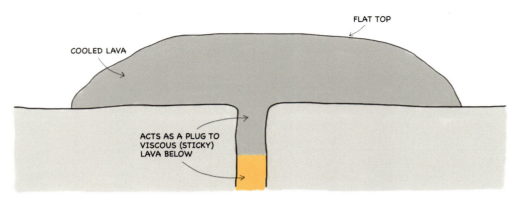

Figure 4.2.14 Lava dome.

Lava domes are a third type of volcano. They form when viscous (sticky, silica-rich) lava erupts. Often, they are one-time events and will only erupt once. The lava slowly emerges and piles up around the vent. As it cools, the outer layer can harden and then shatter, creating slopes of broken lava pieces.

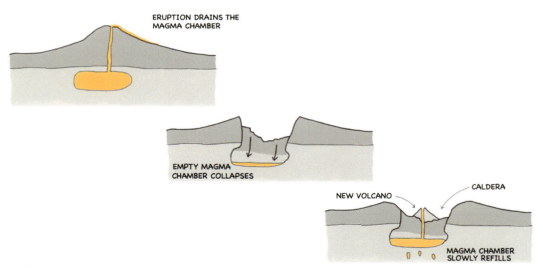

Figure 4.2.15 Caldera.

1. During a volcanic eruption, the magma chamber can empty quite quickly. The unsupported roof of the magma chamber collapses.
2. Over time, the magma chamber may refill, and new volcanoes might appear within the caldera.

Figure 4.3.15 shows a collapse caldera. Another type, the explosive caldera, is created when an eruption is so powerful that it blasts off the bulk of the volcano, leaving an enormous scar of a crater.

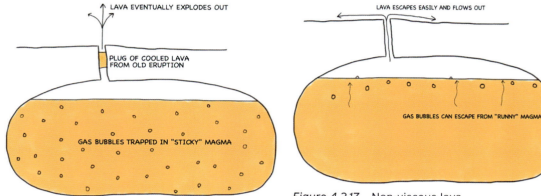

Figure 4.2.16 Viscous lava.

Figure 4.2.17 Non-viscous lava.

These are simple diagrams to show the build-up of gas in sticky, or viscous, lava. Note the plug in the viscous example. If the lava is stickier, then it is more likely to cool and harden in the vent of the volcano. This plug acts like a champagne cork and helps build the pressure. The non-viscous lava plugs less readily, which makes the build-up of pressure less likely.

Lava Plug Analogy

Lava plugs occur when cooled lava from a previous eruption blocks the vent of a volcano. The sheer volume of solid rock will only be removed once pressure has built up enough below.

Imagine an old, crusty tube of toothpaste. Someone has left the lid off, and the toothpaste near the opening has hardened and created a thick plug. To remove it is going to take more pressure than usual from below, but when the plug is finally removed, it will probably be a messy explosion.

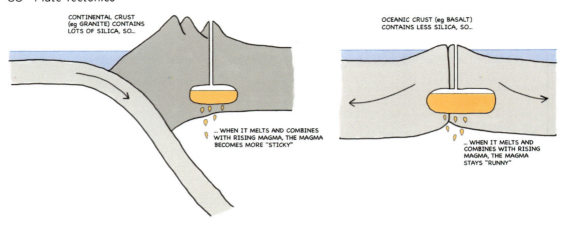

Figure 4.2.18 Silica content.

These diagrams rely on the annotations rather than the actual drawing. They are definitely simplifying the process but should show how magma changes as it rises towards the surface. Another factor is the speed at which the magma rises. If it takes a long time to rise through the lithosphere, then it will change more and likely increase the silica content.

Case Studies

64.0701, -18.2375 Lakagígar Volcanoes, Iceland (mid-ocean ridge)
- 20.7372, -71.3068 Atacama Trench, Chile (ocean trench)
37.8203, -122.5002 Marin Headlands, USA (pillow lava)

Checking for Understanding

- What are the two main types of volcanoes?
- How does a caldera form?
- What is viscous lava?
- How does silica content affect the shape of a volcano?

4.2.10 Volcanic Hazards

Difficulty to draw: ●●●
Difficulty to explain: ●●●

What Students Should Already Know

- Snowfall will occur when temperatures are low enough.
- Snow and ice will melt when temperatures are high enough.
- Evaporation and snowfall are part of the hydrological cycle.

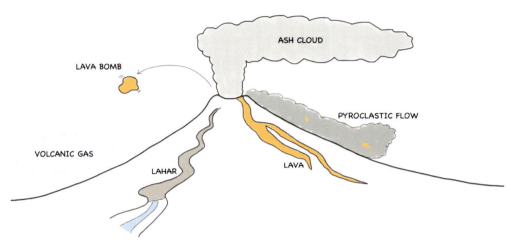

Figure 4.2.19   Volcanic hazards.

Ash is material <2mm in diameter and is created by the explosion of magma. Can cause health issues and affect climate.

Pyroclastic flows are a mix of lava, hot gas, ash, and rock. Can travel at speeds of up to 200km/h. Deadly.

Lava is more of a danger to property than people. Can travel up to 50 km/h. Solidifies into rock when cool.

Lahars occur when volcanic material mixes with water and travels rapidly (up to 60 km/h) downslope. Very dangerous.

Lava bombs are pieces of molten lava that cool as they spin through the air. Often blasted from an exploded plug.

Gas that builds up with the magma include sulphur dioxide (corrosive) and hydrogen sulphide (toxic).

The Explanation

This is an easier one to draw and explain, and students tend to enjoy considering the least-worst hazard they would want to experience. Lahars are a type of mud flow and often follow river valleys, where they continue to pick up water and debris. One of the main gases emitted from eruptions is water vapour, and this can condense to form rain and provide the water for the deadly lahars. Other sources of water for lahars include melted glacial ice or a collapsed crater lake.

Figure 4.2.20 shows how a large eruption can produce enough ash to affect global weather patterns if the volcano spews out large quantities of ash whilst the Earth continues to turn.

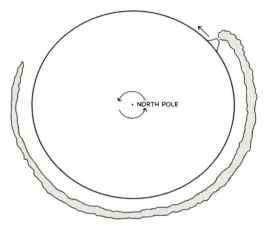

This is a simple-enough diagram to draw, but make sure you know which way the Earth spins on its axis!

Ash particles tend to settle within a few days, but sulphur dioxide can stay in the atmosphere for several years, slowing down incoming solar radiation and causing global cooling.

Figure 4.2.20 Volcanic ash.

Case Studies

46.8442, -121.7578 Mt Rainier, Washington, USA (location of several previous lahars)
19.3165, -155.3628 Kīlauea, Hawaii, USA (lava flows)
50.1076, 6.9263 Strohn, Germany (lava bomb)

Checking for Understanding

- What are six different volcanic hazards?
- Which is the deadliest? Why?
- How can one volcano affect the other side of the world?

4.2.11 Volcanic Explosivity Index

Difficulty to draw: ●○○
Difficulty to explain: ●●○

Plate Tectonics   91

What Students Should Already Know

- Volcanoes erupt when magma is forced to the surface.
- Different volcanic eruptions produce different materials, such lava and ash.
- Some eruptions are more explosive than others.

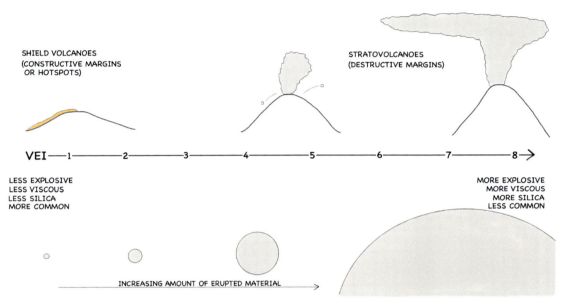

Figure 4.2.21   Volcanic explosivity index.

The Explanation

Start with the central line, with the eight numbers. Each number represents a tenfold increase in the size of the eruption. The scale is based on the amount of material that is ejected and the height of the ash cloud. It is not a perfect system, especially as effusive eruptions like those in Hawaii may produce a large amount of material (lava) but a relatively small ash cloud.

Add the labels at either end about explosivity, viscosity, silica, and occurrence. These can be tailored or omitted according to what has been taught about volcanoes already. Based on these descriptions, you can draw on the three examples of the volcanoes. The amount of erupted material is not drawn to scale but is a useful comparison.

Checking for Understanding

- What is the scale used to measure volcanoes?
- What two factors is it based on?
- Why isn't it a perfect system?

4.2.12 Earthquakes

Difficulty to draw: ●●
Difficulty to explain: ●●

What Students Should Already Know

- The outer layer, the lithosphere, is constantly moving and is divided into tectonic plates.
- These plates are all moving towards, away from, or past each other.

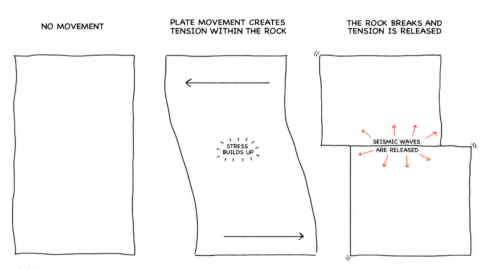

Figure 4.2.22 Earthquakes.

The Explanation

By now students should be familiar enough with the idea of plates rubbing past each other. The friction that builds up and is then subsequently released can be shown using previous diagrams. Commonly, Figure 4.2.8 is used to show why earthquakes occur at transform margins.

Plate Tectonics 93

This diagram aims to show how earthquakes occur after tension builds where rock is subjected to huge pressures, and that this is not always exactly along a plate margin. You can also add a label marked "focus" to show that it is the point of rupture where the earthquake starts.

Earthquakes occur along faults, which are fractures within the rock. Faults are categorised by their angle and the direction of movement. Normal faults result from the blocks of rock being pulled apart, and reverse (or thrust) faults are caused by compression. Where the two blocks slide past each other, it is called a slip-strike fault, and Figure 4.2.8 can be used to show this (but without the reference to lithosphere and asthenosphere).

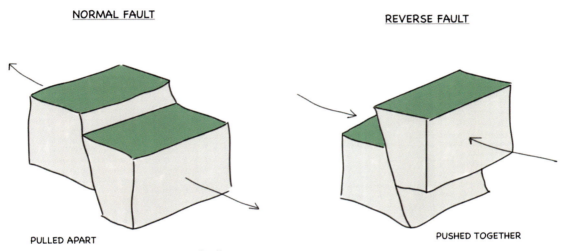

Figure 4.2.23   Normal and reverse faults.

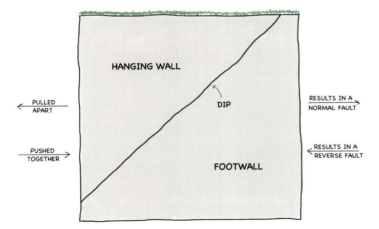

Figure 4.2.24   Hanging wall.

Drawing a dipping fault from the side is another way to show the difference between normal and reverse faults. Note that the arrows correspond with each other on either side.

Earthquake Analogy

Earthquakes occur when huge portions of rock are trying to force their way past each other. Tension builds because they can't just slide past one another. Eventually, they slip past, and seismic waves ripple out from the point where they have suddenly moved.

Ask students if they can click their fingers. Then ask them to do it in slow motion, or at least consider what is happening in slow motion. Thumb and finger are trying to slide past each other but get stuck. Suddenly they can slip past each other, and the tension is released.

Mapping the plate margins and some of the faults found in New Zealand is a good way to show how earthquakes happen at different types of plate margin and along fault lines caused by the constant movement of the plates.

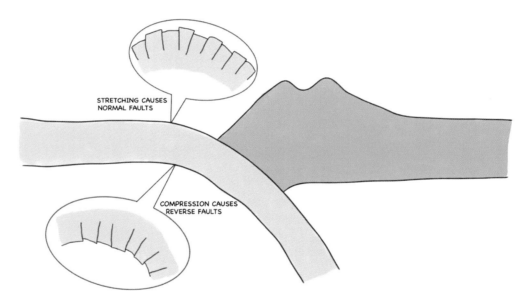

Figure 4.2.25 Faults in the crust.

The many faults found in places like New Zealand are the result of tectonic plates moving together and the immense forces on them causing buckling and folding.

This can be demonstrated by showing students a rubber, and slowly bending it until it reaches breaking point, and small cracks start to appear.

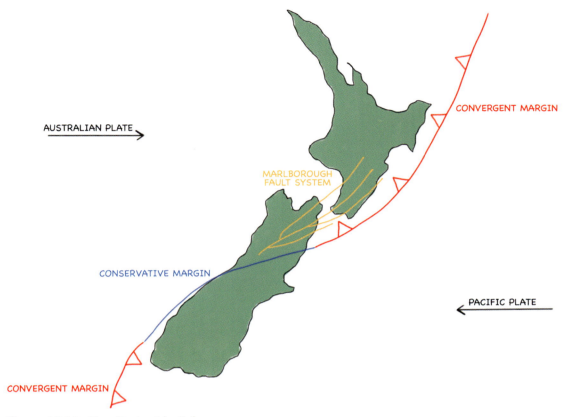

Figure 4.2.26 New Zealand fault lines.

Checking for Understanding

- What causes the tectonic plates to move?
- Explain how it is the release of tension that starts the earthquake.
- What is a fault?
- What is the difference between a normal fault and a reverse fault?

4.2.13 Earthquake Hazards

Difficulty to draw: ●●●
Difficulty to explain: ●●●

What Students Should Already Know

- Earthquakes occur when tension is released after a build-up of friction.
- They occur along faults in the Earth's crust.

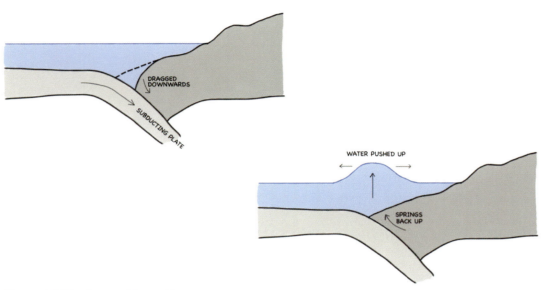

Figure 4.2.27 Tsunami formation.

1. At a subduction zone, the overlying plate is dragged downwards by the subducting plate.
2. Eventually, the plate springs back up. If this occurs under the ocean, water is suddenly forced upwards before it spreads rapidly away in the form of large waves.
3. The waves will travel rapidly across the ocean, at speeds of up to 800 km/h.

The Explanation

Tsunamis occur when large bodies of water are displaced, so the scale of the fault movement is important. Earthquakes of less than magnitude 7.0 generally do not result in a tsunami, because the sea isn't displaced enough from below. The diagrams are the standard subduction zone diagrams, but make sure the first diagram clearly shows the crust being dragged down. A dotted line can be used to show the original position. Figure 4.2.28 shows how the waves bunch together and grow taller as they reach shallow water and are slowed down.

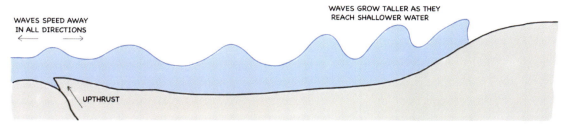

Figure 4.2.28 Tsunami wave.

Liquefaction

If settlements are built on weak or unconsolidated rock, then they may be at risk from liquefaction. The grains within sediments are shaken violently during an earthquake and may lose contact with each other. The rock starts to act like a liquid, and buildings on top can start to sink.

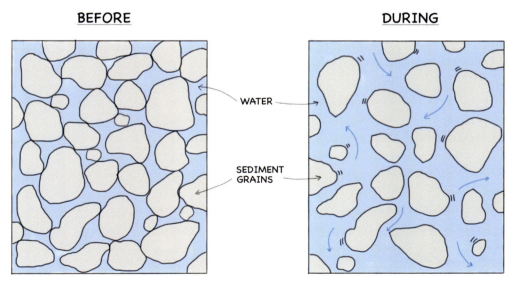

Figure 4.2.29 Liquefaction.

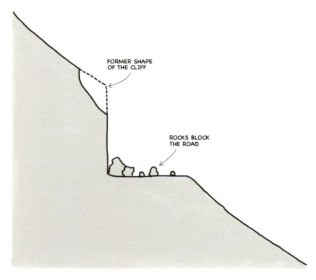

Figure 4.2.30   Rockfall.

Rockfall

The violent shaking of steep, mountainous areas can result in rockfalls, landslides, and mud flows. This diagram shows a rockfall and the potential impact it can have on blocking transport routes, which are needed to provide emergency assistance immediately after an earthquake. Figure 4.4.19 on page 158 shows a landslide, and this can be used, too, as they are also sometimes caused by earthquakes.

Checking for Understanding
- How does a tsunami happen?
- Explain how it is the release of tension that starts the earthquake.
- What is a fault?
- What is the difference between a normal fault and a reverse fault?

4.2.14 Measuring Earthquakes

Difficulty to draw: ● ● ○
Difficulty to explain: ● ● ●

What Students Should Already Know
- Earthquakes occur when tension is released after a build-up of friction.
- They occur along faults in the Earth's crust.

Plate Tectonics 99

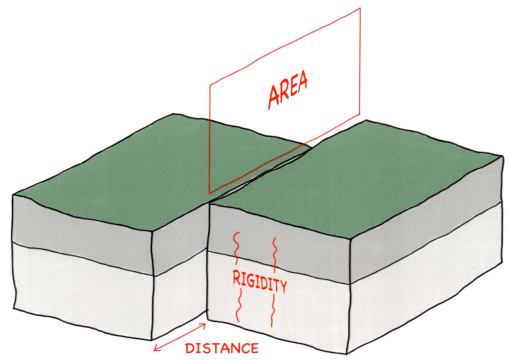

Figure 4.2.31 Moment magnitude scale.

1. Seismologists look at how large the area of the fault is that slipped.
2. They combine this information with the *distance the fault moved* and the *rigidity of the surrounding rock*.
3. Then a formula is used to create the moment magnitude, which is measured on a scale of 1–10.

The Explanation

The diagram is the same as the transform margin shown in Figure 4.2.8. The additions are the three components of the moment magnitude calculation, which can be added on individually during the explanation.

Start with *area*, and remind students about how, when an earthquake happens, there will be a place underground where two masses of rock have suddenly moved past each other. It figures that the larger the two pieces of rock involved, the larger the earthquake. Similarly, the *distance* that they move past each other will also affect the magnitude of the earthquake.

100   *Plate Tectonics*

Both of these factors can be discussed through the "clicking finger analogy" from page 94: a bigger finger and thumb will result in a bigger click. The *rigidity* part might be trickier to understand. Ask students to consider shaking a towel, creating ripples as though shaking the sand out of it. Then ask how different towels made of different materials might be shaken. The different materials will be able to transmit the shaking ripples in different ways. It is the same with different rocks within the crust. Some will produce more shaking than others during an earthquake.

It is the explanation that is the difficult part, because the calculations involved are undergraduate-level geography. Many students will reference the Richter scale for measuring earthquakes. The limitations of the Richter scale, discussed on page 101, are a good way to build up to drawing the moment magnitude scale diagram.

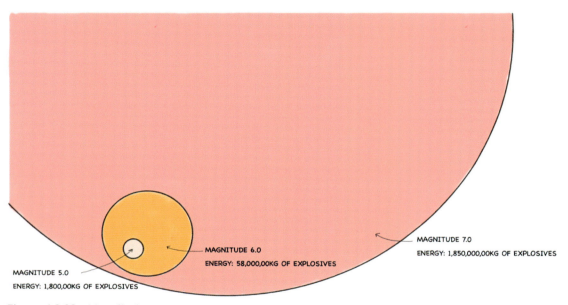

Figure 4.2.32   Magnitude.

Figure 4.2.32 shows a visualisation of the relative energy of different-magnitude earthquakes. Each step along the moment magnitude scale is logarithmic so represents a tenfold increase. This also translates to a roughly 32-fold increase in the energy released. The proportional balls shown in the diagram are not perfectly to scale, but they do show that there is a huge difference between the different points on the scale.

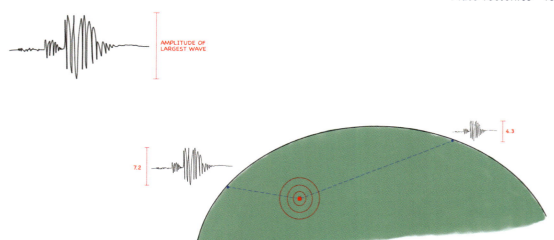

Figure 4.2.33   Richter scale.

The Richter scale just measures the amplitude of the largest wave recorded on a seismometer. However, for larger earthquakes, this is too simplistic.

Figure 4.2.33 shows how two seismometers will record different amplitudes for the same earthquake, depending on the distance.

However, the USGS does still use amplitude of wave (i.e. Richter scale) for <3.5-magnitude quakes.

Checking for Understanding
- How are smaller earthquakes measured?
- What three factors are combined to create the moment magnitude?
- How many times more energy is released after each point on the scale?

4.3 Rivers

4.3.1 Hydrological Cycle   Difficulty to draw: ● ●
                               Difficulty to explain: ● ●

> **What Students Should Already Know**
> - All rivers eventually flow into a sea, lake, or another river.
> - Evaporation is the change of liquid water into a water vapour.
> - Condensation is the change of water vapour into liquid water.

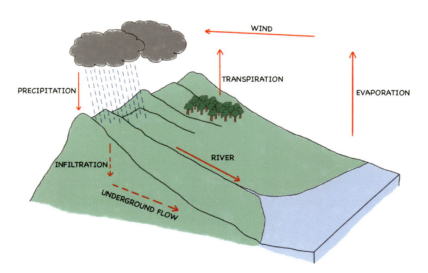

Figure 4.3.1 Hydrological cycle.

1. Water moves from the sea, through the air, onto the land, and then back to the sea.
2. All the movement is caused by either the sun's heat or by gravity.
3. How much water moves and how quickly it moves depend on factors such as the climate, the type of soil, and the shape of the land.

Rivers 103

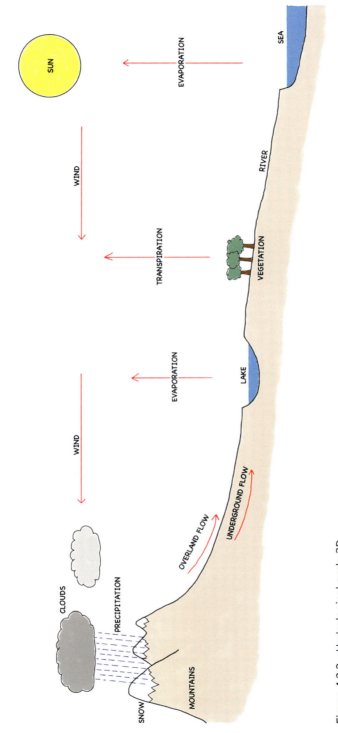

Figure 4.3.2 Hydrological cycle 2D.

The 3D version of the hydrological cycle might be too difficult to draw, so this cross-section profile works well too. This diagram includes both a lake and a sea so could be simplified further by only having the sea.

The Explanation

As an introduction to rivers, discussing the hydrological cycle works well because it shows a "zoomed-out" view of a river and, therefore, where it fits in. Students should be comfortable knowing that a river starts higher up and then runs downhill to the sea. So your drawing should start with the hills, a river, and then the sea. Ask students to think about where the water for the river comes from. Once you agree on rainfall, you can introduce the term *precipitation* and draw on the dark cloud and rain.

Then you can discuss what happens when the rain doesn't land directly in the river. Ask the students to consider what happens if you pour water onto some grass. Where does it go? Explain that some will run over the surface towards the river, and some will soak into the ground. After going through the different ways water can travel towards the sea, finish by connecting the cycle with evaporation, wind, and condensation. Clearly, these are potentially tricky concepts so may well need additional time before you can explain how they fit into the hydrological cycle.

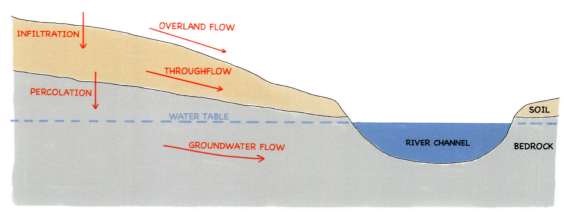

Figure 4.3.3 Groundwater movement.

The hydrological cycle "bigger picture" diagram does not address some of the processes that occur. Zooming in a bit and explaining how the water soaks into the soil and bedrock, and then how it moves down towards the river, can be done using this diagram. Discuss and define the differences between *infiltration* and *percolation*, and then the relative speeds of overland flow, throughflow, and groundwater flow. Emphasise that understanding these processes is really helpful when explaining why some rivers flood more quickly than others. The water table is a dotted line here to show that it is not fixed and will move up or down depending on how much rainwater soaks into the ground.

Rivers 105

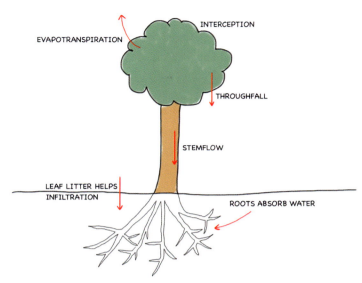

Figure 4.3.4 The role of trees.

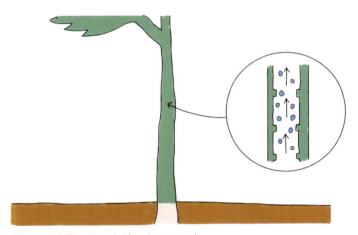

Figure 4.3.5 Vegetation transport.

The role of vegetation is sometimes overlooked in the hydrological cycle, and a simple drawing of a generic tree can help with the explanation of this important element.

It might be worth emphasising how vegetation, or a lack of it, can affect river flooding. Having this diagram is a useful one to refer back to when you cover flooding later.

How a plant transports water is very optional but, if you have time, can be useful. Transpiration can be quite hard to understand for students. The rate at which water is lost from a plant's stomata is related to the surrounding atmosphere's relative humidity. Similarly, different plants lose water at different rates. A succulent plant's thick, waxy coating is why they are well suited to life in a hot desert.

Case Studies

There is no one specific place that can be used to show the cycle, as it occurs everywhere. That said, exploring a river on a map or Google Earth can be a good way to discuss where the different elements might occur.

Checking for Understanding

- What is the hydrological cycle?
- What do these key terms mean: *evaporation, condensation, transpiration, infiltration, percolation, surface run-off, throughflow, groundwater flow*?
- What role do plants play in the hydrological cycle?

4.3.2 Aquifers

Difficulty to draw: ●●○
Difficulty to explain: ●●●

What Students Should Already Know

- Water moves within the hydrological cycle.
- Some water soaks down into underlying bedrock.
- Some rocks can absorb water; some rocks cannot.

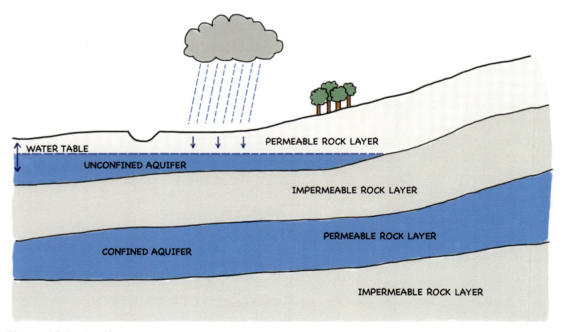

Figure 4.3.6 Aquifers.

The Explanation

This can be a tricky one for students. It might seem odd to consider how some seemingly solid rocks can hold water. There are all sorts of misconceptions about underground lakes and sponges. With this diagram, start by drawing the surface of the land and the rain cloud. Pose the question of what happens to the water when it lands. Having recapped the hydrological cycle, you can discuss what happens to the water that percolates down into the rock layers below. Now, remind students that some rocks are able to absorb water and some cannot. Figure 4.3.7 is a good way to show how a rock's make-up determines its ability to hold water.

Back to the main diagram, draw the different layers and label them as *permeable* or *impermeable*. Show how water that travels down from the surface will do so until it reaches an impermeable layer. Draw the water table as a dotted line, to show that it will move up or down as water is added or removed.

The pressure exerted on confined aquifers by the layers of rock above them means that water can be extracted using a well or borehole. A simple double-line, representing a well, from the surface down to the aquifer can be added to the diagram as part of a discussion about how we extract underground water and how important it is.

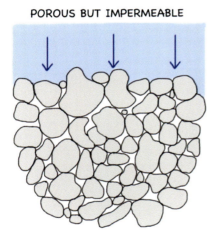 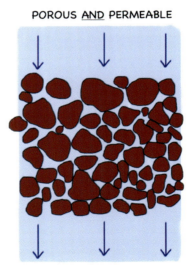

Figure 4.3.7 Porous vs permeable.

Porous or Permeable?

A rock's porosity is the measure of how much water it can hold. The permeability of a rock refers to water's ability to pass through rock. Therefore, a rock can be porous but not permeable if it has lots of pores but they are not connected. Conversely, a rock might contain cracks and joints that allow water to pass through it, but it doesn't have many pores.

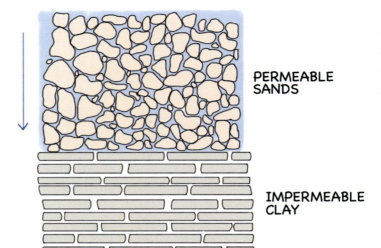

Clay is porous, but because of its layered nature, it does not allow water to pass through. Sand is both porous and permeable, making it a good aquifer.

Figure 4.3.8   Sand vs clay.

Case Study

37.6645, -99.3887 Ogallala Aquifer, Kansas (shows centre pivot irrigation, which relies on underground water extraction; the aquifer is actually enormous and underlies parts of eight US states)

Checking for Understanding

- How does water travel from the surface down into underlying rock?
- What is the difference between a confined aquifer and an unconfined aquifer?
- What does *impermeable* mean?

4.3.3   Drainage Basin

Difficulty to draw: ●●○
Difficulty to explain: ●○○

What Students Should Already Know

- Water moves within the hydrological cycle.
- All rivers eventually flow into a sea, lake, or another river.

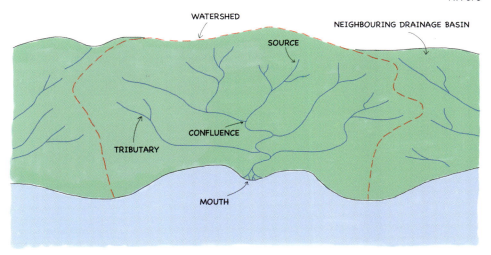

Figure 4.3.9 Drainage basin.

1. All rain falling on the ground that isn't evaporated, or held as ice, will eventually reach a river or stream.
2. The area of land that is drained by a river is called a drainage basin.
3. The edge of each drainage basin is called the watershed.

The Explanation

This is another 3D drawing that can go wrong if you don't practise and can end up looking messy during an explanation! Really, it is a simple drawing that, once you have got the watershed line in the right place, is easy enough to complete. Start with the tops of the hills as the horizon. Part of your explanation should be that the land either side of this drainage basin is going to be other drainage basins so, therefore, drawing hills sloping down either side of your basin is preferable.

Draw the main river channel flowing down into the sea. Then you can discuss what would happen to rain that falls on the surrounding slopes. Add on additional tributaries. If you have got the shape of the hills right, then you can show why the watershed exists where it does (i.e. the top of the hills).

Finally, streams in the neighbouring basins help show how each basin is a contained unit.

Tips and Tricks

Make sure the streams do not start on the actual watershed line, as they need to be fed water from the slopes above before they become streams.

Drainage Patterns

How a network of streams and rivers flows is largely dependent on the geology and topography of the land. Looking at the different patterns can be a good way to practise map skills too.

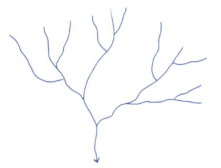

Figure 4.3.10   Dendritic pattern.

Dendritic

Occurs where the river follows the shape of the land and there are not any significant differences in the rock type below.

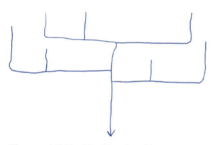

Figure 4.3.11   Trellised pattern.

Trellis

Form often where the underlying rock has been folded to create a number of layers of different hardness.

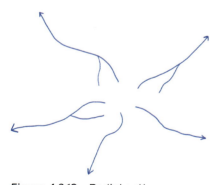

Figure 4.3.12   Radial pattern.

Radial

Develop from a central high point, such as a hill. The streams flow out in all directions.

Rivers 111

Drainage Basin Analogy

A *drainage basin* is the land from which a river drains. All precipitation that lands within a drainage basin will all drain to the same river.

> *Ask students to cup their hands together and imagine there is a river flowing down the middle. All rain that lands within their hands will eventually make its way into that river. Placing two pairs of cupped hands next to each other shows two adjacent basins.*

Case Studies

35.4395, -84.6727 Athens, Tennessee, USA (trellis stream pattern)
-39.2986, 174.0844 Mt. Taranaki, New Zealand (radial stream pattern)
54.3549, -2.4937 Yorkshire Moors, UK (dendritic stream pattern)

Checking for Understanding

- What is a drainage basin?
- What do these key terms mean: *watershed*, *tributary*, *confluence*, *source*, *mouth*?
- What is a dendritic stream pattern?

4.3.4 Long Profile

Difficulty to draw: ● ● ●
Difficulty to explain: ● ● ●

What Students Should Already Know

- All rivers eventually flow into a sea, lake, or another river.
- Some rocks are more resistant (harder) than others.
- A river has more or less energy, depending on how fast it is flowing.

112 *Rivers*

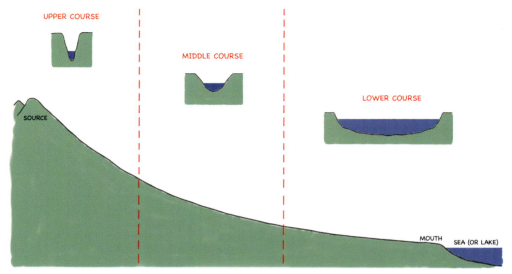

Figure 4.3.13 Long profile.

1. A steeper gradient causes more vertical (downward) erosion. This results in a deep but narrow river valley.
2. As the gradient levels off, more lateral erosion happens, leading to a wider river.
3. A very gentle gradient. Lateral erosion and more water from tributaries lead to a large deep channel.

The Explanation

Exploring the long profile of a river allows students to consider how a river is likely to vary at different points along the course. The main points to note are the difference in gradient from source to mouth, and the naming of the upper, middle, and lower courses.

An additional sketch, Figure 4.3.15, can show how the gradient will change as a river erodes. Emphasise the importance of gradient in determining how much energy a river has. Higher in the upper course, a steeper gradient leads to vertical erosion by downcutting. The lower course has a near-flat gradient, resulting in more lateral erosion.

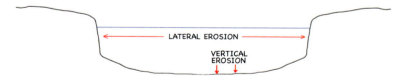

Figure 4.3.14 Lateral vs vertical erosion.

Simple sketch to show the difference between lateral and vertical erosion. This is the sort of diagram that students will find useful to just have in their notes as a reference point.

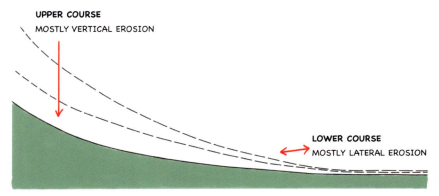

Figure 4.3.15 Changing long profile.

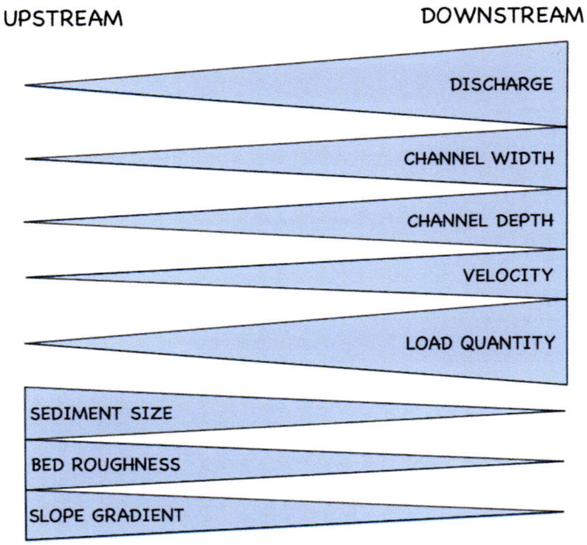

Figure 4.3.16 Bradshaw's model.

Rivers change the land they flow over. Remind students of this with a simple sketch to show what happens to a river's long profile over time. This is an example of encouraging students to think about different timescales. As we focus on processes like erosion and transport, it is easy to only consider these as relatively immediate processes. With all landforms, ask students to predict what the feature might look like in tens or thousands of years.

This is also a good time to discuss other ways that a river might change from source to mouth. Bradshaw's model is a great example of a geographical model that we can use to compare against a real river. Each section of the model can be considered as a hypothesis for how a river might vary. Ideally, this discussion would be part of either fieldwork or map work.

Case Studies

27.5177, 87.1980 Arun River, Nepal (looking downstream provides an excellent view of the changes along a river)

Checking for Understanding

- What are the three stages along the long profile?
- How does the river change from the upper course to the lower course?
- What is vertical erosion?
- What is lateral erosion?

4.3.5 Erosion

Difficulty to draw: ●○○
Difficulty to explain: ●○○

What Students Should Already Know

- The river channel is composed of the riverbanks and river bed.
- Some rocks are more resistant (harder) than others.
- A river has more or less energy, depending on how fast it is flowing.

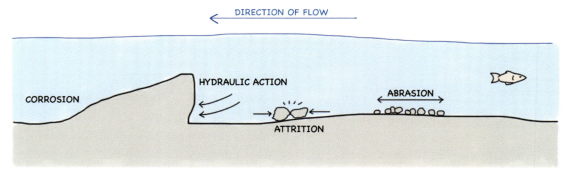

Figure 4.3.17 Types of erosion.

1. Corrosion is the slow dissolving of some minerals found within certain rocks.
2. Hydraulic action is the force of the water acting on the bed and banks of the river.
3. Attrition is the breaking down of rocks in the river as they bash and rub into each other.
4. Abrasion is the wearing away of the bed and banks by the repeated scraping of the river's load.

Rivers 115

The Explanation

Start by asking students to think about what the river bed and banks are made of. Whether the responses are mud or rocks, then you can discuss whether a river could wear it away. Eliciting ideas about the speed of the water or the softness of the riverbanks means you can start to guide the students towards the actual mechanics of how a river could wear the riverbanks away. Look at photos of a river bed, or watch video clips, and ask how those bits of rock came to be there.

A couple of notes for the diagram. Firstly, abrasion is less about individual rocks being flung at a riverbank and more about the "sandpaper effect" of constant rubbing, so try to show that with the double-ended arrow. An addition to the attrition section is to show a sequence of rocks steadily becoming smaller and more rounded over time. Corrosion is often referred to as solution, but the term "solution" is better used for the mode of river transport that carries the dissolved minerals away. Using "solution" is fine, but having the same word for a *river erosion* and *transport* can be confusing.

Erosion Analogies

Abrasion is the river's load scraping away at the river bed and banks.

Consider how sandpaper works. Many individual pieces of sand steadily rubbing back and forth along a surface to make it smoother and worn down.

Attrition is the river's load bashing into itself, making each particle smaller and smoother.

Imagine putting two bricks into a washing machine. They would be smashed around, and little parts would keep breaking off.

Checking for Understanding
- What are the four types of river erosion?
- Why is sandpaper a good analogy for abrasion?
- Why are the rocks in the lower course of the river often smooth and round?

4.3.6 Transport

Difficulty to draw: ● ● ●
Difficulty to explain: ● ● ●

116 *Rivers*

> **What Students Should Already Know**
> - A river erodes and can pick up the eroded material.
> - More energy is needed to carry larger material.
> - A river has more or less energy, depending on how fast it is flowing.

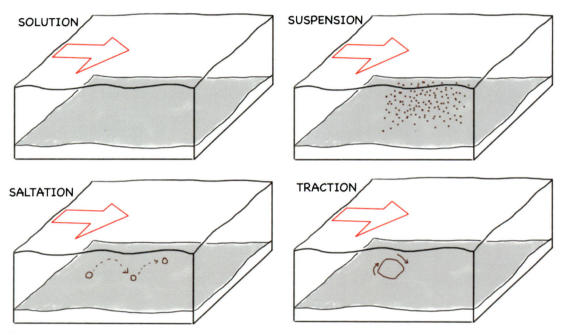

Figure 4.3.18 River transport.

The Explanation

These diagrams are 3D but can easily be drawn 2D. It is a good idea to introduce the key term of load here, and that rivers can carry different amounts and sizes of eroded material, depending on how much energy the river has.

Start with the larger load first, stones and pebbles, and explain how they cannot be picked up but might be slowly rolled along by traction. Rolling like a tractor wheel is one way to remember it! Smaller particles bouncing like salt dropped onto a table is another, albeit tenuous, way of helping remember the term *saltation*. With suspension, ask students to think about why a river might look brown. It isn't actually dirty but is carrying its load in suspension. The final diagram of solution looks incomplete but, of course, needs to show that the process is not visible to the naked eye.

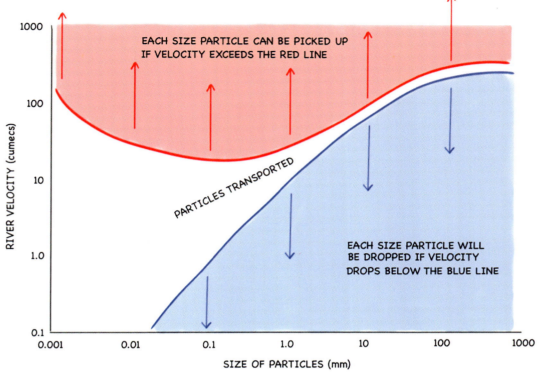

Figure 4.3.19 Hjulström curve.

The Hjulström curve can appear as quite a complex graph, especially as it uses logarithmic scales. However, it can be a good way to show the relationship between erosion, transport, and deposition within a river. It can be simplified by replacing the logarithmic scale with just simple 'increasing velocity' and 'increasing size of particles' along the axes.

Start with the red erosion line. The smallest particles (clay) are sticky and so are actually quite difficult to erode for a river. The line then drops down for sand-sized particles, as they are not sticky and still small enough to be easily picked up by the river current. Then, as expected, larger particles require a higher velocity to be picked up.

Checking for Understanding
- What are the four types of river transport?
- What factor decides how a certain particle is going to be transported?
- What does the Hjulström curve show?

4.3.7 River Flow

Difficulty to draw: ●●○
Difficulty to explain: ●●●

What Students Should Already Know

- Area is calculated by multiplying the length and height of a shape.
- Discharge is the amount of water flowing down a river and generally increases farther downstream.
- Velocity is the speed that the water is moving.

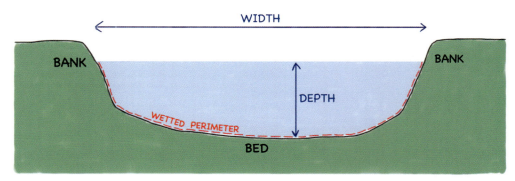

Figure 4.3.20 River cross section.

1. A river's energy is determined by its discharge and its velocity.
2. Discharge increases as tributaries add more water to the river.
3. Velocity is affected by gradient and friction. Friction is less when the river is efficient and has a higher hydraulic radius.
4. Hydraulic radius compares the length of bed and banks with the discharge of the river.

The Explanation

The formula for working out the hydraulic radius (and therefore how efficient the river is) requires students to appreciate how to calculate area, and also to work out the wetted perimeter, which is the length of the river bed and banks that is in contact with the river (i.e. wetted).

The formula for the hydraulic radius is:

$$\text{Hydraulic Radius} = \frac{\text{channel cross-sectional area (depth} \times \text{width)}}{\text{wetted perimeter}}$$

Rivers 119

Knowing the hydraulic radius helps explain when a river is at its most and least efficient. A hydraulic radius below 1 is considered low. The higher the hydraulic radius, the more efficient the river channel is at transporting its load downstream. This is because a higher hydraulic radius means there is more water in the river than is away from the bed and banks, which encourages a faster flow.

This topic can be extended by adding rocks to the river bed of these diagrams. This will increase the wetted perimeter and decrease the cross-sectional area of the river, affecting its efficiency. Upper-course streams that have boulders in and a relatively low discharge can be compared to lower-course, wider channels with only smaller, rounded pebbles.

There are three main ways water flows downstream.

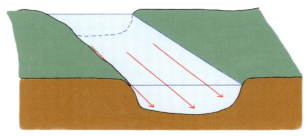

Figure 4.3.21 Laminar flow.

Laminar flow is very rare, perhaps only occurring when floodwater runs over a smooth surface, such as a road.

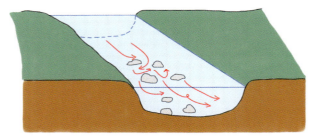

Figure 4.3.22 Turbulent flow.

Turbulent flow occurs because friction with the bed, banks, or rocks causes the water to slow down. Slow water is overtaken by faster water, resulting in a turbulence.

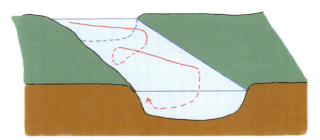

Figure 4.3.23 Helicoidal flow.

Just as water flowing down a plug spirals, water flowing in the fastest part of the river channel can also start to spiral. Helicoidal flow is usually seen when a river meanders, where the fastest flow (the thalweg) is found on the outside of the bend.

Common Misconception

The turbulent water of the upper course is often mistakenly thought of as being the fastest flow. As the following diagram shows, turbulent flow can have a greater maximum velocity due to the steeper gradient, but the constant changing of direction caused by friction and a rough river bed means that a smoother laminar flow would have the greater average velocity.

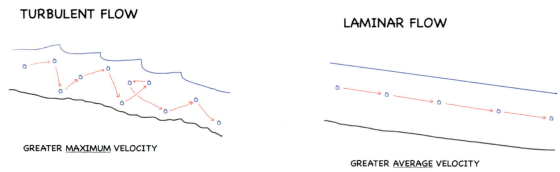

Figure 4.3.24 Average vs maximum.

Checking for Understanding

- What is the wetted perimeter? How do you measure the hydraulic radius?
- What are the three main types of flow?
- Why is velocity greater in the lower course?

4.3.8 Hydrographs

Difficulty to draw: ●●●
Difficulty to explain: ●●●

What Students Should Already Know

- Discharge is the amount of water flowing down a river at a given time.
- Rainfall landing in a drainage basin will eventually make its way down to the river.

Rivers 121

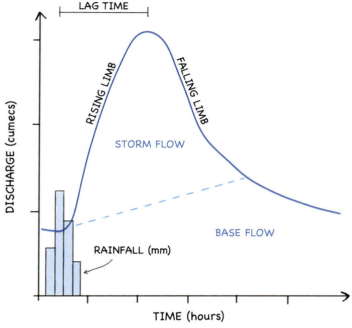

1. Peak rainfall. The worst of the storm, so it indicates how likely a flood is to occur.
2. Rising limb. A steeper line shows a river rising quickly.
3. Peak discharge. The highest water level reached.
4. Lag time. Shorter lag time shows a river that will flood quickly after heavy rainfall.
5. Storm flow. River discharge resulting from the storm. Caused by overland flow and throughflow.

Figure 4.3.25   Hydrograph.

The Explanation

Hydrographs need some context before explaining them. Why are they useful? Why do rivers need to be monitored after heavy rainfall? How much rain is too much rain? Show students images of a river gauge station, ideally one you could locate on Google Earth, so that you can consider what would happen if there was heavy rain over the drainage basin.

Start the drawing of the hydrograph with the x-axis of time. Add on the mini y-axis for rainfall, and add bars for a storm of several hours. Then label the main y-axis as discharge, reminding students about how this is measured with the gauge station. The discharge, as the storm begins, is fairly steady. Show how it will take a few hours before the gauge notices the river discharge increasing, by steadily drawing the rising limb, peaking a few hours later, before descending down again.

Adding the difference between base flow (the normal river level) and the storm flow helps students see how this relates to river flooding.

Factors Affecting Discharge

The discharge of a river is affected by a number of drainage basin characteristics. These factors will affect the shape of a hydrograph. Simple diagrams and hydrographs can show these impacts, and this is a good way to start discussing the factors that lead to some rivers flooding.

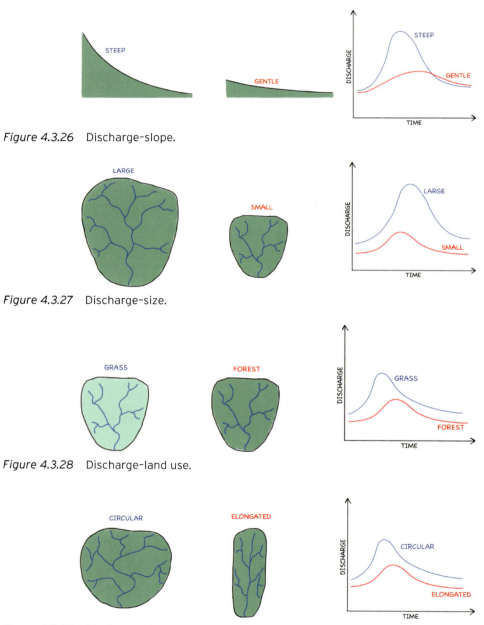

Figure 4.3.26   Discharge-slope.

Figure 4.3.27   Discharge-size.

Figure 4.3.28   Discharge-land use.

Figure 4.3.29   Discharge-shape.

Why Do Some Rivers Flood?

Given that hydrographs are used to show a flood event for a river, this is a good time to consider some of the factors that make a river's hydrograph either look like A (short lag time and high peak discharge) or B (longer lag time and lower peak discharge).

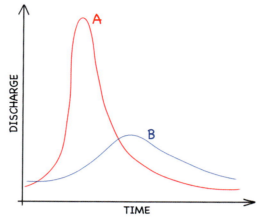

Figure 4.3.30 Comparing hydrographs.

Each simple diagram that follows can be drawn alongside Figure 4.3.30 and annotated to explain why some rivers act like example A and some like example B.

Steep Slopes

The steeper gradient means there is less time for water to infiltrate. The faster overland flow carries water quickly to the river, making a flood more likely.

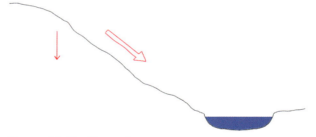

Figure 4.3.31 Steep slope.

Impermeable Surfaces

Concrete or soil compacted by heavy farm machinery prevents infiltration. Rainwater flows quickly over the surface.

Figure 4.3.32 Impermeable surface.

Presence of Vegetation

Plants and trees help prevent flooding. They intercept rainfall, slowing it down. Their roots also increase infiltration. Deforestation, therefore, increases the risk of flooding.

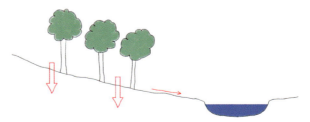

Figure 4.3.33 Vegetation.

Checking for Understanding

- What is discharge? How is it measured?
- What are the following key terms: *rising limb, peak discharge, lag time, falling limb*?
- What drainage basin characteristics can affect the shape of a hydrograph?
- Why are hydrographs useful?

4.3.9 Potholes   Difficulty to draw: ●○○
                    Difficulty to explain: ●●○

What Students Should Already Know

- A river erodes and can pick up the eroded material.
- More energy is needed to carry larger material.
- A river has more or less energy, depending on how fast it is flowing.

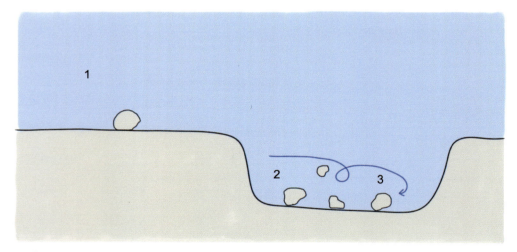

Figure 4.3.34   Potholes.

1. In the upper course, stones and pebbles are transported by traction and saltation.
2. The uneven river bed has dents that trap the stones and pebbles. They scrape the dent, making it deeper.
3. The larger pothole traps more bed load, and abrasion leads to a round pothole forming.

The Explanation

This is a relatively simple feature to explain. If students are comfortable with the ideas of river transport and abrasion, then potholes are straightforward. It is worth noting that potholes are particularly common in the upper course, where the dominant erosion is vertical. The uneven bed load in the upper course causes turbulence that can start the scouring out of a dent in the first place (Figure 4.3.35).

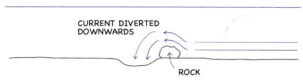

Figure 4.3.35 Vertical erosion.

4.3.10 Rapids and Waterfalls

Difficulty to draw: ●●
Difficulty to explain: ●●

What Students Should Already Know

- Some rocks are more resistant (harder) than others.
- Rivers erode the bed and banks if they have enough energy.
- The upper course is usually steeper and more turbulent.

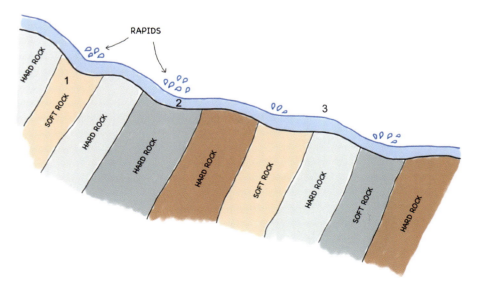

Figure 4.3.36 Rapids.

1. Rapids occur in the steeper upper course of a river, where there are different bands of rock.
2. The softer, less-resistant rock is more easily eroded by processes such as abrasion.
3. The remaining harder rock creates sudden drops in height for the river, which are the rapids.

The Explanation

Remind students about the long profile and what they would expect the upper course to be like (i.e. steeper, rocky, turbulent flow). The key point for rapids is that the underlying rock that makes up the river bed will be made up of different rock types. Having previously learned about erosion, students should know that some rocks are more resistant than others and so will be eroded more quickly.

You can use *softer* or *harder* as the terminology, but *more-* and *less-resistant* would be better. All the rocks underlying a river will be hard, but some may be harder than others!

Teaching rapids links well to waterfalls, so the next discussion point would be for students to consider what might happen if some of the less-resistant rock bands were to continue eroding down. In other words, when does a rapid become a waterfall?

Long Profile Recap

A simple sketch showing the long profile of the river can firstly locate where rapids are likely to occur but then can also be used to show that the underlying bedrock can be made of varying bands of different rock types. These rocks may have been lifted and tilted, resulting in unusual patterns over which the river will have to flow.

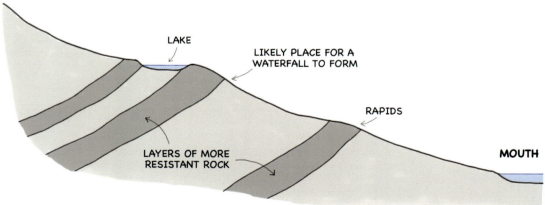

Figure 4.3.37 Long profile bands of rock.

Case Studies

42.7031, -123.9180 Blossom Bar Rapids, Oregon, USA
0.5465, 33.0893 River Nile, Uganda

Checking for Understanding

- Whereabouts do rapids usually occur?
- Why are different rock types important for their formation?
- How do river rapids form?

4.3.11 Waterfalls 1   Difficulty to draw: ● ●
                            Difficulty to explain: ● ●

What Students Should Already Know

- Some rocks are more resistant (harder) than others.
- Rivers erode the bed and banks if they have enough energy.

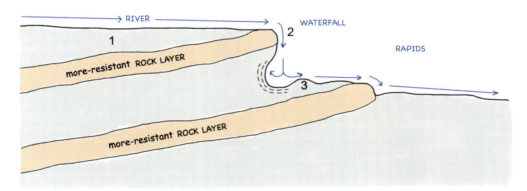

Figure 4.3.38 Cap waterfalls and rapids.

1. Layers of rock that alternate in resistance are eroded at different rates. More resistant rock protrudes as a knickpoint.
2. Water flows over the knickpoint and downwards, eroding the less-resistant rock below.
3. A plunge pool develops which is deepened over time by hydraulic action and abrasion. Over time, the waterfall retreats upstream as the back of the waterfall is eroded further.

128 Rivers

The Explanation

Cap rock waterfalls, as these are known, are the result of differential erosion of the underlying bedrock below the river. As with the explanation of rapids (page 125), more-resistant rock acts as a knickpoint, which leads to a vertical drop in the river. The falling water carves out the softer rock below even further, creating the plunge pool.

As the waterfall retreats farther upstream, a gorge can form, assuming the layers of rock are horizontal. If the climate is relatively arid and there is little weathering of the gorge sides, then it will remain deep and narrow.

Misconception Alert!

These cap rock waterfalls are often the only types taught in schools. This is likely because of their relative simplicity to draw and explain. They are also the standard exam-answer waterfall that are commonly found in almost all textbooks. It is fine to focus on this type but certainly worth highlighting the existence and, indeed, abundance of the other two main types.

4.3.12 Waterfalls 2

Difficulty to draw: ●●●
Difficulty to explain: ●●●

> **What Students Should Already Know**
> - Rivers form part of the hydrological cycle and flow downhill towards a sea, lake, or river.
> - Glaciers flow across the land and create landforms, such as valleys.

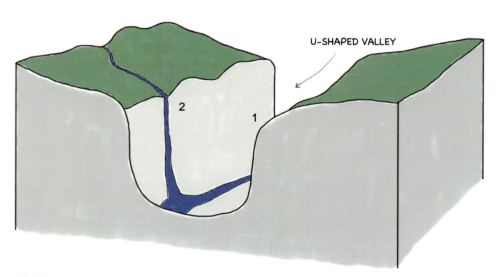

Figure 4.3.39   Hanging waterfall.

1. Over thousands of years, glaciers advance and retreat across the land, carving out large U-shaped valleys.
2. Tributary channels that once led directly to a glacier now flow into the hanging valley.

The Explanation

Hanging valleys may have been covered if you have already taught glaciers. They are probably the most common type of waterfall in the UK but are often overlooked and not taught in schools. If the glacial processes are already understood and students know that retreating glaciers leave behind U-shaped valleys, then the process is relatively simple to explain.

The trickier part is drawing a 3D diagram to show the valley. That said, with a little practise, this is a satisfying diagram to get right. Start by drawing the bottom half of a standard cuboid. The waterfall and river are the last parts to add after you have got the tops of the valleys right.

It might be best explaining it to students using an initial first sketch that shows the glacier in place (Figure 4.7.16 on page 270) before you rub it out, leaving the U-shaped valley.

4.3.13 Waterfalls 3
Difficulty to draw: ●●●
Difficulty to explain: ●●

What Students Should Already Know
- Rivers form part of the hydrological cycle and flow downhill towards a sea, lake, or river.
- Plate movement can create faults and discontinuities in the crust.

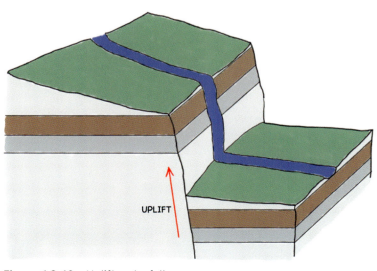

1. Tectonic forces thrust sections of land upwards along a fault line during an earthquake.
2. A river flowing over the fault suddenly has a waterfall that drops over the edge of the fault.
3. Exposed layers of rock show how the two sections of land were once level.

Figure 4.3.40   Uplift waterfall.

130 *Rivers*

The Explanation

This is a difficult one to draw as it is 3D, and it has layers that need to be positioned carefully. Once the layers are added and colour is used to distinguish them, the impact of the uplift is easy to see. Start with the lower portion of the land. This is to highlight that this area is the original position, and that the uplift was vertical and relatively dramatic. Then draw the left-hand, larger side, including the upwards arrow. Add the two layers as you are explaining and show how they help to demonstrate the distance of uplift.

The uplift could be caused by an earthquake that might suddenly thrust the land upwards. It could also be the result of the land more slowly rebounding upwards after a heavy glacier has melted. Uplift of this nature is isostatic and occurred in many areas at the end of the last Ice Age.

Uplift Analogy

Waterfalls can occur when sudden tectonic uplift forces sections of land up above another.

> *Consider two desks or tables next to each other. Imagine a river running over both of them. Suddenly, an earthquake thrusts one of the tables upwards. What happens to the water in the river? A roll of toilet paper can also be used. Likewise, table and toilet paper can be used to show how the waterfalls within a hanging valley form as a glacier retreats.*

Gorges

Gorges are often associated with waterfalls and are commonly found where a waterfall retreats into horizontal layers of rock.

The diagram is 3D so will probably require some practise but really helps give waterfalls and their retreating nature some context.

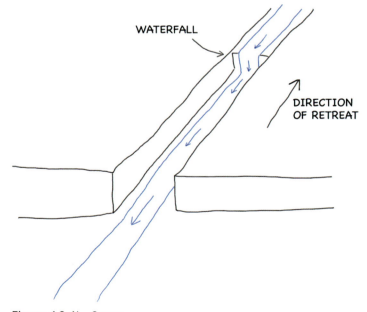

Figure 4.3.41 Gorge.

Case Studies

54.6503, -2.1876 High Force Waterfall, UK (cap rock waterfall and gorge)
0.5465, 33.0893 Yosemite Falls, California, USA (hanging valley waterfall)
63.6155, -19.9886 Seljalandsfoss, Iceland (caused by isostatic uplift)

Checking for Understanding

- What are the three main types of waterfall?
- How can different rock types under a river lead to a waterfall?
- What is a gorge?
- What is a hanging valley?
- How could an earthquake cause a waterfall to form?

4.3.14 Interlocking Spurs

Difficulty to draw: ● ●
Difficulty to explain: ●

What Students Should Already Know

- Some rocks are more resistant (harder) than others.
- Rivers flow downstream from source to mouth.

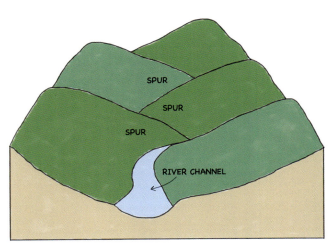

Figure 4.3.42 Interlocking spurs.

132 *Rivers*

A river always takes the path of least resistance down a slope. That means a river tends to go around more-resistant rock. This results in the river having a winding path. The bends around the harder rock become more pronounced as the river erodes the outside bend.

The Explanation

Previous lessons should have covered rocks being different resistance, and students should by now appreciate what the upper course of a river will look like.

Draw the different spurs first, with the river eventually emerging at the bottom. Given that you cannot see all the river in the diagram, you may need to highlight its course around the spurs. The different shades of green are optional and may not be practical, but they help to show the different spurs.

River bends in the upper course can sometimes be misattributed as meanders, so it is worth noting the difference now and when you come to teach about meanders.

> ### Case Study
> 54.3421, -2.5142 Yorkshire Moors, UK (interlocking spurs)

4.3.15 Meanders and Oxbow Lakes

Difficulty to draw: ● ● ○
Difficulty to explain: ● ● ○

> ### What Students Should Already Know
> - A river has more or less energy, depending on how fast it is flowing.
> - Rivers can erode and deposit material.

Rivers 133

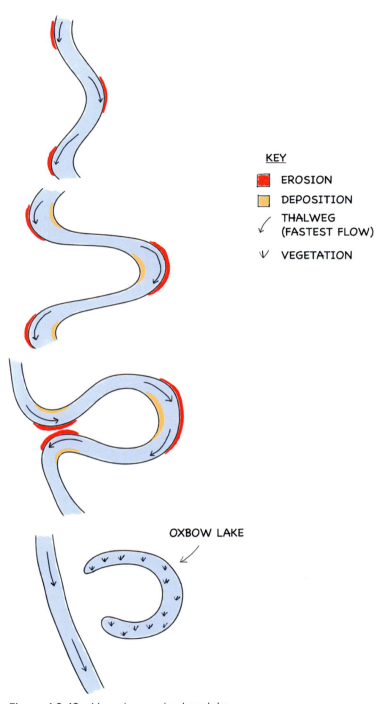

Figure 4.3.43 Meanders and oxbow lake.

1. Turbulent flow prevents a river from flowing straight. Any change in direction results in erosion of the riverbank.

2. The river flows fastest at the outside of bends. This faster water increases erosion there. Slower water on the inside bend causes deposition.

3. Over time, a narrow neck forms between two meanders. Erosion and deposition continue.

4. Eventually, the neck is cut through by the river, creating a shorter path for the river to take. The old meander becomes an oxbow lake that eventually dries up and becomes vegetated.

Meander Cross Sections

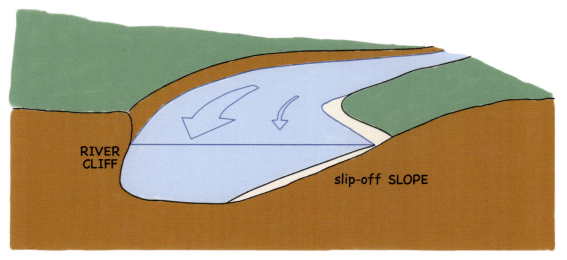

Figure 4.3.44 Meander cross section.

Two of the key features of meanders are their asymmetrical nature and the differences between the outer and inner bends. Therefore, it is worth spending time drawing and annotating a cross section. It can be drawn 3D or 2D. The 3D version has the advantage of being able to draw arrows that show the relative speeds of the current within the meander.

Start by drawing the 2D front of the cross section, ensuring the asymmetrical shape is obvious. Additional labels showing where erosion and deposition occur could also be added.

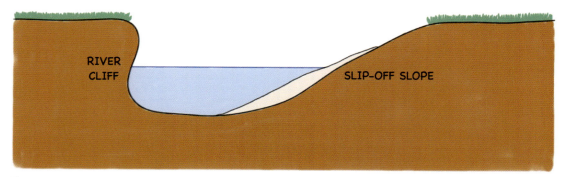

Figure 4.3.45 Meander cross section 2D.

Tips and Tricks

The presence of helicoidal flow within the meander could also be added, but this may just over-complicate the diagram. Helicoidal flow is more than just a corkscrew motion and should show the current at the surface moving to the outer edge, and then descending at the river cliff before moving back up the point bar. It is not easy to draw!

Thalweg

The thalweg is the fastest flow within the river channel. It is useful because it can help show where erosion occurs as a river meanders.

The word *thalweg* comes from the German *thal* (meaning "valley") and *weg* (meaning "way"), so it literally means "valley way." This refers to the idea that it is the deepest part of the river valley, which will have the fastest flow.

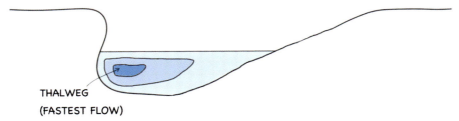

Figure 4.3.46 Meander thalweg.

Pools and Riffles

Although meanders are constantly moving, they do tend to follow certain patterns.

Alternating areas of deep water (pools) and shallower sections (riffles) are caused by erosion and deposition.

The distance between two meanders is usually ten times the width of the channel.

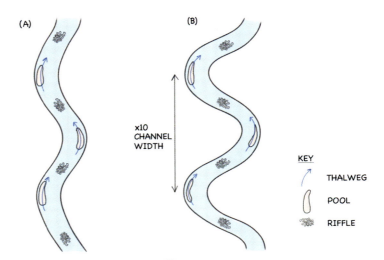

Figure 4.3.47 Pools and riffles.

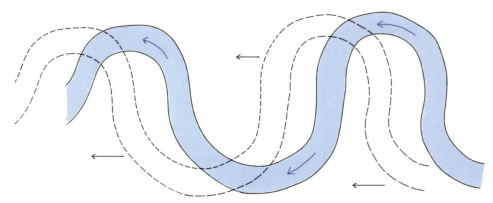

Figure 4.3.48   Meander migration.

Meander Migration

As meanders operate within the relatively soft material of a flood plain, they can move quite quickly.

Drawing a meander alongside a dotted outline of it in a future position helps show this movement.

Case Studies

-3.4413, -67.4805 Jutai River, Brazil (meander migration and oxbow lakes)
52.5212, -3.3995 River Severn, UK (point bar and river cliff)

Checking for Understanding

- What is a *meander*? How does it become an oxbow lake?
- Whereabouts do meanders occur?
- What are pools and riffles?
- Why do meanders have asymmetrical cross sections?

4.3.16 Floodplains and Levees

Difficulty to draw: ● ●
Difficulty to explain: ● ●

What Students Should Already Know

- The lower course of the river is flatter, and the river is wide and deep.
- A flood is when rivers overspill their banks.
- Deposition occurs when rivers lose energy.

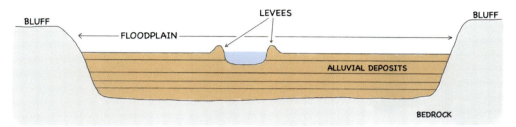

Figure 4.3.49   Floodplain and levees.

1. As rivers repeatedly flood over time, deposition occurs on the surrounding land.
2. Floodwater can only carry large particles a short distance, so these are deposited next to the river, building up as levees.
3. The finest particles, carried in suspension, are deposited furthest, creating flat, fertile land called the floodplain.

The Explanation

The diagram is easy enough, but the explanation can cause some confusion if not delivered carefully. Sequencing of lessons is important for topics such as floodplains because students will need prior knowledge to help construct their understanding.

Start by reminding students where on the long profile floodplains are found. Recap the gentle gradient of the lower course and, assuming you have covered them, discuss the nature of meanders and how and why they are able to shift position over time. The idea being that getting them to appreciate the softer make-up of the floodplain helps to see how they could be formed by repeated flooding and deposition. Other relevant prior knowledge is how a river transports and then deposits material. Heavier material is deposited first; lighter material can be carried in suspension for longer distances.

Case Study

51.8224, 5.5100 Meuse River, Netherlands (notice the land either side of the river is lower)

Checking for Understanding

- Where on the long profile are floodplains usually found?
- How are they formed?
- What are *levees*?
- Why are floodplains usually ideal for farming?

4.3.17 Braided Channels

Difficulty to draw: ● ● ○
Difficulty to explain: ● ● ●

What Students Should Already Know

- Sand and gravel are carried along by saltation and traction.
- Deposition occurs when rivers lose energy.
- A river has more or less energy, depending on how fast it is flowing.

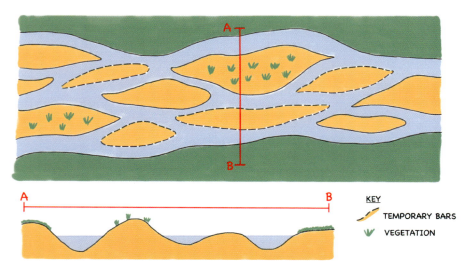

Figure 4.3.50 Braided channel.

1. Some rivers carry lots of material along, such as sand and gravel. It transports it by saltation and traction.
2. If the discharge drops, then the sand is deposited as small islands.
3. Some islands are temporary and can easily be washed away. Some are more permanent and stay long enough for vegetation to grow.

The Explanation

Students need to be confident on discharge, transport, and deposition if they are going to understand how and why braided channels form. It is definitely worth spending time reviewing these before starting the explanation. A good place to start with the explanation of braided channels is how sand is carried and then dropped by a river. For example:

How can a river carry material? It has a high-enough discharge and enough energy.
How does a river transport sand? Saltation and traction.
Why does a river lose energy? The discharge decreases.
What happens if the river loses energy? It will deposit the sand.
What would that look like? Little piles of sand would form on the river bed.
We can also distinguish braided rivers from other rivers, such as meandering rivers, by the steeper gradient, whereas meandering rivers tend to have more gently dipping slopes.

Although braided channels could also be made up of gravel and other material, sand is probably the one that is most relevant to students. If you have any sand, then putting it in a tray and showing it can easily be shifted by pouring water over it can help.

For the diagram, draw the main channel first, then add the islands. Drawing some as dotted lines distinguishes the temporary from permanent. Sandbars that are larger, and therefore less likely to be washed away, are more likely to have plants settling and growing. The roots of the plants, however small, can help hold the sand in place, which then helps more sand that is being transported along.

Other points to note in your explanation are that braided channels usually form along steeper gradients than meanders, and that braided channels require a variable discharge to encourage the regular deposition of material. This is why braiding often occurs along rivers that are fed by seasonal glaciers or snowmelt.

Like meanders, braided channels are always shifting; however, they are very mobile, and the islands' size and location will change far more quickly than meanders.

Case Study

-43.3026, 171.9685 Waimakariri River, New Zealand (fed by snowmelt and glacial run-off)

Checking for Understanding

- Where on the long profile are braided channels usually found?
- What are they made of?
- Why are some islands temporary and some more permanent?

4.3.18 Deltas

Difficulty to draw: ●●○
Difficulty to explain: ●●●

What Students Should Already Know

- Deposition occurs when rivers lose energy.
- Rivers can transport different-size particles, depending on how much energy the river has.
- Rivers flow downhill from source to mouth.
- Many rivers eventually flow into a sea or lake.

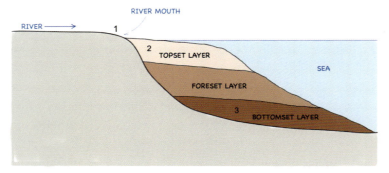

Figure 4.3.51 Delta cross section.

1. At the river mouth, the rapid drop in velocity leads to deposition.
2. The heaviest particles are deposited nearest the mouth, in the topset beds.
3. The finest particles are able to be carried the furthest. They form the bottomset beds.

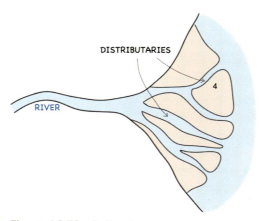

Figure 4.3.52 Delta plan.

4. Deposition blocks the channel, which splits into several smaller distributaries.

The Explanation

It is worth drawing two diagrams for deltas: cross section and plan view. The plan view is the most familiar and can be compared to various real-life examples, but the cross-section diagram can seem confusing.

Start by reminding students about the long profile and asking students what they think happens when the river reaches the sea. What will the river be carrying by then? What happens to the velocity of the river?

Next, draw the river, noting the location of the mouth, and then draw an exaggerated drop when it reaches the sea. Draw on the three layers. Ask students to think about when a river deposits different-sized materials. As the river reaches the relatively still body of water of the sea, the largest particles drop first, and the finest particles travel furthest. Label on the layers in order.

The plan view of the distributaries can be framed in comparison to braided channels covered previously. In braided channels, discharge drops when snow or glacial meltwater finishes at the end of spring. Compare this to deltas. Why does discharge drop here? What other similarities are there to braided channels?

Figure 4.3.53 Long profile sketch.

Teaching about river features is often best done by starting in the upper course and working downstream. So reminding students of the long profile of the river is a good way to recap what has gone before and is also a useful way of discussing how the river discharge might have changed, as well as asking students to consider what happens when a fast-moving river reaches a relatively stationary body of water.

Case Study

46.2282, 48.4755 Volga Delta, Russia

142　*Rivers*

Checking for Understanding

- Why do rivers slow down when they reach the sea?
- What happens when a river slows down?
- What are the different layers of a delta?
- What are distributaries?

4.4 Coasts

4.4.1 The Coastal Zone   Difficulty to draw: •
   Difficulty to explain: ••

> **What Students Should Already Know**
> - The Earth's surface is made up of land and ocean.
> - Where the land and sea meet is called "the coast."

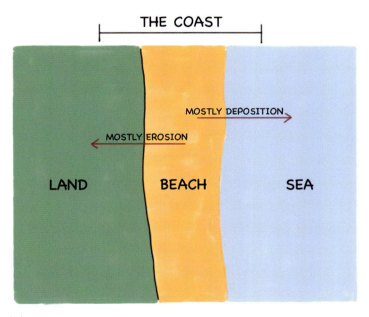

Figure 4.4.1 Coastal zone.

1. The zone where the land and the sea interact and affect each other.
2. If erosion is the main process, the coastline will move inland.
2. If deposition is the main process, the coastline will move out to sea.

144 Coasts

The Explanation

The usual answer to 'what is the coast?' is: "where the land meets the sea." However, it is more complicated, and is the reason we tend to refer to the coast as a zone where the land and sea interact. Over time, that zone might migrate inland if erosion dominates, or it might move out to sea.

A simple diagram, like Figure 4.4.1, can be drawn by teacher and students with an explanation to help define "the coast."

Useful Distinction

Coast or coastline: the narrow zone affected by coastal processes.
Shoreline: the shifting line of contact between the land and sea.

4.4.2 Wave Formation   Difficulty to draw: ●●○
Difficulty to explain: ●●○

> **What Students Should Already Know**
> - Coasts are the dynamic zones where land meets sea.
> - That zone sometimes retreats inland; sometimes it moves out to sea.

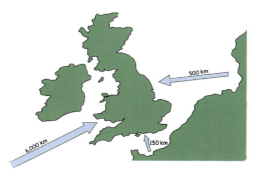

Figure 4.4.2 Fetch.

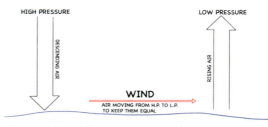

Figure 4.4.3 High pressure and low pressure.

1. Rising air in areas of low pressure is replaced by incoming air from areas of higher pressure.
2. The greater the difference between the low pressure and high pressure, the stronger the wind.
3. The stronger the wind is, and the longer it blows for, then the larger the waves will be.
4. Wind that blows over a longer distance will generate larger waves. The distance the wind blows is the fetch.

The Explanation

The size of waves is determined by three factors:

1) The strength of the wind blowing
2) The duration of the wind
3) The fetch (the distance of open sea over which the wind blows)

Fetch can be illustrated by a simple sketch map of the UK, or any island, with the distances to the nearest land marked around it. In this case, wind that blows from the south-west produces the largest waves because the fetch can be 1000s of kilometres long. Winds from the south tend to produce smaller waves as the wind only blows from France across a shorter distance.

The additional wind diagram shows how wind is simply the movement of air from an area of high pressure to an area of low pressure. You don't need to think about how wind forms to study waves, but it might be a good time to recap the topic.

Tips and Tricks

The fact that it is energy moving forwards and not the water itself can be quite tricky to understand. If any students have bobbed up and down in the sea, they will have experienced wave energy passing them but not actually moving them along.

Case Study

-8.7048, 115.1638 Kuta Beach, Bali, Indonesia (Why is this a popular location for surfers? In which direction does the wind need to blow from to create the largest waves?)

Checking for Understanding

- What is *wind*?
- What are the three factors that determine how powerful waves can be?
- What is *fetch*?

4.4.3 Wave Structure

Difficulty to draw: ● ●
Difficulty to explain: ● ● ●

> **What Students Could Already Know**
> - Wind blows over the sea to create waves.
> - That zone sometimes retreats inland; sometimes it moves out to sea.

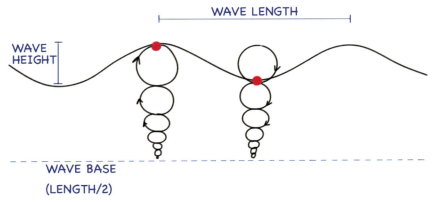

Figure 4.4.4 Wave structure.

1. Wind blows over the surface of the sea and drags along individual water particles.
2. These move in a circle, returning to their original position. They also cause other water particles below to move too.
3. Below a certain point (the wave base), this knock-on effect is no longer felt.
4. Waves are measured by the distance between crest and trough (height) and between two crests (length).

The Explanation

Figure 4.4.4 shows the structure of a wave when it is out in deeper water. The key message is that it is friction from the wind that causes water particles on the surface to move. This friction, plus downward wind pressure, causes the particles to oscillate. Each particle (shown by the red dot) moves forwards on the wave crest and backwards in the wave trough. In this way, the water itself does not move forwards; rather, it is energy that is transmitted forwards through the water. The disturbance at the surface of individual water particles has knock-on effects, hence the decreasingly smaller circles below. The wave base (below which the movement of the waves is not felt) should be half of the wave length. Try to make sure the relative distances are roughly accurate on the diagram.

Wave Motion Analogy

Waves out in the deep sea do not move forwards. Instead, it is the energy that is moving forwards through the water.

> *Imagine a group of students lying down underneath a large carpet or rug. As they all roll along the floor underneath it, the carpet will bob up and down but will also stay still.*

4.4.4 Breaking Waves

Difficulty to draw: ● ●
Difficulty to explain: ● ●

What Students Could Already Know
- Wind blows over the sea to create waves.
- That zone sometimes retreats inland; sometimes it moves out to sea.

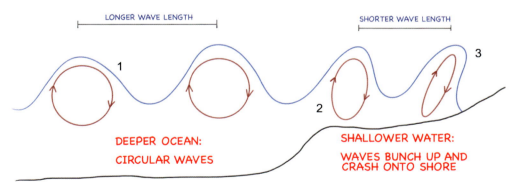

Figure 4.4.5 Breaking waves.

1. In deeper water, a wave's orbit is circular.
2. On reaching shallow water, waves drag on the bottom and bunch together.
3. As the bottom of the wave slows down, the top of the wave topples forwards, and it crashes onto the shore.

The Explanation

Whilst out in deep water, the smooth orbital motion continues. Waves generated by wind can travel for great distances across oceans in long straight lines. These are called swell waves and can maintain most of their energy. When waves reach shallow water, the orbital motion is disrupted by the seabed. The waves drag along the bottom, slow down, and the wave length decreases. The waves bunch together, the wave height increases, and the wave topples over as it breaks onto the shore.

Useful Key Terms

- Storm waves: waves that are generated by a local storm.
- Swell: waves generated far away that can be seen as undulations as they travel across oceans.

Constructive vs Destructive Waves

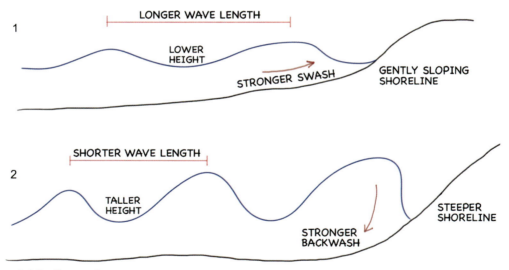

Figure 4.4.6 Types of waves.

1. Constructive Waves
   Longer wave length, lower wave height, arrive to shore less frequently, move material onto the shore (swash > backwash).
2. Destructive Waves
   Shorter wave length, higher wave height, arrive to shore more frequently, move material off the shore (backwash > swash).

The Explanation

As the wave breaks, water that rushes up the beach is called the swash. The water then returns to the sea as backwash. The relative strength of the swash and backwash is one of the factors that help shape the coastline. Tall waves that break onto a steep beach generate plenty of down-force, so there is less energy to create a strong swash. They do, however, have a strong-enough backwash to remove material from the beach. These are destructive waves. If a wave is shorter and spills onto a gently sloping beach, its energy is directed up the beach as swash. These are constructive waves, as they carry more material onto the beach than they remove.

Figure 4.4.7 shows how the nature of the beach material can affect what happens to the backwash. A wave breaking onto a compact sandy beach will see relatively little water percolate down into the sand. Therefore, the backwash will be stronger and head back directly to the sea. Conversely, a pebble beach, with the larger spaces between the stones, allows a breaking wave to percolate. This reduces the power of the backwash, making the wave less destructive.

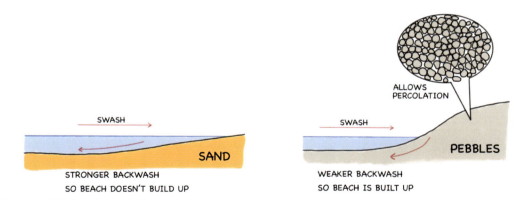

Figure 4.4.7 Sand vs pebbles.

Misconception Alert

It is often thought that a coast will either have destructive or constructive waves. In reality, a coastline usually experiences both constructive and destructive processes at varying times of the year. For example, during a typical summer, a beach may build up due to calmer weather conditions that make deposition favourable (constructive waves). Winter storms later in the year would not only produce larger waves but would also have the summer's beach to erode (destructive waves). That sediment is removed from the beach but likely just deposited offshore, perhaps as a bar. The following summer, that sediment may be returned onto the beach. So it is a combination of weather conditions and the availability of sediment that makes waves either construct or erode. The point being that it is not so simple to just say a coast has either destructive or constructive waves. The wave sizes of the summer and winter months may actually be quite similar, but if there is more or less beach sediment available, then those similar-sized waves will be considered either constructive or destructive. It is the waves and beach constantly working to find an equilibrium.

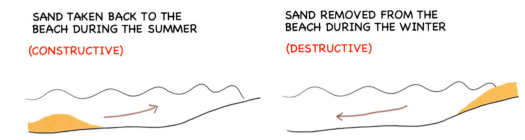

Figure 4.4.8   Summer vs winter.

Case Studies

21.5827, -158.145 Northern Oahu, Hawaii (Why are the waves so good for surfing?)
-4.0011, 39.7380 Mombasa, Kenya (There is a coral reef that runs parallel to the coast. The large ocean waves break at the reef, meaning, that by the time they arrive at the shore, they have less energy and are constructive in nature. Much of the beach is made up of coral fragments that are broken off by the larger waves and then deposited because the waves have lost their energy. Only during the largest storms do big waves bypass the reef and have an erosive effect on the coast.)

Checking for Understanding
- What are the three factors that determine the size of waves?
- How is energy transmitted by waves?
- What happens when a wave breaks?
- Why are some waves destructive and some constructive?

4.4.5 Tides

Difficulty to draw: ● ● ●
Difficulty to explain: ● ● ●

What Students Could Already Know

- Wind blows over the sea to create waves.
- That zone sometimes retreats inland; sometimes it moves out to sea.

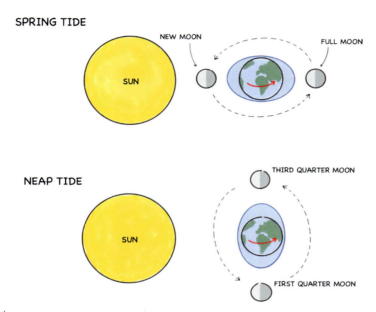

Figure 4.4.9 Tides.

The Explanation

The moon and, to a lesser extent, the sun exert a gravitational pull onto the surface of the Earth as it rotates. This effectively pulls all the oceans and seas towards the moon whilst the Earth rotates underneath. The tricky part is explaining why there are two bulges. The first bulge is clearly because the water is attracted to the moon. The second bulge, on the other side of the Earth, is to do with how the Earth is also affected by the moon's gravitational pull. The shape of the Earth is squeezed and squashed, which results in there being another bulge on the other side.

The diagram shows the two extremes of the tides. The spring tide has the largest tidal range (the difference between high and low tide), because the moon and sun are aligned and pulling together. During a neap tide, the moon and sun are at right angles and counteract each other.

Whilst explaining it, draw the two versions but take each position of the moon in turn (new moon, first quarter moon, full moon, third quarter moon).

152 Coasts

4.4.6 Marine Erosion

Difficulty to draw: ●○○
Difficulty to explain: ●●○

What Students Could Already Know

- Waves break onto the coast. Some waves carry more energy than others.
- All coasts are different and will be affected by waves in different ways.
- Some rocks are more resistant than others.

Abrasion/Corrasion

1. Waves hurl sand, pebbles, and boulders against the base of the cliff.
2. Repeated wave movement also causes the same material to rub like sandpaper on the seabed.

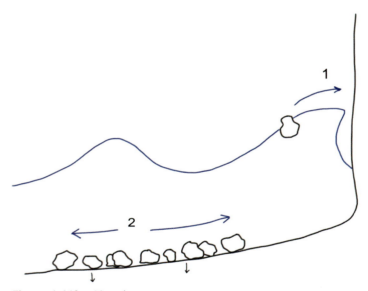

Figure 4.4.10 Abrasion.

The Explanation

Abrasion, also known as corrasion, is the most effective type of marine erosion. However, it does depend on the nature of the cliff. More-resistant cliffs will erode more slowly than softer rocks. However, a more-resistant cliff may also provide more eroded pebbles and boulders that can be used during the abrasion process. If there are different layers of hard and soft rock, then the softer layers will erode back to form caves at sea level. Arrows should be added to the diagram to help show the relevant movements.

Hydraulic Action

1. Water thrown against the cliff is forced into cracks, where it traps and compresses air bubbles.
2. When the water retreats and the pressure is released, the air expands and can explode, which, over time, can cause stresses and more cracks to occur.

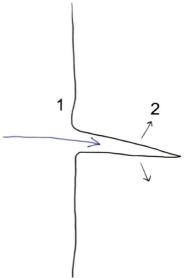

The Explanation

It is both the force of the water and the "air explosions" that erode the rock. The force of a large wave can be up to 50 kg/cm². It is also sometimes called wave quarrying.

Figure 4.4.11 Hydraulic action.

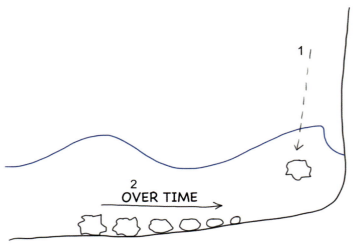

Attrition

1. Pebbles and boulders that have been eroded fall to the base of the cliff.
2. Repeated wave action bashes them into each other. Over time, they become smaller and more rounded.

Figure 4.4.12 Attrition.

The Explanation

As eroded material is hurled against the shore and each other, they are constantly chipped away and rounded to form the smooth pebbles found on many beaches. This type of erosion is different from the others in that it does not affect the actual coastline.

Corrosion

1. Usually occurs where water collects as pools on ledges.
2. There needs to be a local source of acidity. This could be from limpets, or sewage run-off.
3. Most common on cliffs that are rich in calcium carbonate, such as limestone.

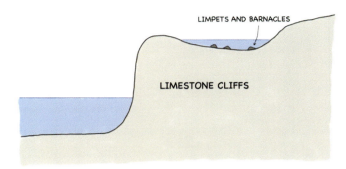

Figure 4.4.13   Corrosion.

The Explanation

A common misconception is to name the fourth type of erosion as "solution" and to describe how "certain minerals within rocks are dissolved by acids within the seawater." Seawater is not naturally acidic, and not all rocks contain the requisite minerals. Seawater can dissolve certain minerals if there is a local source of acidity, such as factory affluents or sewage run-off. Studies have also shown that limpets and barnacles excrete acids which can erode limestone cliffs. As per the diagram, try to show the water having pooled on a ledge rather than simply splashing onto a cliff face from a wave.

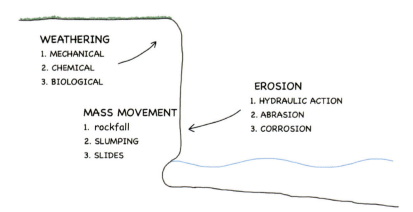

Figure 4.4.14   Weathering vs erosion vs mass movement.

Figure 4.4.14 is a useful way to introduce or remind students that marine erosion almost always works with both weathering and mass movement. The diagram shows the three processes and roughly where they operate. Types of weathering are covered in more detail in "Rocks and Weathering." The types of mass movement can be found on page 156.

Similarly, this diagram can be used to show the various types of marine erosion. It could either simply be used to highlight whereabouts each one occurs or could be developed to include more detailed annotations about each one.

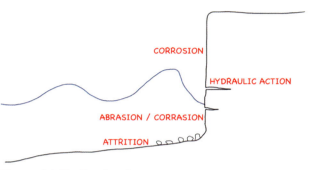

Figure 4.4.15   Erosional processes.

Case Study

50.6122, -2.1369 Kimmeridge Bay, UK (Whereabouts would each type of erosion happen?)

Checking for Understanding

- What does erosion do to a cliff?
- What are the four types of erosion?
- When does corrosion happen?
- Why is attrition different from the others?

4.4.7 Mass Movement

Difficulty to draw: ● ●
Difficulty to explain: ● ●

What Students Should Already Know

- Erosion and weathering act together to weaken and break off pieces of the coast.
- Some rocks are more resistant than others.

Slumping

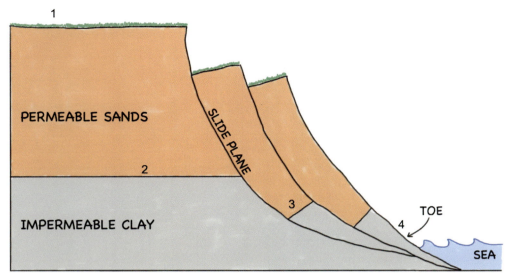

Figure 4.4.16 Slumping.

1. Heavy rain saturates the soil, which adds weight to the cliff.
2. Water slowly moves down into the rocks below until it reaches rock it cannot be absorbed into.
3. When the weight of the cliff is too much, it will slump down.
4. Sea waves erode the base of the cliff, which helps make the cliff unstable.

The Explanation

Slumping is common along coastlines made of softer, less-resistant materials. Rocks that are more permeable absorb rainwater, which adds weight to the slope, as well as providing a lubricant for the movement. Slumping is also known as a rotational slide due to the concave nature of the downwards movement.

Individual portions of the collapsed slope remain relatively undisturbed as the ruptures tend to follow internal weaknesses, such as joints or fractures. The resultant blocks are often tilted inwards, thus collecting rainwater and increasing the likelihood of further failure.

Weathering, such as freeze thaw and carbonation, acts on the cliff face, which will also decrease the sheer strength of the slope.

Figure 4.4.17 shows how water is able to percolate down through some materials but not others, depending on the rock's composition.

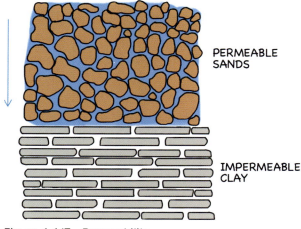

Figure 4.4.17 Permeability.

The diagram might be difficult to draw, but it is a useful addition for students to include if you want them to explain how geology can affect mass movement.

Marine erosion and weathering operate in the coastal zone. Where there are cliffs or any slope down to the sea, there is likely to be some form of mass movement. *Mass movement* can be defined as the downslope movement of material under the influence of gravity. At the coast, we tend to see slumping, slides, and rockfalls. It is primarily the nature of the local geology that determines the type of mass movement. Other factors include the presence of water, vegetation cover, as well as levels of weathering and erosion.

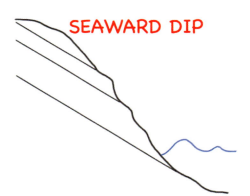 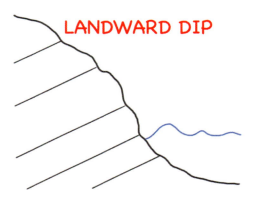

Figure 4.4.18 Seaward vs landward dip.

Figure 4.4.18 shows how some cliffs can be made up of different layers of rock. Tectonic pressures can tilt these layers, resulting in some coasts that are more or less susceptible to different types of mass movement. Layers that dip towards the sea are more likely to slump or slide.

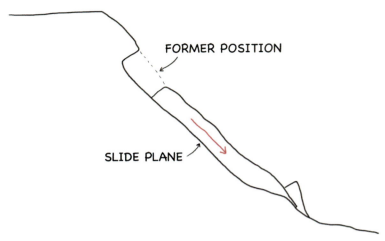

Figure 4.4.19 Slides.

1. Heavy rain saturates the soil, which adds weight to the cliff.
2. A section of soil and/or rock moves downslope along a slide plane.
3. Wave erosion at the base of the cliff helps weaken the cliff.

The Explanation

A slide occurs when one section of soil or rock moves, as a whole, downslope. Most likely to happen if the layers of rock that make up the cliff are all sloping down towards the sea. As with slumps, a slide happens along a slide plane, which is often lubricated after heavy rain, and may be between permeable and impermeable layers of rock.

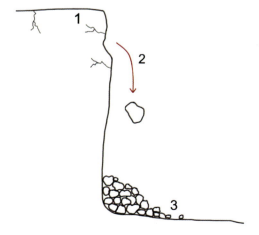

Figure 4.4.20 Rockfall.

Fall

1. Rocks within the cliff are weakened, often by freeze thaw.
2. A mass of rock falls down the cliff.
3. Broken rocks collect at the base as a scree slope.

The Explanation

A very simple diagram to show the steep nature of the cliffs involved. Falls usually occur on exposed rock faces, where joints and cracks are subjected to weathering or erosion. A scree slope (or talus slope) can form at the base, made up of fallen rocks.

Factors Affecting Mass Movement

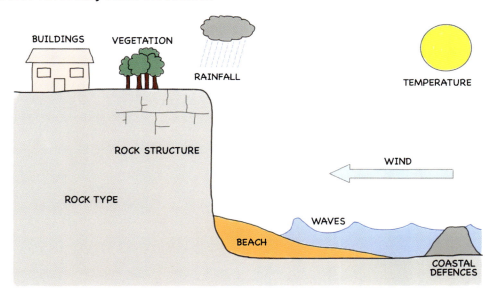

Figure 4.4.21   Factors affecting mass movement.

The different factors that affect coastal mass movement can be shown on one diagram, such as Figure 4.4.21. Note that this is a very generic diagram for all types of mass movement. In reality, the factors that affect a slide might be different to the factors that affect a rockfall.

For this diagram, start with the outline of the cliff. Draw on the waves to show the sea and then start discussing and adding the different factors with the students.

Temperature: will determine the type of weathering on the cliff face.
Rainfall: water lubricates any potential slip planes and can add weight to the cliff.
Vegetation: roots may help bind the soil together, or the roots could help dislodge rocks.
Wind: affects wave size and strength and may also bring certain types of weather.

Waves: larger waves will cause more marine erosion at the base of the cliffs.
Beach: by absorbing the waves' energy, a beach can protect a cliff from marine erosion.
Rock type and structure: some rocks are more easily weathered and eroded than others.
Buildings: they can add weight to the top of a cliff, making it more likely to collapse.
Coastal defences: usually designed to stop the wave from breaking onto a cliff.

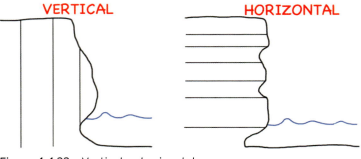

Figure 4.4.22   Vertical vs horizontal.

Figure 4.4.22 shows that rockfalls are more likely to occur when the layers of rock within a cliff are vertically or horizontally aligned.

If horizontal layers of rock erode at different rates, then more resistant layers can be undercut, leading to overhangs.

Case Studies

32.9996, -117.2777 Solana Beach, California (Why does slumping occur here and not rockfall?)

37.8593, 20.6241 Shipwreck Beach, Greece (What evidence is there of erosion and mass movement?)

Checking for Understanding
- What are the three types of mass movement?
- How does a slide happen?
- How do the layers of rock within a cliff affect mass movement?
- What factors can make mass movement more likely?

4.4.8 Transport

Difficulty to draw: ● ○ ○
Difficulty to explain: ● ○ ○

What Students Should Already Know

- Winds are responsible for the direction and strength of waves.
- The swash of a wave can carry material up onto a beach; backwash can remove material from a beach.
- Waves perform three main roles: erosion, transport, and deposition.

Longshore Drift

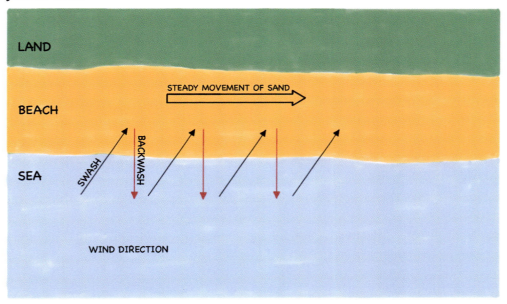

Figure 4.4.23 Longshore drift.

1. Prevailing wind is at an angle to the beach. Waves also arrive in this direction.
2. Swash moves up the beach in the same direction, carrying sediment.
3. Backwash is only controlled by gravity so moves directly back down to the sea.
4. As a result, sand steadily moves along the beach.

The Explanation

Prevailing winds determine the direction that waves usually break onto a beach. If they break at an angle, the swash of the waves will carry sand and other particles up the beach in the direction of the wind. Backwash is not influenced by wind direction and will run straight back down into the sea. In this way, over time, the sand and other particles are steadily carried along the shore in a zigzag motion. The waves break at a rate of 7 per minute; that equates to around 10,000 swashes in a 24-hour period!

An interesting addition to this diagram is to add a groyne (just draw a simple solid line, along the beach, at a right angle to the shoreline) and consider what will happen to the beach.

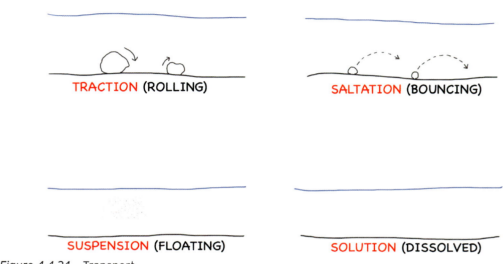

Figure 4.4.24 Transport.

As with river transport, the four ways in which material is carried along within the sea is determined by the material's weight.

- Traction: the heaviest particles are rolled along the seabed. These probably only move along when a particularly large wave pushes them.
- Saltation: particles of sand and small pebbles are picked up and bounced along.
- Suspension: very small, light particles of silt/mud float along. They are what make the water look cloudy.
- Solution: minerals dissolved by the seawater. Invisible to the naked eye, they might be deposited when pooled water evaporates, leaving behind the minerals.

Transport Analogy

Waves transport different-size particles, depending on their weight and the wave's strength.

Traction rolls pebbles along like a tractor wheel. Saltation bounces particles like grains of salt dropped onto a table. Suspension is the reason large rivers like the Thames appear "dirty." Sugar dissolved into a cup of tea is travelling in solution.

Case Study

40.5828, -73.6657 Long Beach, New York (What evidence is there for longshore drift?)

Checking for Understanding

- What is the difference between *swash* and *backwash*?
- Why does sediment move along a coastline?
- What are the four ways that materials are transported by the sea?

4.4.9 Cliff Development

Difficulty to draw: ● ●
Difficulty to explain: ● ●

What Students Should Already Know

- Marine erosion and weathering work together to break down rocks.
- The swash of a wave can carry material up onto a beach; backwash can remove material from a beach.
- Waves perform three main roles: erosion, transport, and deposition.

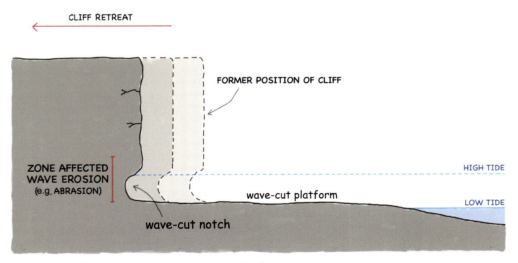

Figure 4.4.25 Cliff development and wave-cut platforms.

1. A cliff is subjected to erosion at the base, and a wave-cut notch is carved out.
2. At the same time, weathering from above weakens the cliff.
3. Eventually, the cliff collapses and the coastline steadily retreats inland.
4. As the cliff retreats, it leaves behind a relatively smooth wave-cut platform.

The Explanation

Cliffs are a common erosional feature along many coastlines. There are many different shapes and heights, and this variety results from a number of factors, such as rock type and the impacts that waves and weathering will have. The zone affected by marine erosion is determined by the tidal range. As the cliffs retreat farther inland, the width of the platform increases, which dissipates wave energy and so slows the rate of erosion of the wave-cut notch.

Drawing Tips

Like other diagrams that show former positions (in this case, the former position of the cliff), try drawing a rough sketch lightly with a pencil first. Then, as you show the retreat of the cliff, rub out the original lines of the cliff and notch. This might end up looking messy, but being able to demonstrate the shifting positions of the cliff in this way can be helpful. Then you can put this sketch to one side and draw a neater version, like Figure 4.4.25. The former positions as dotted lines should then make more sense to students.

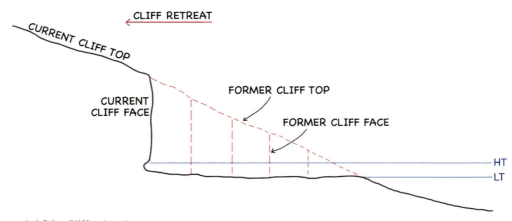

Figure 4.4.26 Cliff retreat.

Changing Cliffs

Depending on what level of detail you are teaching to, using Figure 4.4.26 is an interesting way to zoom out and consider how a cliff can change. The standard diagram of Figure 4.4.25 assumes that the land is flat, but in reality, coastal landscapes are varied, and each will react differently to erosion and weathering. Figure 4.4.26 shows what happens to a coastline that slopes down towards the sea, and how the cliff will increase in height over time as a result. Equally, students could consider what would happen if the land sloped the other way, or if the rock type changed, or if sea levels changed. It is important to ensure that we don't just teach the standard model of a geographical feature without reminding students that the reality in most places rarely fits the model!

Which Is the Dominant Process?

At this stage, students should have considered the three processes of erosion, weathering, and mass movement. A good question to pose to students is what happens if erosion is much more dominant than weathering and mass movement. So there are powerful waves, but the rock type is such that weathering has little impact. In the first of these two simple sketches, we can see that any material that breaks off from the cliff is quickly removed by the waves. In the second diagram, there is considerable weathering and mass movement, resulting in a build-up of material at the base of the cliff. This fallen material will also protect the cliff base from further wave action.

EROSION > MASS MOVEMENT   **MASS MOVEMENT > EROSION**

Figure 4.4.27   Erosion vs mass movement.

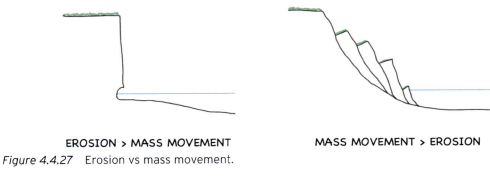

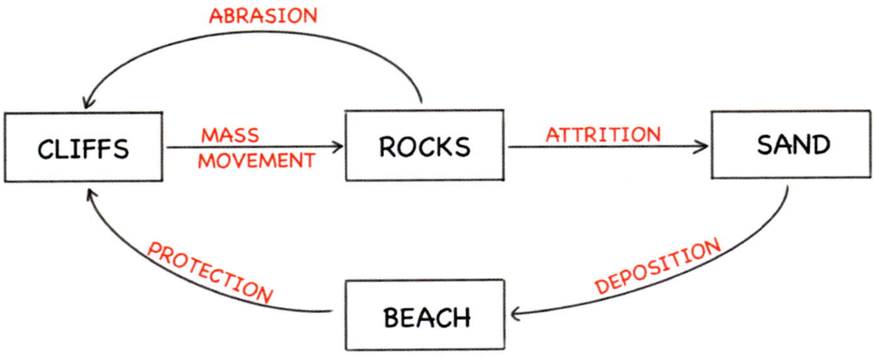

Figure 4.4.28   Balance.

Figure 4.4.28 shows an interesting way to consider some of the processes that happen at the coast, and how they affect each other.

Case Study

50.6122, -2.1369 Kimmeridge Bay, UK (How did the wave-cut platform develop?)

Checking for Understanding
- Which three processes are involved in cliff retreat?
- What is a wave-cut notch?
- Why does a cliff retreat inland?

4.4.10 Headlands and Bays

Difficulty to draw: ●○○
Difficulty to explain: ●●○

What Students Should Already Know
- Erosion and weathering act together to weaken and break off pieces of the coast.
- Some rocks are more resistant than others.

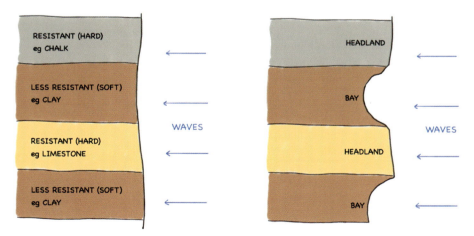

Figure 4.4.29 Discordant coastline.

1. Discordant coastlines are made of rock layers that are perpendicular to the coast.
2. Less-resistant rocks are eroded more quickly than more-resistant rocks.
3. As a result, a series of headlands and bays forms.

The Explanation

If a coastline is made up of different layers of rock, then erosion will occur at variable rates according to how resistant the different rocks are. If the layers of rock run perpendicular to the coast, such as in Figure 4.4.29, then a series of headlands and bays will form. This is a discordant coastline.

The headlands are then also affected by wave refraction, which focuses erosion onto the sides of the headland, as well as leading to deposition in the bays. The way that wave refraction can affect headlands is shown on page 168.

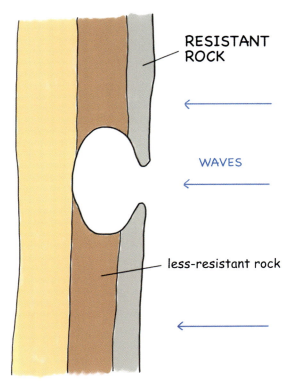

Figure 4.4.30 Concordant coastline.

1. Concordant coastlines are made of rock layers that are parallel with the coast.
2. Waves breach the resistant rock.
3. The waves erode the less-resistant rock behind more easily.

The Explanation

Layers of rock that run parallel to the coastline (Figure 4.4.30) create a concordant coastline. The key point to emphasise is that if/when waves erode through the first layer to the less-resistant rock behind, then the rate of erosion will increase and the resultant bay will continue to expand behind the relatively small opening. Wave refraction is partially responsible for the erosion at the sides of the bay.

Case Studies

50.6353, -1.9398 Swanage, UK (What evidence is there of a discordant coastline?)
50.6174, -2.2468 Lulworth Cove, UK (What evidence is there of a concordant coastline?)

Checking for Understanding

- What is a *discordant coastline*?
- What is a *concordant coastline*?
- Why does a headland form?

4.4.11 Wave Refraction

Difficulty to draw: ●●●
Difficulty to explain: ●●○

What Students Should Already Know

- Winds are responsible for the direction and strength of waves.
- A *headland* is a protrusion of land, usually made of more-resistant rock.
- Waves slow down when they reach shallow water.

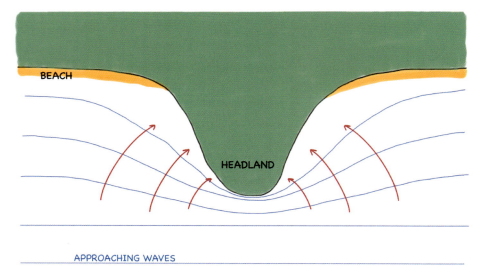

Figure 4.4.31   Wave refraction.

1. Waves approach the coastline. As they reach the shallow water around a headland, that part of the wave slows down.
2. The rest of the wave front swings round towards the headland.
3. By the time the waves reach the bay, they have slowed, and deposition occurs.

Coasts   169

The Explanation

As waves approach the coastline, they slow down upon reaching shallow water (due to friction with the bottom). A wave front can be very long, so if one part of the wave is slowed down by the shallow water around a headland, the rest of the wave front will bend and swing around into the headland.

Useful Key Term

Orthogonals: drawn at right angles to the wave fronts show the direction of wave movement.

Wave Refraction Analogy

A wave approaches the coast in a long line. When one end of that line reaches shallow water, it slows down, whilst the rest of the line of wave keeps going and curls round.

Imagine a line of 20 students all holding hands and walking quickly from one end of the sports hall to the other. They are moving quickly, but the students at one end of the line are having to slow down to climb over some obstacles. If the students keep holding hands, the whole line of students will swing round into the obstacles.

Case Study

6.4186, 81.6183 Yala, Sri Lanka (Notice how the waves bend around the headland.)

Checking for Understanding

- How do waves approach a coastline?
- Why might they slow down?
- What is an orthogonal?
- How can wave refraction act upon a headland?

4.4.12 Caves, Arches, and Stacks

Difficulty to draw: ● ●
Difficulty to explain: ● ●

What Students Should Already Know

- Erosion and weathering act together to weaken and break off pieces of the coast.
- A headland is a protrusion of land, usually made of more-resistant rock.

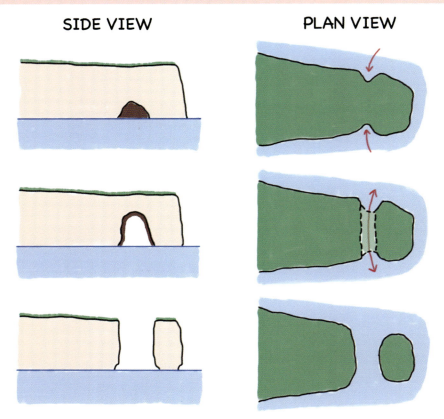

Figure 4.4.32 Cave-arch-stack sequence.

1. Waves erode the sides of a headland, creating a cave.
2. Eventually, the back of the cave is broken through to form an arch.
3. Continued erosion leads to the roof of the arch collapsing, leaving a stack behind.

The Explanation

Weaknesses in the headland are picked out by wave erosion, and any faults or cracks are enlarged. Abrasion and hydraulic action are the main erosional processes but are aided by weathering from above. Headlands are usually harder rocks, anyway, so tend to be affected by rockfalls (rather than slumping or slides). Other features such as blowholes and geos are also found.

Coasts 171

When drawing this diagram, draw the top two boxes first rather than drawing all three of one of the views. Whilst the side-view version is the one usually shown in textbooks, the plan view is a really useful addition to the explanation.

Case Study

51.3870, 1.4418 Kingsgate, UK (What will eventually happen to this arch?)

4.4.13 Bars and Berms

Difficulty to draw: ●●
Difficulty to explain: ●●

What Students Should Already Know

Waves perform three main roles: erosion, transport, and deposition.

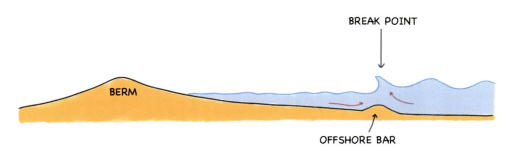

Figure 4.4.33   Bars and berms.

Bars are formed just offshore where steeper waves that break meet the outgoing swash. The meeting of these two occurs where the waves break, hence the proper name for these features: break-point bars. If the waves are not steep enough, then there will not be enough backwash for them to form.

Berms are ridges of sand found at the top of some beaches. They are usually just out of reach of high tides and are created when larger storm waves push material farther up the beach than normal.

Changing Profiles

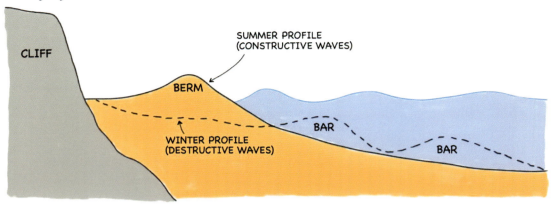

Figure 4.4.34 Changing profiles.

The profile of a beach can change quite quickly. Storms can generate powerful waves that are able to remove almost all the sand from a beach, almost overnight. Many beaches will have seasonal profiles, where calmer constructive waves will push sediment up onto a beach to create a higher profile. Winter storms tend to produce destructive waves that drag the same material back offshore.

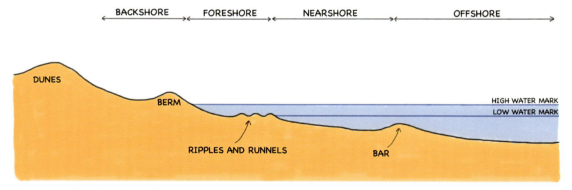

Figure 4.4.35 Beach profile.

The beach zone can be divided into four sections, as denoted in Figure 4.4.35.

Backshore: the area above the high tide mark. Only affected by waves during larger storms.
Foreshore: the area between the high and low tide marks.
Nearshore: the area beyond the low tide mark that is shallow enough for the seabed to be affected by the waves.
Offshore: the area deep enough for the seabed not to be affected by wave action.

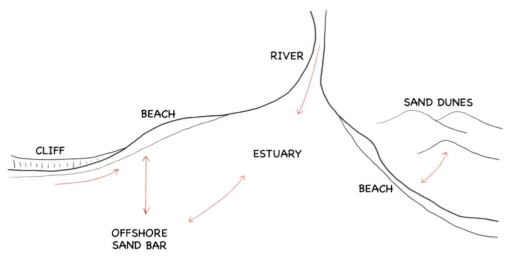

Figure 4.4.36 Sediment supply.

Bars, berms, and other depositional landforms rely on a supply of sediment; otherwise, eventually they would disappear. Figure 4.4.36 shows a simple sediment cell, which can be thought of as a closed system, in that it has inputs (sediment sources) and outputs (sediment sinks). As a result, the relationship between the different components is crucial. For example, were the river to be dammed, the two beaches would lose an important source of sediment. Likewise, stopping longshore drift with groynes on one beach could result in a thinning beach farther down the coast. It is for this reason that the coastlines of England and Wales are divided into sediment cells to help with coastal management.

Case Studies

53.9739, -10.1270 Dooagh Beach, Ireland (How did this beach disappear 30 years and then reappear overnight?)

53.5741, 0.1098 Spurn Head, UK (Where does the sediment for this spit come from?)

Checking for Understanding

- How does a berm form?
- How does a break-point bar form?
- Why do some beaches look different throughout the year?
- What are the four zones on a beach?
- What is a sediment cell?

4.4.14 Spits and Salt Marshes

Difficulty to draw: ●●○
Difficulty to explain: ●●○

What Students Should Already Know
- Waves perform three main roles: erosion, transport, and deposition.
- Rivers flow out into the sea.

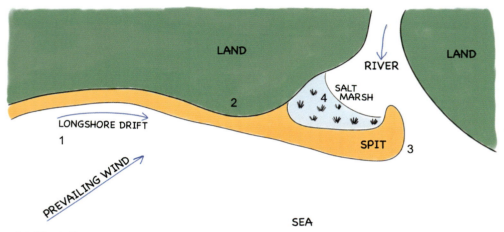

Figure 4.4.37 Spit.

1. Longshore drift, driven by prevailing wind, moves sediment along the coastline.
2. Where the coastline changes direction, the sediment continues to be deposited.
3. A hooked, or recurved, end can be shaped by wind changes or wave refraction.
4. Low-energy environment behind the spit where finer sediment is deposited.

The Explanation

Spits are one of the most common depositional features and often form where longshore drift operates across the mouth of a river. Sediment continues to be deposited out into open water in the direction of the drift. If the spit develops across the mouth of a river, it may result in diverting its flow.

Where the spit attaches to the land is called the proximal end; the other end that juts out into the sea is called the distal end. Many spits have a hooked, or curved, end, and this is usually due to wave refraction bending round the end.

Coasts 175

In the calm, still waters behind the spit where neither longshore drift nor the river is moving the water, deposition of the finest particles occurs. This can result in a salt marsh forming. Where a spit has grown across a bay, it is known as a bar. Figures 4.4.38 and 4.4.39 help to show how deposition of these particles can happen.

Deposition

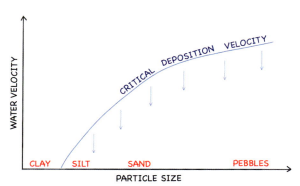

Figure 4.4.38 Deposition.

Waves will transport sediment if they have enough energy. As wave velocity reduces, so does the size of particles it can carry reduce. Figure 4.4.38 shows how the largest pieces (pebbles) are the first to be deposited. The relationship on the graph is fairly linear, apart from the finest particles (clay). These are so fine that even in still water, they will remain in suspension.

That said, a chemical process called flocculation does occur, whereby the finest particles join together. Thus, they become heavy enough to settle.

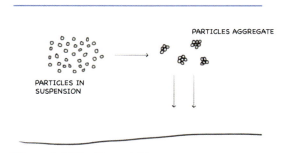

Figure 4.4.39 Flocculation.

Case Studies

-40.5088, 172.8262 Farewell Spit, New Zealand (In which direction is the longshore drift?)

53.6076, 0.1323 Spurn Head, UK (Why has a salt marsh developed here?)

Checking for Understanding

- Where does a spit form?
- Why is longshore drift important?
- How does a salt marsh develop behind a spit?
- What is flocculation?

4.4.15 Coastal Dunes

Difficulty to draw: ●●○
Difficulty to explain: ●●●

What Students Should Already Know

- Prevailing winds are those that blow persistently and constantly from one direction.
- Beaches can become exposed at low tide.

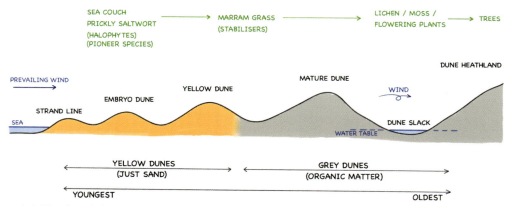

Figure 4.4.40 Coastal dunes.

1. Prevailing winds blow dry sand onshore at low tide. Sand grains bounce along until stopped by an obstacle.
2. As the grains accumulate into a dune, they can be anchored by halophytic plants.
3. As more plants grow then decay, a soil forms. The dune turns from yellow to a more organic grey.
4. Dunes farthest inland are the oldest. Over time, the soil deepens so more permanent vegetation can take root.

The Explanation

The key ingredients to dunes forming are the prevailing wind and the supply of dried sand from a large tidal range. Once sand starts regularly blowing onshore, any obstacle (driftwood, rock, litter) can provide the basis for a dune to form. Embryo dunes are very fragile and prone to movement.

Halophytic (salt-tolerant) plants are also crucial in initially helping stabilise the dunes and then providing the requisite humus for a soil to develop. As a soil develops further, it can hold more water and become a suitable environment for other plant species. Also, as mature dunes are farther from the sea, the salt content in the soil reduces.

A dune slack can occur when winds erode a dune and a marshy depression forms between the dunes. They are fragile environments and prone to damage from tourism. If the stabilising vegetation is lost, the loose sand can easily be blown away by the wind.

Salt grains are bounced along by saltation. This is an aeolian (wind) form of transport. Sands that do not dry out at low tide cannot be picked up by the wind and will not travel. Dunes often start at the top of a beach, where the strand line of washed-up driftwood and other materials form a suitable obstacle.

Figure 4.4.41   Obstruction.

Case Studies

44.4768, -1.2514 Plage de Vivier, France (Why have sand dunes formed here?)
53.0979, 0.3233 Gibraltar Point, UK (Why is this WW2 defence post, built to defend the coastline, so far from the sea?)

Checking for Understanding
- Where does a spit form?
- Why is longshore drift important?
- How does a salt marsh develop behind a spit?
- What is flocculation?

4.4.16 Coral Reefs

Difficulty to draw: ●●●
Difficulty to explain: ●●●

> **What Students Should Already Know**
> - The tropics contain warmer seas than other parts of the world.
> - Sea levels can rise and fall over time.

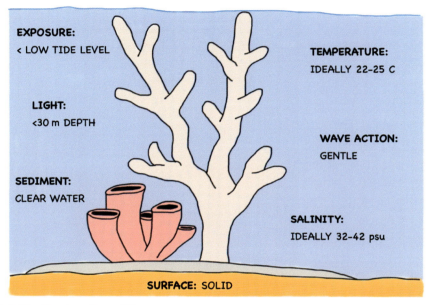

Figure 4.4.42 Coral reef conditions.

1. Coral reefs are made up of many different species of animals called polyps. They live in large communities on structures made of excreted calcium carbonate.
2. The polyps are home to tiny algae that photosynthesise and provide food for the polyps. These also provide the colour.
3. Both the polyps and the algae are very sensitive and need very specific conditions to thrive. Otherwise, the algae die, and the polyps lose their food source.

The Explanation

This is more of a drawing than a diagram, and the sheer variety of coral types means you can be liberal with the drawing, as long as they look vaguely coral-like! The important part is the annotations around it, showing the specific conditions required for the algae to thrive.

A gentle wave action is required to provide oxygen to the polyps. The water needs to be clear of sediment so that sunlight can reach the algae. Similarly, shallower water allows more sunlight to reach the coral.

The algae's proper name is zooxanthellae, which is a great term for students to try to learn.

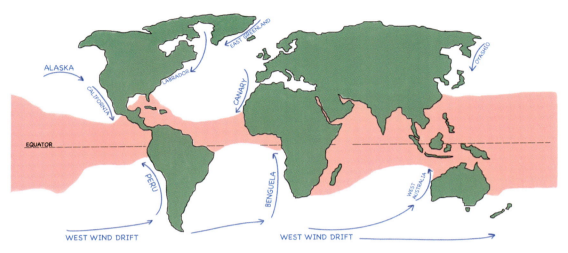

Figure 4.4.43 Coral reef distribution.

The map showing coral distribution highlights two main features. Firstly, it is the warmer waters that corals need in order to grow and survive. The second point is the influence that cold currents can have on the distribution.

These currents have been taken from the map in Figure 4.5.47 on page 217, which shows the major ocean currents.

Types of Reefs

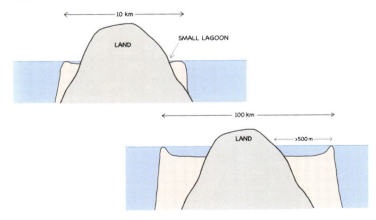

Figure 4.4.44 Coral reef types.

1. The most common type of reef is a fringing reef. They grow close to the shore and sometimes have a small lagoon between the reef and the shore.
2. A barrier reef is farther from the shore and forms a larger, deeper lagoon.

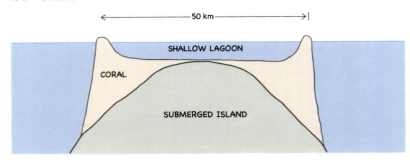

3. Formed once an island has completely submerged, an atoll will surround a protected lagoon of calmer water.

Figure 4.4.45 Atoll formation.

The Explanation

The sequence of diagrams shows one theory of reef development, in that an island (often volcanic) steadily submerges into the sea. Note that it could either be the island submerging or the sea level rising. Fringing reefs and barrier reefs can be distinguished by the width of the lagoon they each create. Over 500 m and it is considered a barrier reef.

The only "live" parts of the reef are those that are pointing upwards, which continue to grow as the sea level rises. The rest of the reef structure is made from the calcium carbonate deposited by the polyps of the reef.

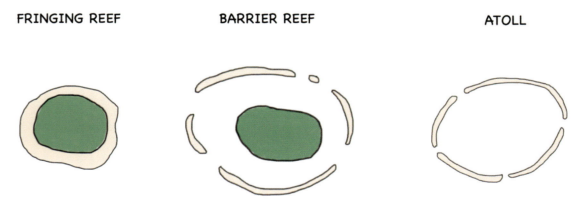

Figure 4.4.46 Coral formation plan.

Drawing the three types in plan view also helps to show the differences.

Case Studies

-8.2547, 127.9916 Toenwawang, Timor-Leste (fringing reef)
16.8567, -88.0726 Belize coastline (barrier reef)
-7.0202, 52.7372 Alphonse Island, Seychelles (atoll)

Checking for Understanding

- What are some of the conditions required for coral to grow?
- Why does coral need clear water?
- What is the proper name for the algae?
- What are the three types of reef?

4.5 Weather and Climate

4.5.1 Layers of the Atmosphere   Difficulty to draw: ● ● ●
Difficulty to explain: ● ● ●

What Students Should Already Know
- The Earth is surrounded by an atmosphere that extends up to space.
- That 1 km equals 1,000 m.

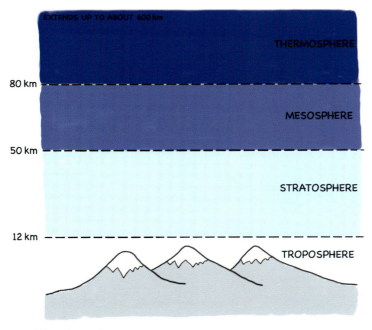

Figure 4.5.1   Layers of the atmosphere.

The Explanation

This diagram provides important context for where weather happens. It shows that the layer in which all our weather happens is relatively small. Some students may have only heard of the *stratosphere*, so it is useful to show the order. Drawing the mountains on will also give some sense of scale. Similarly, aeroplanes and clouds can be added. With this diagram, you can also discuss how most of the atmosphere's water is found in the troposphere and why that results in most of the clouds being found here. The layers of blue shading are optional but just help distinguish them and show the gradual move towards the darkness of space. In reality, the colours of the different layers would depend on the angle of the sun and the varying presence of different aerosols and water droplets.

4.5.2 Temperature

Difficulty to draw: ●
Difficulty to explain: ● ●

What Students Should Already Know

- The sun gives off heat energy that reaches us through the atmosphere.
- Some surfaces get hotter in the sun than others.

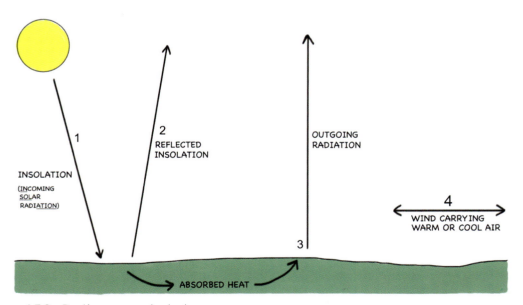

Figure 4.5.2 Daytime energy budget.

184 *Weather and Climate*

1. The sun's energy reaches the Earth as shortwave radiation, known as *insolation*.
2. Some of it is reflected back into the atmosphere.
3. The Earth's surface absorbs some of the insolation. It is then re-emitted back as *longwave radiation*.
4. Winds may also bring in heat from nearby or remove some of the heat.

The Explanation

This diagram and the following night-time energy budget (Figure 4.5.3) are important ways to show how the energy from the sun is the main driver of our weather. Without this energy, clouds, wind, humidity, and rain would not happen in the same way. Students should gain from this diagram the appreciation that each place will receive a certain amount of sunlight, and the amount that stays or leaves the area will affect the weather.

The simple nature of the diagram allows for discussion about what factors could affect the different elements. For example, how would cloud cover affect this diagram? How would lots of snow affect the diagram? How would longer summer days compare to shorter winter days? Don't expect to be able to fully explain these ideas with this diagram, but they are questions that help set up future lessons.

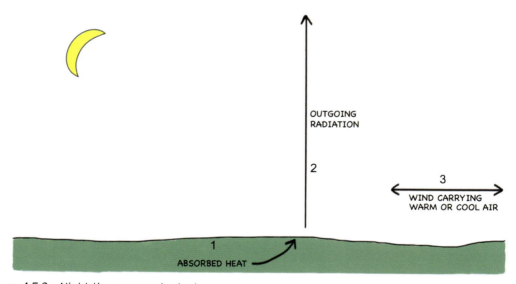

Figure 4.5.3 Night-time energy budget.

1. Heat energy absorbed during the day is slowly released at night.
2. The outgoing heat is longwave radiation.
3. Any wind will also affect the amount of heat energy in the area.

Figure 4.5.4 Clouds and radiation.

The presence of clouds has an impact on the ability of radiation to both reach the Earth's surface as shortwave radiation and then to leave it as longwave radiation.

Different types of cloud affect insolation differently, but the simple version is that more cloud cover prevents insolation reaching the surface, but then it can also trap radiation in, effectively cancelling its impact out.

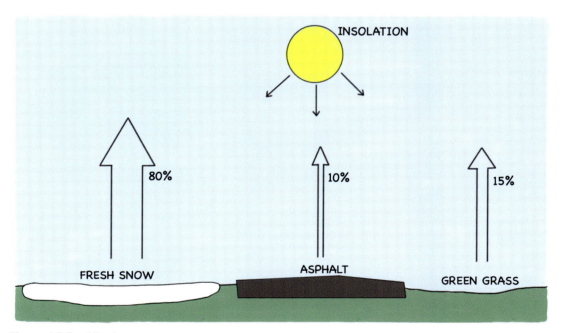

Figure 4.5.5 Albedo.

186 *Weather and Climate*

Albedo is just another name for *reflectivity*. The albedo of a surface, therefore, determines whether that surface will absorb more or less of the sun's heat. This is important not only for the impact the surface will have on local weather conditions but also on a wider scale for the Earth's ability to cope with global warming. Students may know that the concrete around a swimming pool might be too hot to walk on in the summer heat but the grass right next to it is fine. They may also know that lighter-coloured clothing keeps you cooler in the summer. These are just examples of albedo.

Students could draw this on graph paper. Provide them with a list of different surfaces and their albedos and task them with drawing the surface as well as drawing proportional arrows for their albedo.

Case Studies

49.2586, -123.1683 Vancouver, Canada (Which areas will have high or low albedo?)
-65.6869, 103.8799 Conger Ice Shelf, Antarctica (Melting ice shelf. Ice [high albedo] is being replaced by ocean [low albedo]. What impact will this have on global warming?)

Checking for Understanding

- What is *insolation*?
- What happens to heat from the sun when it reaches the Earth's surface?
- How can wind affect how much heat there is in an area?
- How can clouds affect the amount of heat in a place?
- What is *albedo*?

4.5.3 Air pressure

Difficulty to draw: ● ○ ○
Difficulty to explain: ● ● ○

What Students Should Already Know

- Insolation reaches the ground and warms it.
- Temperature decreases with altitude.

Weather and Climate 187

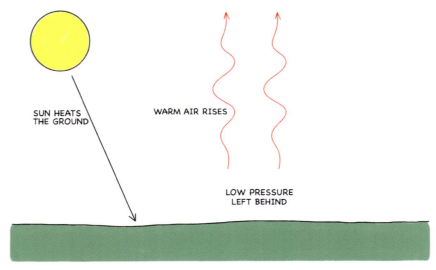

Figure 4.5.6 Low pressure.

1. Insolation heats the ground.
2. The ground then heats the air above it via *conduction*.
3. The warmed air rises via *convection*.

The Explanation

An easy misconception for students is to associate low pressure with cold weather, and therefore, the idea of *low pressure* being generated by the sun's heat can seem counterintuitive. The annotations mention conduction and convection, but these can be omitted, depending on students' prior knowledge. The low-pressure diagram could be added to by showing how it can lead to cloud formation, and the *high pressure* could include a sun to show the opposite: that descending air will result in clear skies.

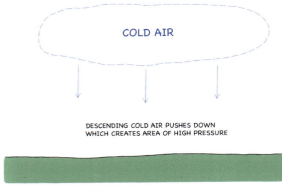

1. Cold air sinks because it is denser than the air around it.
2. The weight of the descending air squashes the air below it, creating high pressure.

Figure 4.5.7 High pressure.

Using the balloon analogy shows how adding more air into a space will create higher pressure. This is also a neat way to demonstrate how wind is simply the movement of air particles from an area of higher pressure to lower pressure.

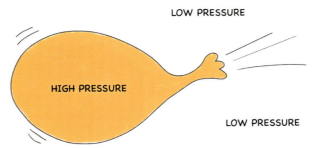

Figure 4.5.8 Balloon.

Figure 4.5.9 shows how air particles within a parcel of air that is warmer will start to move around. This expands the parcel of air, making it less dense than the surrounding air. As it is less dense, it will rise.

Similarly, cooled air contracts, which makes it denser and liable to sink.

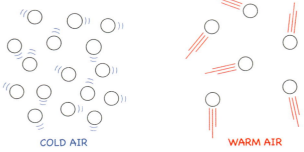

Figure 4.5.9 Air particles.

Warm and Cold Air Analogy

Warm air is less dense, so the particles move around more freely. Cold air is denser and moves less.

> *When it is a sunny day in the playground, students will run around more. When it is a colder day, they tend to huddle in groups and don't run around so much.*

Checking for Understanding
- Why does air rise when it is warmed?
- What happens to cooler air?
- How do differences in air pressure cause wind?
- Why do high pressure conditions cause clear skies?

4.5.4 Wind
Difficulty to draw: ●○○
Difficulty to explain: ●●○

What Students Should Already Know

- Warmed air rises, creating an area of low pressure.
- Cool air sinks, creating an area of high pressure.

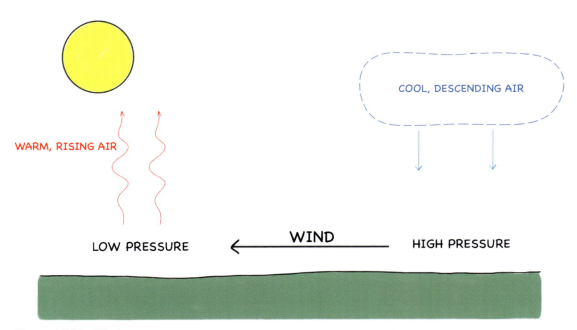

Figure 4.5.10 Wind.

1. Rising air in areas of low pressure is replaced by incoming air from areas of higher pressure.
2. The greater the difference between the low pressure and high pressure, the stronger the *wind*.

The Explanation

Another simple diagram that just needs to show the two different areas of high and low pressure. Students are often surprised that something like the wind is just the movement of air between two places. Start with the low pressure, and then describe how air moves in to fill the space left by the recently departed air. Colours help show the difference between the warmth of the rising air and the cooler descending air. The balloon analogy (Figure 4.5.8 on page 188) is another way to show how wind moves.

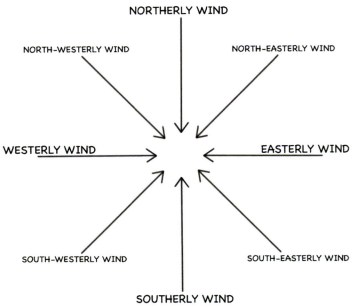

A common mistake from students is to incorrectly name winds by the direction they are travelling to. This version of the compass rose is a useful reference point for students to include in their notes.

Figure 4.5.11 Wind direction.

Checking for Understanding
- What happens to air at low-pressure areas?
- Why does air descend at high-pressure areas?
- True or false? Air travels from low pressure to high pressure?
- In which direction is an easterly wind moving?

4.5.5 Coriolis Force

Difficulty to draw: ●●○
Difficulty to explain: ●●●

What Students Should Already Know
- Wind moves from areas of high pressure to low pressure.
- The Earth is divided into two hemispheres.
- The Earth turns on its axis.

Weather and Climate 191

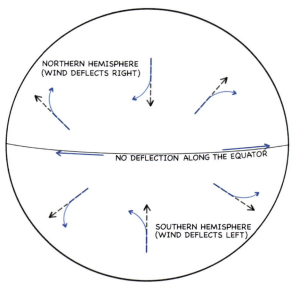

1. Whilst the Earth spins on its axis, winds blow in the air above.
2. This means that whilst the wind may travel in a straight line, its progress on the land looks curved.
3. In the northern hemisphere, this curve is always to the right. In the Southern Hemisphere, it is always to the left.

Figure 4.5.12   Coriolis.

The Explanation

This is best explained using a globe and a whiteboard marker. Draw a simple vertical line down the globe from the North Pole to the equator. Then draw another similar line whilst the globe is slowly spinning. The resultant line should curve to the right.

This diagram represents the globe, so the equator drawn as a slight curve helps provide an element of perspective. Draw the straight lines of the wind as dotted lines, and then full lines to show the deflection.

Figures 4.5.14 and 4.5.15 then show how winds moving from high pressure to low pressure are subjected to *Coriolis force* and the impact that has on weather patterns.

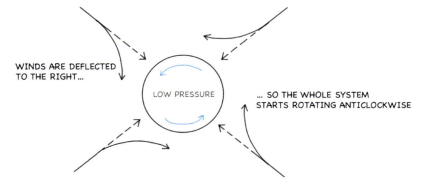

Figure 4.5.13   Coriolis on hurricanes.

192 *Weather and Climate*

Once the idea that the Coriolis force deflects winds has been established, it can be combined with a reminder that winds flow from areas of high pressure to low pressure. Draw a central circle of low pressure. Draw the winds flowing directly in towards the middle, but draw them as a dashed line. Ask students why you have drawn it dashed. Because Coriolis causes winds to be deflected. Redraw the lines curving to the right. Then you can show how the whole low-pressure system starts to rotate. This can be repeated with high pressure, where the winds flow away from the centre.

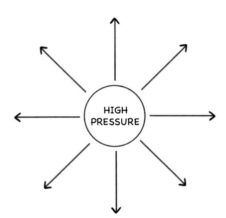

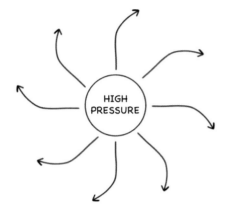

Figure 4.5.14 Wind into high pressure.

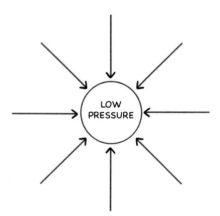

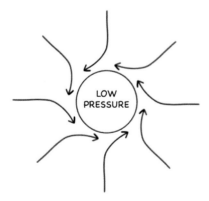

Figure 4.5.15 Wind into low pressure.

Weather and Climate 193

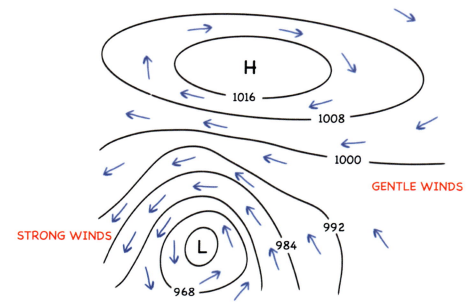

Figure 4.5.16   Isobars.

An extension to discussing winds and Coriolis is to use a map of *isobars* to see how the winds move around areas of differing air pressure. It is also worth noting how closely spaced isobars show where winds will be strongest due to the greater pressure gradient.

Checking for Understanding
- The Coriolis force deflects air which way in the northern hemisphere?
- True or false: air flows into an area of low pressure.
- Which direction does air flow around an area of high pressure?
- Why does air flow anticlockwise around an area of low pressure?

4.5.6 Rain
Difficulty to draw: ●
Difficulty to explain: ●●

What Students Should Already Know
- The sun's energy warms the ground.
- Warm air rises.

194 Weather and Climate

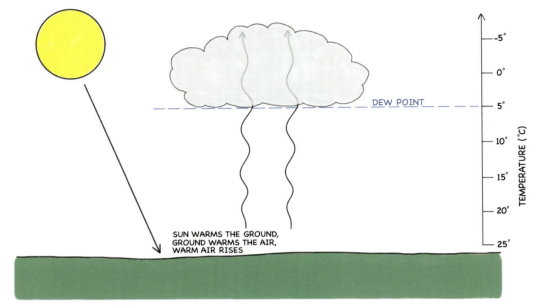

Figure 4.5.17   Dew point.

1. Insolation heats the ground, which, in turn, warms the air above it.
2. The warmed air parcel rises. All air contains some moisture, which is also carried up.
3. The atmosphere is cooler the higher you go. This cools the rising parcel of air.
4. When the parcel of air drops below a certain temperature (called *dew point*), water vapour condenses to form clouds.

The Explanation

Draw the ground and the sun, and remind students that insolation warms the ground, which warms the air above. Students should know that it is cooler the higher you go (because it is farther from the warmed ground), and so the parcel of air starts to cool too. As a parcel of air cools, it contracts, which means it can hold less moisture. Eventually, it will contract enough and become saturated. The temperature at which saturation occurs is called dew point. If the air continues to cool below dew point, then the water vapour within it will condense to water droplets, which are what a cloud is made up of. If enough water droplets join together, they will become too heavy to stay afloat and fall as rain. The following diagrams can be used to help explain the condensation process in more detail.

Figure 4.5.17 shows *convectional rainfall* forming. The two other main types of relief and frontal rainfall are just different ways of getting moist air to rise and cool down. These are shown on pages 197-199.

Weather and Climate 195

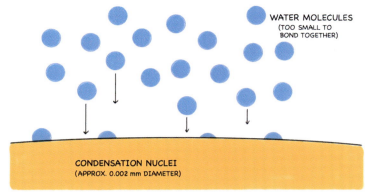

Figure 4.5.18 Condensation.

Condensation cannot happen unless there are tiny particles in the air (e.g. smoke or dust) for the water molecules to attach themselves to.

The tiny particles act as condensation nuclei. They are hygroscopic, which means they have an affinity for water.

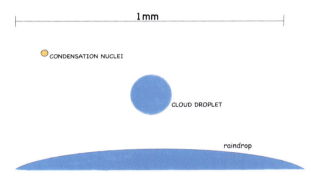

Figure 4.5.19 Relative sizes.

It can be difficult to comprehend the relative sizes of terms like condensation nuclei and cloud droplet, so this image can help give some context. Students staring at 1mm on a ruler and trying to imagine a cloud droplet 1/10th of that can start to appreciate why clouds stay afloat!

Figure 4.5.20 shows the process of coalescence, whereby smaller cloud droplets collide and join together. This is the main way that rainfall occurs. The other theory involves ice crystals forming at high altitudes before melting into raindrops as they fall.

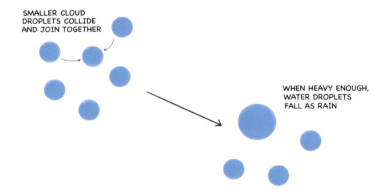

Figure 4.5.20 Collision theory.

196 *Weather and Climate*

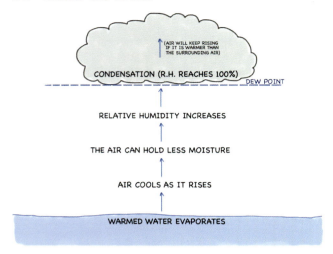

Figure 4.5.21 Condensation flow diagram.

Figure 4.5.21 is a good way to summarise how rising air cools and the water vapour it carries condenses to form clouds. This diagram looks simple but contains several fairly complicated processes. It is a good way to check for understanding and identify any areas for review.

Misconception Alert!

Students can sometimes think that dew point is a height rather than a temperature. This is often down to how it is drawn on diagrams as a line above sea level. Whilst it is true that dew point is reached when rising air reaches a certain height, it is only because that particular height is where the temperature has dropped down to the dew point for those local conditions.

Dew forms when the air close to cold ground also cools down. The cooled air cannot hold as much water vapour, so the water vapour condenses onto nearby surfaces, such as grass and leaves, as liquid droplets.

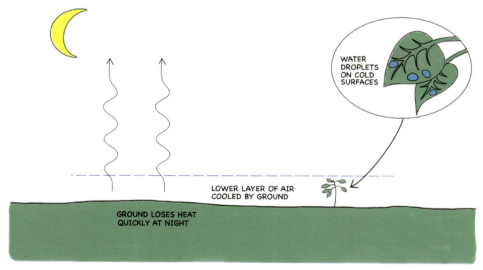

Figure 4.5.22 Dew.

Weather and Climate 197

Checking for Understanding

- What happens to air temperature as you get higher in the atmosphere?
- True or false: dew point is a height above sea level.
- What happens to water vapour when it condenses?
- Put these in order of size: cloud droplet, raindrop, water molecule.
- Why do cloud droplets eventually fall as raindrops?

4.5.7 Relief Rainfall

Difficulty to draw: ●
Difficulty to explain: ●

What Students Should Already Know

- Raindrops are formed when cloud droplets join together.
- Cloud droplets form when air is cooled below dew point.
- Dew point is reached when air rises to a cool-enough altitude.

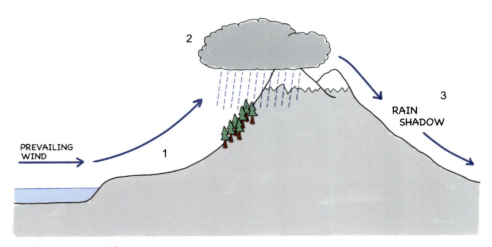

Figure 4.5.23 Rain - relief.

1. Moist air is blown towards a mountain and forced to rise.
2. Once it reaches dew point, the water vapour condenses into cloud droplets, which eventually fall as rain.
3. The air, which is now "dry," having lost its moisture as rain, descends, creating dry conditions.

198 *Weather and Climate*

The Explanation

All three types of rainfall are a result of the vertical uplift of moist air. The generation of the clouds and raindrops is the same for all three, so it is important that students are confident in understanding the processes of rising air, dew point, and condensation. Once they appreciate that it is all about getting the moist air high enough to cool down, then they can start to see how the different types of rainfall are just different ways of getting the air to rise.

The diagram for *orographic*, or relief, rainfall is quite simple. Note the trees on the rising air side. These are there in opposition to the rain shadow side to highlight the lack of rainfall on the far side of the mountain. Try to keep the base of the cloud relatively flat to help reinforce the idea of the rising air having cooled to dew point at a certain height.

Case Study

29.7255, 82.0202 Tibetan Plateau, Tibet (huge rain shadow caused by the Himalayas)

4.5.8 Frontal Rainfall

Difficulty to draw: ● ● ○
Difficulty to explain: ● ● ○

What Students Should Already Know

- Raindrops are formed when cloud droplets join together.
- Cloud droplets form when air is cooled below dew point.
- Dew point is reached when air rises to a cool-enough altitude.
- Warm air rises above cooler air.

Weather and Climate 199

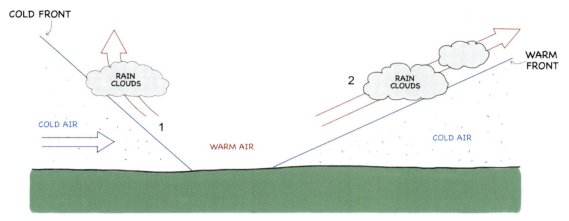

Figure 4.5.24 Rain - frontal.

1. When cold air moves towards warm air, it pushes the warm air up. The rising air eventually cools, and clouds will form.
2. When warm air moves towards cold air, it is forced up and over it because it is less dense.
3. The rising air eventually cools, and clouds will form.

The Explanation

This may look like a complicated diagram, but it can be broken down into stages and made simple. Remind students that warmer air is *less dense* than cold air and so will rise over the colder air. Draw the mass of cold air on the right-hand side of the diagram. Then label the warm air in the middle of the diagram and discuss what would happen if wind blew the warm air into the cold air. Draw the warm front (so-called because it is the warmer air moving into the cooler region) and remind students of what happens when air rises.

The second part of the diagram can be framed as "Now, what happens if some cooler air is to be blown into this warmer air?" Draw the cold front (so-called because it is the colder air moving into the warmer region) at an angle to denote the cold air forcing its way underneath. The blue dots within the cold air are just there to help distinguish it from the portion of warm air.

Page 203 has a number of diagrams and suggestions for how to explain the different types of fronts.

200   *Weather and Climate*

4.5.9 Winter Weather   Difficulty to draw:
Difficulty to explain:

> **What Students Should Already Know**
> - Water will freeze to ice if subjected to cold-enough temperatures.
> - Ice will melt to water if it is warmed above 0°C.

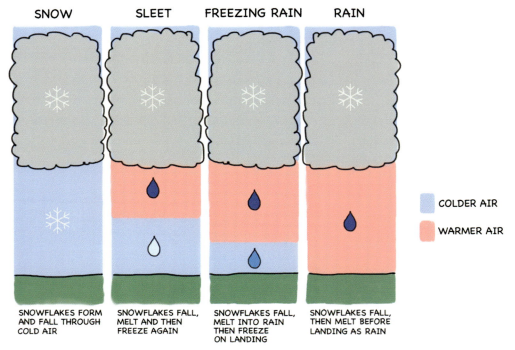

Figure 4.5.25   Cold precipitation.

The Explanation

Remind students about how cloud droplets form when water vapour condenses as the air is cooled below dew point. Snowflakes form when very cold water vapour condenses as an ice crystal rather than a cloud droplet. If the snowflake falls though cold air all the way to the ground, it will remain a snowflake. If a snowflake falls but melts on the way down and then refreezes again, it will land as sleet. If it falls and melts and lands as rain on frozen ground, then it is known as freezing rain. If a snowflake falls and melts, then it will land as rain.

Figure 4.5.26 Snow formation.

This diagram helps consider how different conditions affect the individual snowflakes.

Apart from temperature, as shown here, the different ways that a snowflake might fall then rise, melt then refreeze, affect the way a snowflake develops.

The unique journeys snowflakes take from cloud to ground are the reason each snowflake is different.

Another useful consideration in the formation of snow is the amount of the moisture in the air. A newly formed ice crystal needs to melt in air moist enough for the edges of the crystals to stick together to form snowflakes. If snow falls through very cold but dry air, it will form powdery snow that does not stick together.

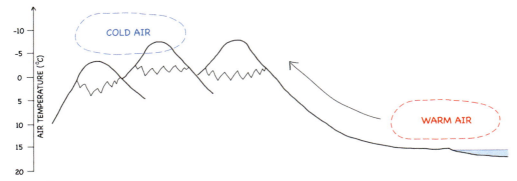

Figure 4.5.27 Snow.

Checking for Understanding
- What happens to water vapour if it condenses in very cold conditions?
- What happens to snowflakes if they pass through warm air on the way down?
- Why does sleet occur?

4.5.10 Hail Difficulty to draw: ●●○
  Difficulty to explain: ●●○

What Students Should Already Know
- Water will freeze to ice if subjected to cold-enough temperatures.
- Ice will melt to water if it is warmed above 0°C.

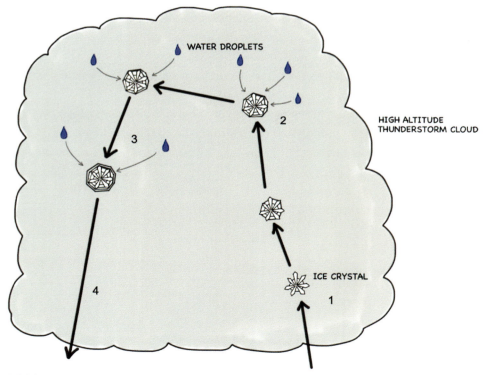

Figure 4.5.28 Hail formation.

Weather and Climate 203

1. Ice crystals form when water vapour freezes around a speck of dust.
2. The ice crystals are continuously moved up and down through the cloud by updrafts and gravity.
3. Throughout this, the outer layer repeatedly melts and refreezes. More water vapour attaches and also freezes.
4. This repeats until the ice crystal is too heavy and falls as a hailstone.

The Explanation

One way to frame this explanation is to review how large rain clouds are generated from rising air. Then ask students to consider what would happen if the cloud were to move into very cold air.

The key to this diagram is ensuring that the ice crystals are shown to be growing with additional layers as more water vapour freezes onto them. The ice crystals do not need to be intricate drawings but could be simpler concentric circles, showing the different layers.

Checking for Understanding

- Why does air rise?
- Why do ice crystals form instead of water droplets?
- What causes the crystals to move around within the cloud?
- Why do hailstones eventually fall from the cloud?

4.5.11 Fronts

Difficulty to draw: ● ●
Difficulty to explain: ● ●

What Students Should Already Know

- Warm air rises, and cold air sinks.
- Different parts of the world have different local weather conditions.
- Wind is air moving from one place to another.

204 Weather and Climate

Figure 4.5.29 Meeting fronts.

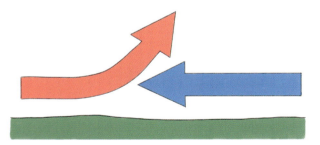

Figure 4.5.30 Meeting fronts 2.

The Explanation

An air mass is a large volume of air which all has a similar temperature and humidity. These are generated due to local conditions and can then be moved by wind to different places. When two of these air masses meet, they form a front.

Some are moist and warm, whilst some are cold and dry. Those that form over land are called continental air masses, and those that form over the sea are maritime air masses. There are also several others, categorised by their origin and characteristics. These include tropical maritime and polar maritime.

The map shows two typical air masses that meet over the UK. The colder air from the north meets warmer, moister air formed over the Atlantic Ocean. You can either sketch the UK, or any other place, or provide students with a map. Figure 4.5.30 then shows how the warmer air is forced up and over the cold air.

Weather and Climate 205

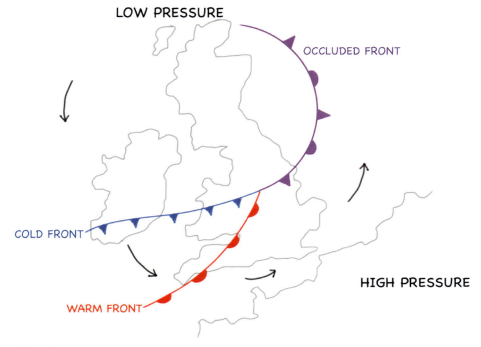

Figure 4.5.31 Fronts.

The edges of different fronts are shown on weather maps by the symbols shown by the images in the following. The red semicircles of the warm front show where warmer air is moving in to replace colder air. The blue triangles of a cold front show where colder air is moving in to take the place of warmer air. Both of these, plus the slightly more complicated occluded front, are explained further on page 206.

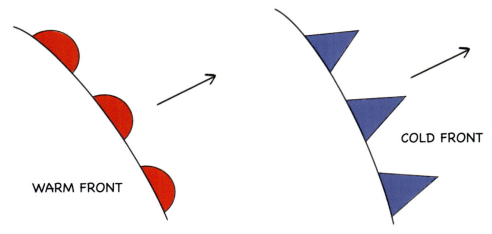

Figure 4.5.32 Fronts map.

206 *Weather and Climate*

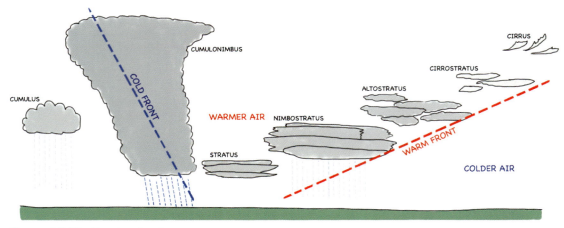

Figure 4.5.33 Passing fronts.

Figure 4.5.33 shows the typical progression from the formation of a warm front being followed by a cold front. Start by drawing the colder air on the right-hand side. Remind students that should warm air be pushed towards it, the warmer air would rise up over the warm front. Depending on whether you have covered types of cloud, you can either discuss how different types of cloud form at different heights along the front, or you could simplify the diagram by just drawing a generic rain cloud. Either way, remind students that it is the rising of air that leads to condensation and rainfall, and therefore this is how frontal rainfall happens. The cold front shows how when cold air is pushed into warmer air, it is forced underneath; hence, the angle of the front is much steeper.

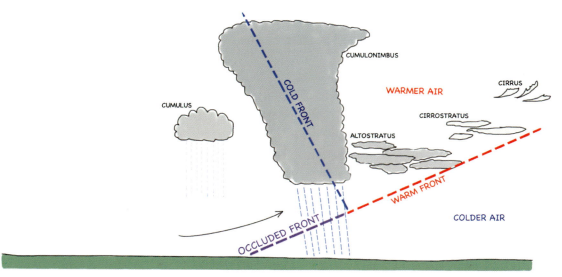

Figure 4.5.34 Occluded front.

Weather and Climate   207

The second diagram shows what happens when the cold front catches up with the warm front. Where the two meet, an occluded front is formed. You can see from these diagrams why, for example, the appearance in the sky of cirrus clouds may indicate that a warm front may be approaching.

The old rhyme "Mackerel sky, not 24 hours dry" refers to how altocumulus clouds will often turn into altostratus clouds, which are then likely to produce rain because of the arrival of a warm front.

Checking for Understanding

- What is an *air mass*?
- What happens when two air masses meet?
- What is an *occluded front*?

4.5.12 Humidity

Difficulty to draw: ●●
Difficulty to explain: ●●●

What Students Should Already Know

- Water can exist in three phases: gas, liquid, or solid.
- A change of temperature can lead to a phase change.
- Warmer air will expand because the molecules move faster and spread out.

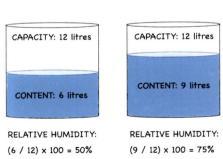

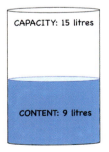

Figure 4.5.35   Relative humidity.

1. All air contains some moisture. It is usually measured as a percentage of what the air could contain.
2. If the amount of water moisture increases (e.g. through evaporation), then the percentage increases.
3. Or if the parcel of air expands (e.g. when it is heated), then the percentage would decrease.

The Explanation

Start by asking students to consider a parcel of air. That is actually quite hard to do, so give the parcel a size (e.g. the classroom). Then they will have a reference point once you start considering how the parcel of air can change size or have moisture added or removed.

The three images show a container with liquid water, rather than invisible water vapour, so you will need to remind students that the same maths applies but the water is in the form of vapour rather than liquid. The drawings don't have to be 3D, but it does help to show volume if they are. Ideally, draw the amounts relatively accurately (so that a relative humidity of 75% shows the container three-quarters full).

Figure 4.5.36 shows how temperature change affects the relative humidity. It is also a helpful supporting diagram for discussing how clouds form when moist air rises, then cools, and the water vapour condenses.

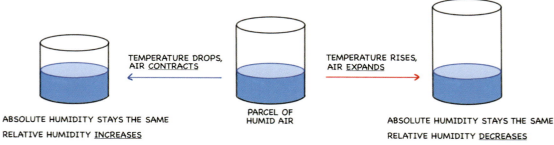

Figure 4.5.36 Relative humidity and temperature change.

As a parcel of air rises, it cools down. This causes the air to contract. The amount of moisture in the air remains the same. This causes the relative humidity to increase. It helps explain why relative humidity is usually higher during the night and then decreases throughout the morning. The sun warms the air, making it able to hold more moisture.

Some Useful Key Terms to Use

Relative humidity: the amount of water in the air, compared to how much the air could carry.
Absolute humidity: the actual amount of water vapour carried in a given volume of air.
Carrying capacity: the total amount of water vapour that the air can carry at that temperature.
Saturated air: air that has reached its carrying capacity (i.e. it is full of water, so is at 100% humidity).
Dew point: temperature that air drops to before reaching carrying capacity.

Checking for Understanding

- In what state does the air carry water?
- What happens to air when it is warmed?
- What is *relative humidity*? How is it measured?
- What happens to the relative humidity of a parcel of air when it is cooled?

4.5.13 Clouds
Difficulty to draw: ● ●
Difficulty to explain: ● ●

What Students Should Already Know

- The atmosphere is divided into different layers.
- Clouds form when air cools to dew point and water vapour condenses into cloud droplets.

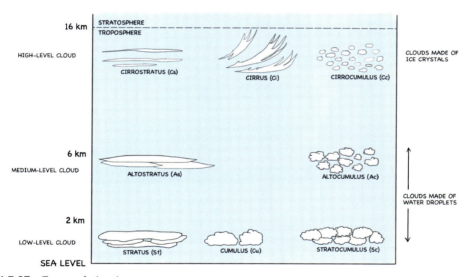

Figure 4.5.37   Types of clouds.

1. Cumulus clouds are fluffy and usually have a flat base. They are formed by localised uplift of warmed air.
2. Stratus clouds are layers of clouds. They occur where there is only some vertical uplift of air.
3. Cirrus clouds occur at high levels, where condensation creates ice crystals rather than cloud droplets.

210 *Weather and Climate*

The Explanation

Draw the outline box almost as though it is a graph. Explain as you draw it that clouds are usually divided into the three types: cumulus, stratus, and cirrus. They are also classified according to the height: low-, medium-, and high-level clouds. Start with the three main types (Cu, St, and Cs), drawing them on and describing their characteristics. The others are all variations of those three.

The other useful prefix is *nimbo-*, which denotes the rain-bearing version of the clouds. Figure 4.5.38 shows the features of a cumulonimbus cloud, which is also a useful one to include, especially if you will be studying tropical storms.

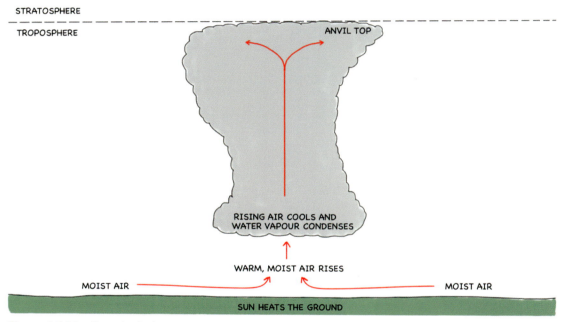

Figure 4.5.38 Cumulonimbus.

The diagram and processes are very similar to the diagram showing how convection creates clouds (Figure 4.5.17 on page 194). You could start with that diagram, and then consider what would happen if there were lots of moist air available and the ground was particularly warm. The moist air would just continue to rise until condensation occurs.

Classic photos of cumulonimbus clouds show the distinctive flat "anvil" top, which occurs when the cloud rises all the way up to the tropopause (the boundary between the troposphere and the stratosphere). The air stops rising here because the stratosphere is warmer than the air below. The heavy rainfall caused by these large clouds is down to the sheer volume of water that forms with so much condensation.

Checking for Understanding

- What are the three main types of cloud?
- Which type of cloud is fluffy?
- How high are cirrus clouds often found?
- What does *nimbo-* mean?

4.5.14 Fog   Difficulty to draw: •
Difficulty to explain: ••

> **What Students Should Already Know**
>
> Clouds form when air cools to dew point and water vapour condenses into cloud droplets.

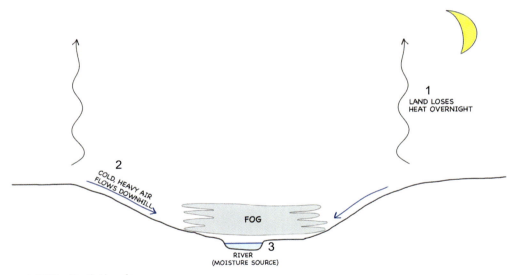

Figure 4.5.39   Radiation fog.

1. On calm, clear nights, the land can cool down very quickly.
2. The cold ground cools the air above it, which "flows" down and collects on the valley floor.
3. If there is moisture in the air, such as from a river or from rain during the day, it will condense to form radiation fog.

The Explanation

If students can explain how cooled air condenses to form clouds, then the formation of fog should be easy enough. Fog is essentially a cloud, but at ground level. Remind students that clouds form when air is cooled to below dew point. Fog forms in the same way: because the air near the ground has been cooled to below dew point. Valleys are susceptible to fog forming because of how the cooled air is relatively dense and so flows downhill. Figure 4.5.40 shows how advection fog forms. Again, the process of moist air being cooled is the same; it is just a different mechanism for getting moist air to be cooled.

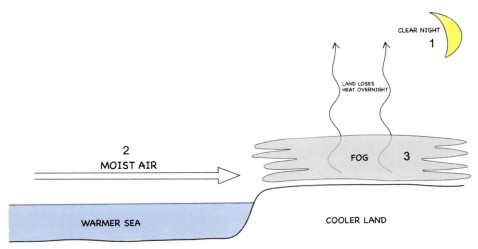

Figure 4.5.40 Advection fog.

1. On calm, clear nights, land can cool down very quickly.
2. Moist air is carried from the sea onto cooler land, where it is cooled down to below dew point.
3. Below dew point, the air becomes saturated, so water vapour condenses to water droplets.

When discussing condensation with students, it is always worth reminding them that the opposite process, evaporation, will occur when the temperature rises above dew point. That is, water droplets will turn into water vapour, and the fog or cloud will disappear. This is why fog is more common early in the morning. As the morning goes on and temperatures increase, the air expands and becomes able to hold more moisture.

Useful Distinction

Fog and mist are formed the same way, through condensation, but fog is when you can see less than 1,000 m, whereas it is mist if you can see more than 1,000 m.

Checking for Understanding

- Why does the ground cool more quickly on a cloudless night?
- What makes the air cool down?
- What is dew point?
- What condenses, the air or the water vapour?
- Name two types of fog.

4.5.15 Factors Affecting Climate

Difficulty to draw: ●●●
Difficulty to explain: ●●

> **What Students Should Already Know**
> - Energy from the sun reaches the Earth's surface, providing warmth.
> - Earth is surrounded by an atmosphere.
> - The distance from the equator can be measured using latitude.
> - The climates of different places around the world are caused by a number of different factors: latitude, time of year, distance from the sea, altitude, aspect, and ocean currents.

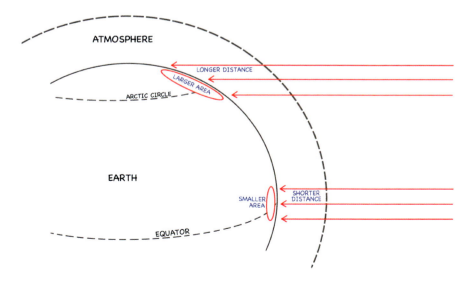

Figure 4.5.41   Temperature – latitude.

214 *Weather and Climate*

1. At higher latitudes, the sun's rays have a thicker amount of atmosphere to pass through before reaching the Earth's surface. The Earth's curve also means that the sun's rays are spread over a larger surface area, making them less intense.
2. At the equator, the sun's rays pass through a shorter amount of atmosphere and reach the Earth's surface at a vertical angle, focusing on a smaller area of land.

The Explanation

This is a difficult diagram to draw freehand, so use a compass to ensure you maintain the same thickness of atmosphere. Similarly, try to ensure that the three lines you draw for the sun's rays are the same distance apart. This will help show the difference in land area that the sun's rays cover when they reach the Earth's surface.

This is a good time to check whether students understand latitude and how it helps show distance from the equator. Figure 4.5.50 helps show how latitude is calculated.

Time of Year

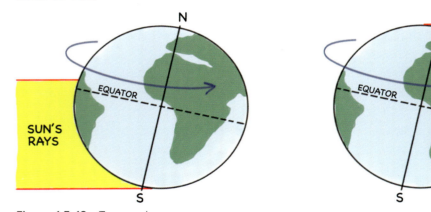

Figure 4.5.42   Temperature – seasons.

1. The Earth is tilted on its axis, so for half of the year, the northern hemisphere is tilted away from the sun. The days are shorter, and the angle of the Earth's surface means the sun's rays are spread over a wider surface area.
2. In June/July/August, the days are longer and the northern hemisphere is tilted towards the sun, meaning, the sun's rays are more vertical when they reach the surface.

The Explanation

The focus of the sun's rays is exaggerated, as they would also reach the other hemisphere, too, so perhaps change the label "sun's rays" to "more intense heating" for both images. The impact of the seasons can be nicely demonstrated using a tilted globe and a torch. As with

Weather and Climate 215

many geographical concepts, these diagrams work best after the concept has been shown using a practical demonstration, video, or series of photos.

This might also be a good opportunity to review some of the differences between the hemispheres and how the length of days is different throughout the year. Figure 4.5.43 looks at what happens on the June solstice, which usually falls around June 21. This helps explain why the Arctic and Antarctic Circles exist, as well as why the length of the day changes more with higher latitudes.

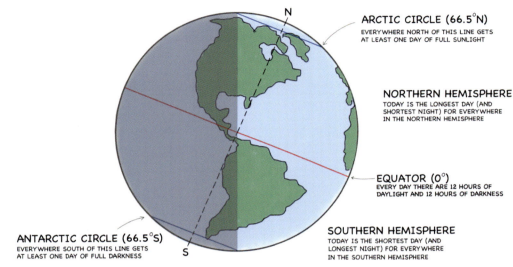

Figure 4.5.43   June solstice.

Distance from Sea

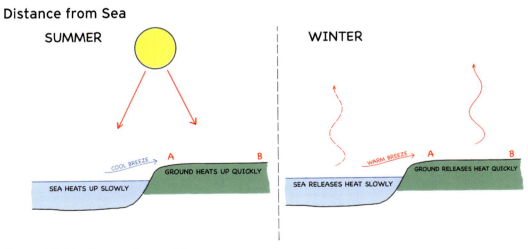

Figure 4.5.44   Temperature – distance.

1. Water heats up more slowly than land. So in the summer, coastal areas feel cooler from being next to the relatively cool sea.
2. Land loses heat more quickly than sea. So in the winter months, coastal areas feel warmer from being next to the relatively warm sea.

The Explanation

This is known as the maritime influence. It is caused by the sea having a greater specific heat capacity. More energy is required to warm the sea to a given temperature than to warm the land, so the sea takes longer to warm up. However, it also means that the land cools down more quickly.

Altitude

Air temperature decreases with altitude. The rate of decrease is around 6.5°C for every 1,000 m.

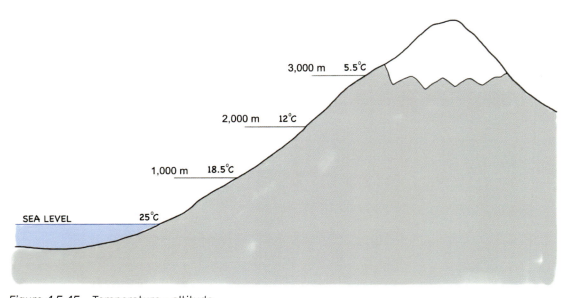

Figure 4.5.45   Temperature – altitude.

Aspect

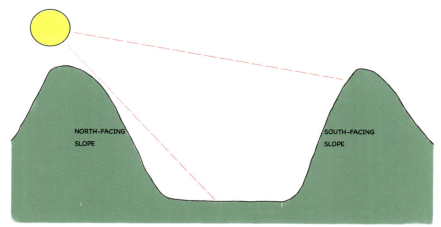

Figure 4.5.46 Temperature – aspect.

The aspect of a place is the direction in which it faces. In the northern hemisphere, a slope that faces the south will receive more sunshine, and therefore heat, because of the lower angle of the sun. A north-facing slope will be shaded for the same reason. The opposite is true in the Southern Hemisphere, whereas the impact of aspect in the tropics is negligible because the sun is near vertical.

Ocean Currents

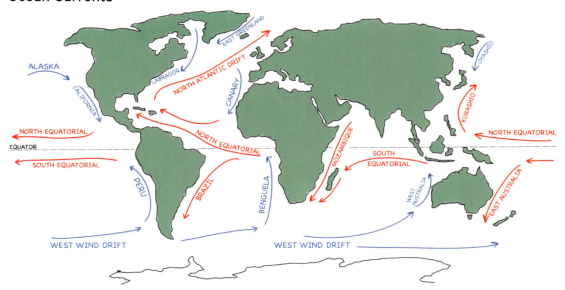

Figure 4.5.47 Temperature – currents.

218 *Weather and Climate*

An interconnected system of warm and cold currents flows around the oceans. Generally speaking, warm currents are those that originate in the tropics, and they take warmer water towards the poles. Cold ocean currents are those that carry water away from the poles. These currents influence the climates of coastal areas. For example, the UK is at a similar latitude to colder places in Canada and Russia but is kept warmer by the North Atlantic Drift. There are other, smaller currents, but this map shows a good range and also helps show how energy is distributed around the world by ocean currents.

Checking for Understanding

- What is the difference between *weather* and *climate*?
- How can latitude affect the temperature of a place?
- Which heats up more quickly: sea or land?
- By how much does the temperature decrease with every 1,000 m ascent?
- How does a place's aspect affect its temperature?
- How can ocean currents affect the climate of a coastal town?

4.5.16 Global Circulation

Difficulty to draw: ● ● ○
Difficulty to explain: ● ● ○

What Students Should Already Know

- Energy from the sun reaches the Earth's surface, providing warmth.
- The distance from the equator can be measured using latitude.
- Wind is the movement of air from areas of high to low pressure.
- Low pressure = rising air = clouds and rain. High pressure = sinking air = clear skies.

Weather and Climate 219

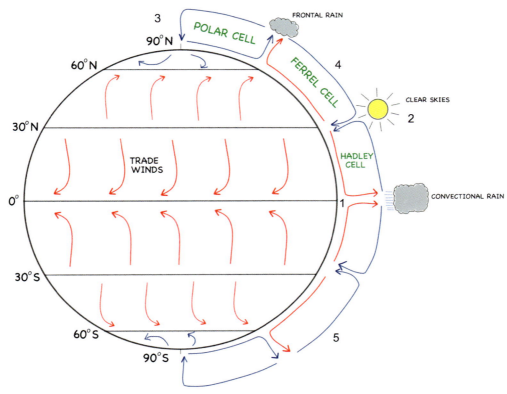

Figure 4.5.48 Tricellular model.

1. Intense heating from the sun at the equator causes air to rise and creates low pressure. Rain falls as a result.
2. The rising air is pushed north, away from the equator. At height, it cools and starts to descend around 30°N. This creates high pressure and clear skies.
3. At the North Pole, the cold air descends, creating high pressure. Wind blows southwards until it warms up around 60°N and starts to rise, creating low pressure.
4. The rising and falling of air, along with the winds between high and low pressures, creates cells called the Hadley cell and the polar cell. These don't stretch to meet each other so cause a third cell, the Ferrel cell, to operate.
5. The cells and the winds that blow from the areas of high to low pressure are replicated in the Southern Hemisphere too.

The Explanation

This takes time to draw neatly but is somehow very satisfying to draw and teach. Perhaps because it looks fairly complicated, but the light bulb "Aha!" moment from a student once

220 Weather and Climate

they connect the different parts is great. Use a compass to draw the outline of the Earth, and mark on the main lines of latitude. Figure 4.5.50 is a good supporting diagram to explain how latitude works.

Before drawing the main diagram, ask students to consider which parts of the Earth are hottest and which are coldest. Then use Figure 4.5.49 to ask why, in that case, isn't there one large cell of wind moving from the high pressure at the poles to the low pressure at the tropics. Explain that the Earth is too large for that, and so smaller cells form as a result.

As per the annotations, start the main diagram with the Hadley cell, showing how it causes the daily thunderstorms over the tropical rainforests and cloudless skies over the Sahara and Middle East. Then move to the polar cell, starting with how cold conditions cause air to sink, which leads to high pressure.

The Ferrel cell is caused by the other two (use the analogy of a cog being turned by two others) so is perhaps the harder one to understand. Drawing the winds blowing from the different pressure zones helps remind students that the Earth is 3D, and this diagram is just a slice through cells that wrap around the whole planet. Ideally, the winds are drawn showing the influence of the Coriolis force.

Mark on the rising air at the equator and sinking air at the poles. Draw on the air moving from high to low pressure as surface winds and then complete the cell with the higher-level winds.

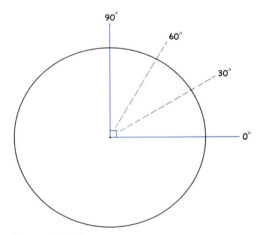

Figure 4.5.50 Teaching latitude.

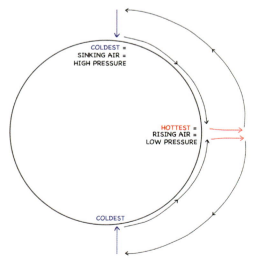

Figure 4.5.49 Simple global model.

Draw a circle with a compass and use a protractor to mark off the angles. Use a ruler to show where the angled lines meet the Earth's surface.

Weather and Climate

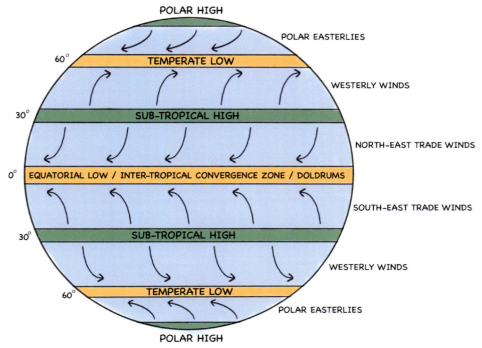

Figure 4.5.51 Global pressure belts.

Figure 4.5.51 is a clear way to just show the major pressure bands and winds without the processes involved. A common mistake from students is to label winds according to which direction they are blowing to, rather than from, so this also helps correct any misconceptions.

Checking for Understanding
- Where on Earth is the sun's radiation the strongest?
- Why is there an area of low pressure around the equator?
- Why does air sink at the poles?
- Why does wind blow from the North Pole southwards?
- What is the *Hadley cell*?
- Why is there an area of high pressure around 30°N and 30°S?
- Whereabouts does the Ferrel cell operate?

4.5.17 Tropical Storms

Difficulty to draw: ●●
Difficulty to explain: ●●

What Students Should Already Know

- Clouds form when air cools to dew point and water vapour condenses into cloud droplets.
- The Coriolis force causes winds to deflect to the right in the northern hemisphere.

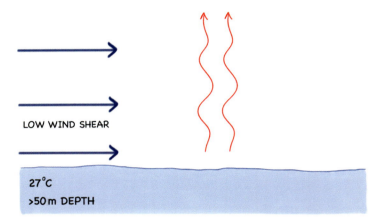

Figure 4.5.52 Hurricane formation 1.

1. Warm, moist air over the ocean rises to create an area of low pressure. There should be low wind shear to stop the storm from breaking apart.

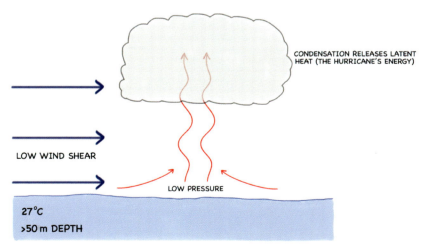

Figure 4.5.53 Hurricane formation 2.

2. Cumulonimbus clouds form. More moist air arrives to replace the rising air.

Weather and Climate 223

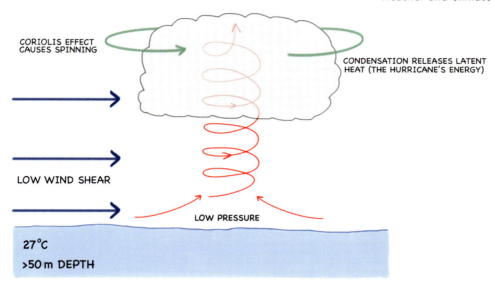

Figure 4.5.54 Hurricane formation 3.

3. Coriolis causes the whole storm system to rotate, but only when it is large enough. Air continues to rise, and the storm keeps growing.

The Explanation

The formation of tropical storms needs to be sequenced carefully. Start simply by reminding students about what happens when moist air rises. Explain that all hurricanes and cyclones start in the same way a "normal" cloud forms, but if the conditions are right, some can keep growing and develop into a tropical storm.

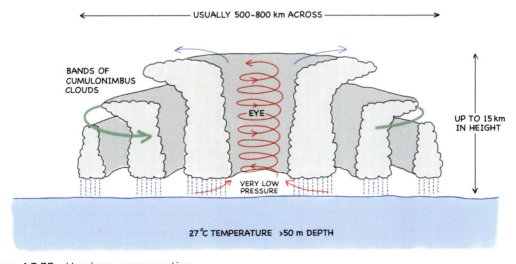

Figure 4.5.55 Hurricane cross section.

Using the three diagrams helps keep the explanation clear. Figure 4.5.55 can then be used to show the characteristics and specific features of a tropical storm, and Figure 4.5.56 helps to locate the formation of hurricanes. It is worth highlighting that *hurricanes*, *typhoons*, and *cyclones* are just different names for the same process.

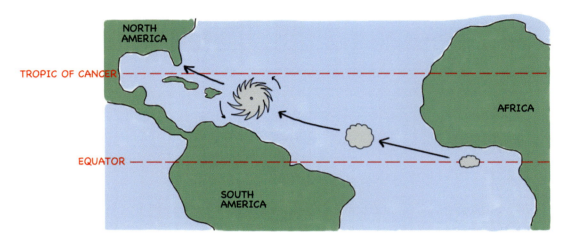

Figure 4.5.56   Hurricane map.

Figure 4.5.56 helps to show how an area of low pressure off the west coast of Africa can develop into a hurricane. Using a map like this also helps show the latitudes that hurricanes can form within: too close to the equator and Coriolis is not strong enough; too far north and the water is not warm enough. The westward path is also an important characteristic and is due to the way the Earth spins. The spin of the hurricane is caused by the Coriolis force and can be explained using Figure 4.5.12 on page 191.

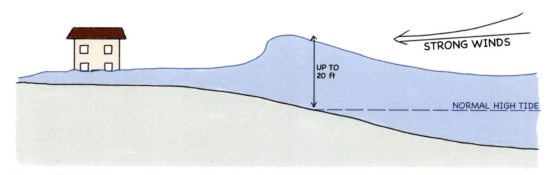

Figure 4.5.57   Storm surge.

Weather and Climate 225

The greatest risk to life from hurricanes and other tropical storms is not the strong winds; it is from storm surges. The powerful winds push the seawater onto the coast, creating huge surges of water that can engulf coastal settlements. However, the most powerful winds do not generate the worst storm surges. The surge will be highest when it combines with a high tide, when the water is channelled by bays and inlets, and when the storm approaches at a right angle to the coast.

Storm Surge Analogy

The strong winds of a hurricane blow water towards the coast, pushing it far inland and resulting in coastal flooding.

> *Imagine a cup of tea, or a bowl of soup. When you blow over the surface, the ripples that you create are like a mini storm surge. Hence the expression "storm in a teacup."*

Checking for Understanding

- What is the difference between a *hurricane*, a *cyclone*, and a *typhoon*?
- What temperature does the sea need to be for a hurricane to form?
- Why can't a hurricane form on the equator?
- What is the calm area in the centre of a hurricane called?
- Why do most hurricanes spin anticlockwise?
- What makes some storm surges so dangerous?

4.5.18 El Niño   Difficulty to draw: ● ●
Difficulty to explain: ● ● ●

What Students Should Already Know

- Rising air causes low pressure and rain. Sinking air causes high pressure and clear skies.
- The climates of different parts of the world are caused by a combination of factors.
- Trade winds are caused by the Hadley cells and blow from east to west between the tropics and the equator.

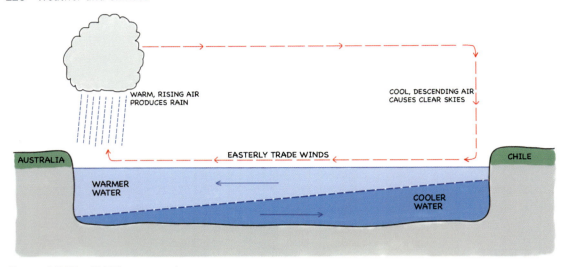

Figure 4.5.58 El Niño - normal.

1. In normal years, trade winds blow warm water from east to west. Near Australia, the warm, moist air rises to create rain.
2. Cooler water is pushed east. The cool, sinking air completes a cell of air movement.

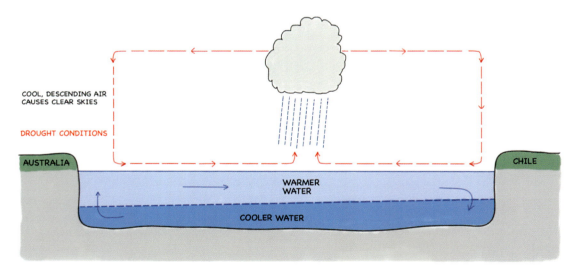

Figure 4.5.59 El Niño.

3. During El Niño years, the easterly trade winds weaken. The warm water sloshes back east. The rising air and rainfall follow, leaving Australia dry.
4. The change in water temperature off the coast of Chile reduces fish numbers and negatively affects local fishing industries.

Weather and Climate 227

The Explanation

El Niño is not fully understood by climate scientists. The patterns and impacts can be seen, but the causes of the weakening trade winds are still being investigated. These uncertainties are worth highlighting to students.

Start the first diagram with the easterly trade winds. These might have been covered already during a lesson on global circulation, and the cause of the wind can be reviewed using page 221. Then add the warmer water being focused in the west. This naturally leads to the rising air and rain, which makes the rest of the diagram simple to complete.

Begin the second diagram with the rebalancing of the warmer and cooler water. Without the trade winds pushing warmer water, it "sloshes" back east. The rain cloud and rainfall are in the centre for this diagram, but note that the rain might be farther east, depending on where the warmer water is found as it moves east.

Checking for Understanding

- What direction do trade winds move in the Pacific Ocean?
- Why does the air rise in the west Pacific?
- Where is the area of higher pressure in normal years?
- What causes the water to slosh back east during El Niño years?

4.5.19 Greenhouse Effect

Difficulty to draw: ● ●
Difficulty to explain: ● ●

What Students Should Already Know

- The sun's energy warms the ground.
- Burning fossil fuels releases carbon dioxide into the atmosphere.

228 Weather and Climate

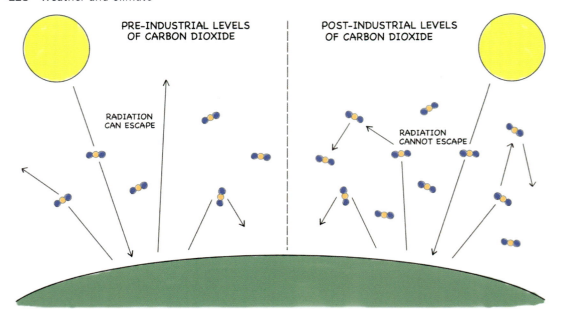

Figure 4.5.60 Greenhouse effect.

1. The sun gives off shortwave radiation, which passes through the atmosphere to warm the ground.
2. The warmed ground releases the energy as longwave radiation, which rises and heads back out to space.
3. If the longwave radiation meets any CO_2, it is absorbed and then released out again in a new direction.
4. If there is additional CO_2 in the atmosphere, it keeps the longwave radiation in the atmosphere, causing it to warm up.

The Explanation

This diagram is in response to the common but misleading "blanket" of greenhouse gases diagram. That suggests that the gases form in a layer high up in the atmosphere and reflect the heat back down to Earth. Showing the CO_2 molecules helps to not only explain how they absorb and then release the longwave energy but also show that the greenhouse gases are everywhere, not just a layer in the sky.

It is important that students know that the incoming solar radiation (known as insolation) is shortwave, and the outgoing is longwave. The difference explains why the incoming radiation is not affected by the presence of carbon dioxide. Figure 4.5.61 helps show how the CO_2 reacts to the radiation.

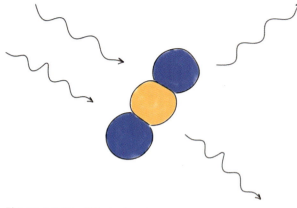

Figure 4.5.61 CO_2 molecules.

The CO_2 will absorb the longwave radiation once it has been radiated from the Earth's surface, and then re-emit it. It could be re-emitted in any direction, potentially to another CO_2 molecule. Therefore, the more CO_2 there is in the atmosphere, the more likely the heat is to become trapped in the atmosphere as it passes from one CO_2 molecule to another rather than leaving the atmosphere and heading back out to space.

Checking for Understanding
- Why doesn't the incoming solar radiation become trapped by carbon dioxide?
- What are some of the sources of carbon dioxide?
- What happens when longwave radiation reaches a CO_2 molecule?
- Why do more CO_2 molecules result in more radiation being trapped in the atmosphere?

4.6 Ecosystems

4.6.1 Features of an Ecosystem

Difficulty to draw: ●●○
Difficulty to explain: ●●○

> **What Students Should Already Know**
> - Plants use sunlight for photosynthesis.
> - Plants and animals need water to survive.
> - They also need nutrients in food to live and grow.

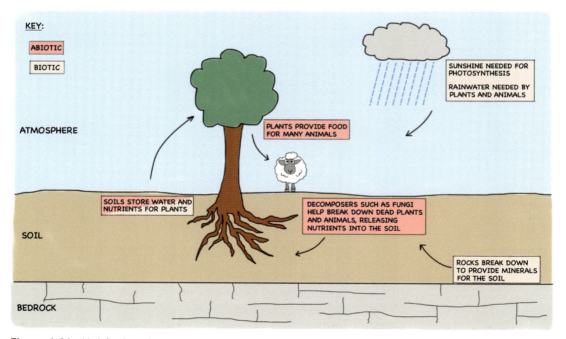

Figure 4.6.1   Nutrient cycle.

Ecosystems 231

1. Water and sunlight are essential to the ecosystem. Plants and animals need both to survive.
2. During decomposition, nutrients are released into the soil. Rocks also provide the soil with some minerals.
3. Plants absorb nutrients from the soil and use them to grow. The nutrients will be passed on to animals when they eat the plants.

The Explanation

As an introduction to the topics, much will depend on students' prior knowledge. They will need to appreciate that all living organisms need water and nutrients, as well as the role that sunlight plays in plant growth. These basics are crucial, and it is important to spend time checking if these building blocks of knowledge are in place first.

Start by drawing the tree and asking what a tree needs to survive and grow. Then label on the sunlight, rainfall, and nutrients. The weathering of rocks and subsequent release of minerals may need some clarification. Then draw an animal (doesn't have to be a sheep!) and discuss what it needs to survive and grow.

Identify which of the parts are living (biotic) and non-living (abiotic), and discuss how the ecosystem is all these different parts.

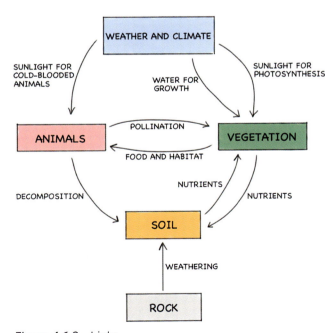

Figure 4.6.2 Links.

Figure 4.6.2 shows the different parts of the ecosystem and how they interact. This is easier to complete with students once you have gone through the "drawing" version. Discuss the importance of systems diagrams like this in geography and how they are used to show connections.

232 *Ecosystems*

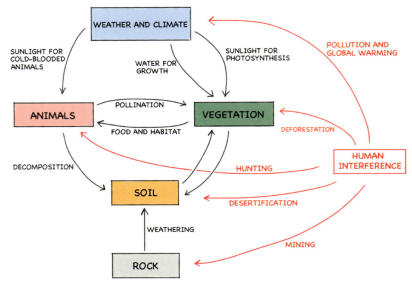

Figure 4.6.3 Links – human impact.

Then Figure 4.6.3 can be used as an extension to show how, by understanding an ecosystem's components, we can assess the impacts of human activity on different parts. This diagram could be given to students partially completed and then annotated together.

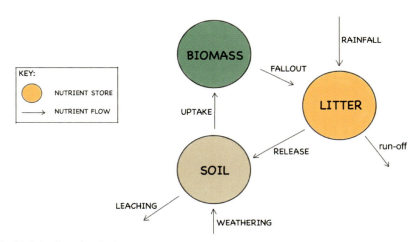

Figure 4.6.4 Nutrient cycle circles.

Figure 4.6.4 is a useful way of showing how nutrients are moved within the different parts of an ecosystem. The relative sizes of the three circles will change depending on the nature of the ecosystem.

Checking for Understanding

- What is the difference between *biotic* and *abiotic*?
- What are *nutrients*?
- What happens to nutrients in plants and animals when they die?
- Where does soil get its nutrients from?

4.6.2 Food Chains and Nutrient Cycling

Difficulty to draw: •
Difficulty to explain: ••

What Students Should Already Know

- Ecosystems are made up of biotic and abiotic parts.
- Each part is connected, and some parts depend on others.

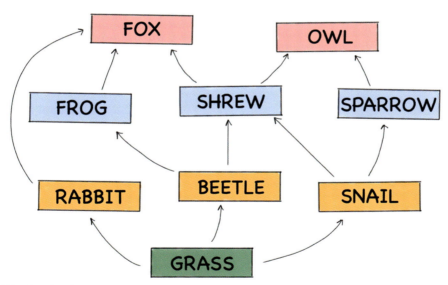

Figure 4.6.5   Food web.

1. Grass is a producer, which means it converts the sun's energy by photosynthesis.
2. Herbivores eat the grass and consume the energy and nutrients.
3. Carnivores feed on herbivores. New grass will eventually get the nutrients again when the animals die and decompose.

The Explanation

Start with grass, and then just choose one of the animals that might eat it (e.g. a rabbit). Draw the arrow showing the movement of energy from the grass to the rabbit. Then add the fox to create a simple food chain.

A food web is a combination of food chains and how they are related and overlap. Then discuss which other animals might eat the grass, and add more accordingly. Remind students about how nutrients and energy will be taken on by the consumer. The arrows show the flow of energy as it passes from one organism to another.

The role of decomposers is not shown here, and that can be added by drawing arrows down from all the animals back into the grass.

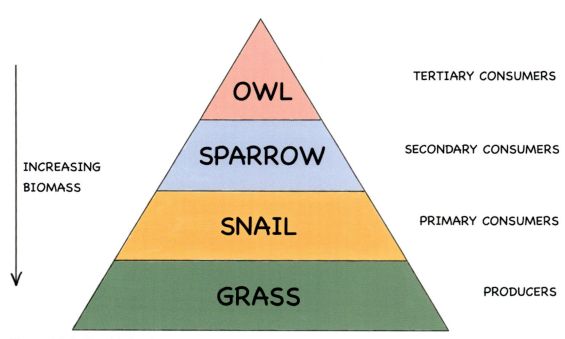

Figure 4.6.6 Trophic level.

Figure 4.6.6 shows the relative numbers of each level within the food web. Energy is lost as you move up the pyramid. One reason for this is that consumers do not actually consume all their food. For example, the snail uses energy to build its shell. However, the sparrow will not eat the shell, and therefore, some of the energy is left behind.

Ecosystems 235

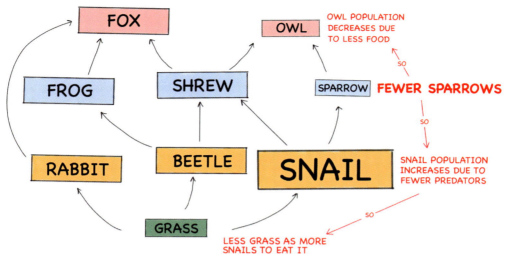

Figure 4.6.7 Food web – imbalance.

Food webs allow us to think about the knock-on impacts of affecting one species. For example, in Figure 4.6.7, we can consider what would happen if the population of sparrows were to decline. There are more annotations that could be added, such as, for example, the impact on rabbits if the snails ate all the grass.

Checking for Understanding
- What is a *producer*?
- What is a *consumer*?
- In a food web, what do the arrows show?

4.6.3 Global Distribution of Biomes

Difficulty to draw: ● ●
Difficulty to explain: ● ●

What Students Should Already Know
- The climate of a place will influence the type of ecosystem that develops there.
- Distance from the equator is marked by latitude.

236   Ecosystems

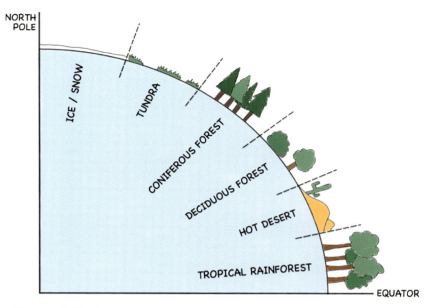

Figure 4.6.8   Biomes – latitude.

1. Distance from the equator determines the type of biome.
2. Rainforests and deserts are found at lower latitudes.
3. Tundra is found at higher latitudes, where it is so cold that little vegetation is able to grow there.

The Explanation

This is best used alongside a map showing the worldwide distribution of the different biomes. There are plenty of different versions available (just search "global distribution of biomes" into a search engine), but choose one that matches the biomes you will use for this diagram. Alternatively, you could adapt the diagram to match a map. For example, some maps won't have coniferous forest but will have taiga instead.

Use a protractor to draw the curve of the Earth, and given the nature of the diagram, this is a good time to recap latitude and how it is calculated. Figure 4.5.50 on page 220 will help explain it.

This diagram could also be extended by adding the relevant parts of the tri-cellular model (see Figure 4.5.48 on page 219) or how the sun's rays are more concentrated onto the lower latitudes (Figure 4.5.41 on page 213).

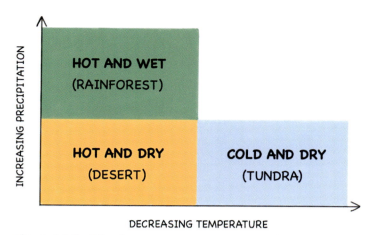

Figure 4.6.9 Climate zones.

Figure 4.6.9 is an interesting way to look at the general trends of the different biomes and the relative importance of temperature and rainfall in determining the location of the major biomes.

Figure 4.6.10 provides a good research task for students. Give students the blank triangle, perhaps even with the labels, but no diagrams. Then students can look up the different biomes (using the following case studies) and add in the relevant average temperatures and rainfall to see whether the places fit with the pyramid's layout. Students can complete the pyramid with a simple image of each biome.

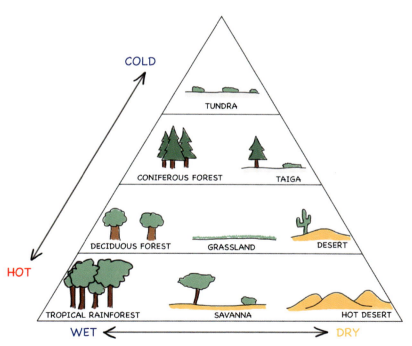

Figure 4.6.10 Biomes – pyramid.

238 *Ecosystems*

Case Studies

65.3458, -114.0305 Northwest Territories, Canada (tundra)
63.1444, 46.5097 Siberia, Russia (coniferous forest)
57.2408, 161.3634 Kamchatka Peninsula, Russia (taiga)
47.5115, 2.0839 Orléans, France (deciduous forest)
39.4561, -104.5280 Colorado, USA (temperate grassland)
3.3103, 116.1865 Kayan Mentarang National Park, Malaysia (tropical rainforest)
-2.0055, 38.7589 Tsavo National Park, Kenya (savanna)
-23.8516, -69.0649 Atacama Desert, Chile (desert)

Checking for Understanding

- What is a *biome*?
- What are some examples of different biomes?
- Why are different biomes located at different latitudes?

4.6.4 Distribution: Latitude

Difficulty to draw: ●●○
Difficulty to explain: ●●○

What Students Should Already Know

- Distance from the equator is marked by latitude.
- The tri-cellular model describes areas of high pressure and areas of low pressure.
- High pressure leads to clear skies; low pressure leads to rising air and rainfall.

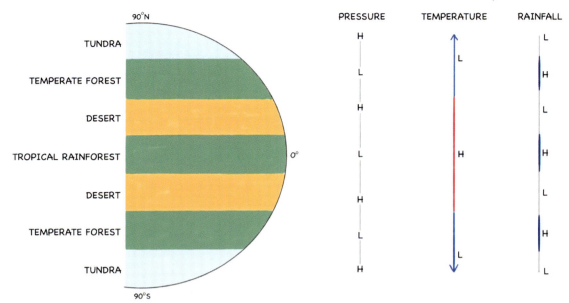

Figure 4.6.11 Latitude and biomes.

1. The Earth is divided into different biomes (or major ecosystems).
2. Where there is high pressure, there is little rainfall. Latitudes of low pressure receive rainfall.
3. Those latitudes closer to the equator are warmer than those latitudes closer to the poles.

The Explanation

This diagram relies on students being confident in explaining the tri-cellular model and how that leads to areas of higher and lower pressure. The relevant diagram and explanation are found on page 219. Figure 4.6.12 also shows just the Hadley cell and how it results in both rainforest and hot deserts.

Use a compass to draw the semicircular Earth. It works well to draw this on lined paper, so that the layers of biomes can be shaded in neatly. Go for two lines per biome.

Assuming students can identify the areas of high and low pressure from the tri-cellular model, mark those on, along with the temperature line, and the varying rainfall line. The combination of the rainfall and temperature lines should be enough to allow for explanation of why the different biomes exist where they do.

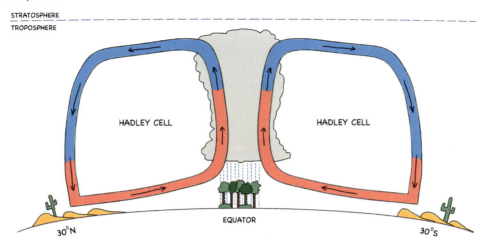

Figure 4.6.12 Hadley cells.

This should be more of a recap than an introduction to the Hadley cells. Intense heating from the sun causes air to rise over the equator, which then cools and produces the daily rainfall associated with the tropical rainforests. As the now "dry" air moves out and away from the equator at height, it is cooler and so descends around 30°N and 30°S. The descending air results in clear skies, no rain, and desert conditions.

> **Case Studies**
>
> -23.8516, -69.0649 Atacama Desert, Chile (desert)
> 3.3103, 116.1865 Kayan Mentarang National Park, Malaysia (tropical rainforest)

> **Checking for Understanding**
> - How does the Hadley cell operate?
> - Why does low pressure result in rainfall?
> - Why does high pressure result in clear skies?
> - What is the climate like where tundra is found?

4.6.5 Distribution: Rain Shadow

Difficulty to draw: ●●
Difficulty to explain: ●●

Ecosystems 241

What Students Should Already Know

- When moist air is forced to rise, clouds and rain are likely to form.
- When air descends, it creates an area of high pressure, characterised by clear skies.

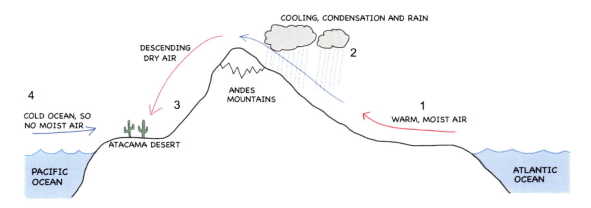

Figure 4.6.13   Dist – rain shadow.

1. Air, warmed by the sun, carries moisture from the Atlantic Ocean onto the land.
2. It is forced upwards over the Andes mountains, where it cools and rain clouds form.
3. The now-dry air continues down the other side of the mountains. It is descending, so there are no clouds or rain.
4. Air that arrives from the Pacific Ocean is cold, so there has been little evaporation.

The Explanation

Prior to using this diagram, you should have shown students where the major biomes are located and discussed the role that latitude plays in their location. This diagram explains one of the reasons for deserts forming and uses the Atacama Desert as an example.

As with other diagrams, little features such as the exaggerated snow cap, the oversized clouds, and the cacti can help highlight certain aspects of your diagram. The coloured arrows also convey the idea of warmer air being cooled as it ascends the mountains.

Case Study

-23.8516, -69.0649 Atacama Desert, Chile (desert)

242 *Ecosystems*

Checking for Understanding

- On which continent is the Atacama Desert located?
- Why is the air blowing in from the Atlantic Ocean moist?
- Why do clouds form?
- Why doesn't the air from the Pacific Ocean bring any rainfall?

4.6.6 Distribution: Ocean Currents

Difficulty to draw: ●○○
Difficulty to explain: ●●●

What Students Should Already Know

- Water vapour will condense when it is cooled down enough.
- Ocean temperatures will affect the temperature of the overlying air.
- During the day, winds usually blow from the land out to sea and then switch direction at night.
- Warmed air can hold more water vapour, which is why fog will evaporate later in the morning.

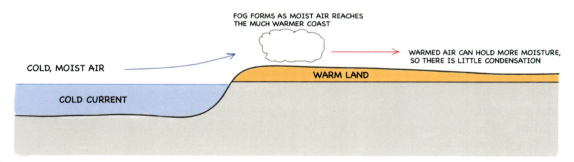

Figure 4.6.14 Dist – cold currents.

1. Air that has been warmed by the land meets cold air from over the ocean. Fog forms.
2. The fog is blown onto the land by the ocean breeze.
3. By mid-morning, the air has been warmed again enough for the fog to disappear.
4. So a coastal desert might be damp from fog but never experiences rainfall.

The Explanation

The point of this diagram is to show how even though there might be a cold current, and even though fog does regularly form, a desert can remain hot and dry. The Atacama Desert is, again, a good example of this phenomenon.

The fog is also the main supply of moisture for the plants and animals that live in these deserts. Indeed, some of the species found are adapted specifically to get their water from fog. For example, the darkling beetle of the Namib Desert will stick its bum in the air each morning to let the fog condense onto it before the moisture drips down its back into the beetle's mouth.

The diagram is simple to draw. Start with the difference in temperature between the land and the sea. During the day, wind usually blows from the land out to sea before returning at night. This is due to the differences in heat capacity, and Figure 4.5.44 on page 215 can be adapted to help this explanation. This is the mechanism by which the fog is first created and then returns to the land for the morning. You may also want to use Figure 4.5.44 to remind students about air's ability to hold certain amounts of moisture at certain temperatures. This is the reason that when the air warms up throughout the morning, it can hold more water vapour and so the fog evaporates.

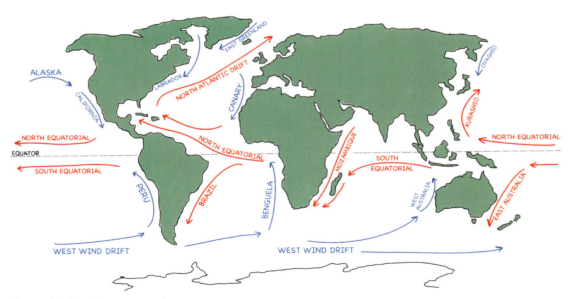

Figure 4.6.15 Ocean currents.

The map of ocean currents is a good starting point for discussing the impacts of the currents. Ask students to compare a map of the currents with a map of biome distribution, and to look for places where deserts occur next to cold ocean currents. They should spot

244 *Ecosystems*

the Atacama and Namib Deserts, which are two good examples to use. Remember that each biome is affected by multiple factors, not just latitude and ocean currents, so any biome that doesn't quite fit the "model" is likely explained by something else, such as the presence of mountains or a local prevailing wind.

Case Studies

-23.8516, -69.0649 Atacama Desert, Chile
-24.9563, 15.0410 Namib Desert, Namibia

Checking for Understanding

- How does fog form?
- Why do coastal winds change direction at night-time?
- What other factors, apart from ocean currents, can affect a place's climate?

4.6.7 Tropical Rainforests

Difficulty to draw: ● ● ●
Difficulty to explain: ● ● ●

What Students Should Already Know

- Tropical rainforests are one of the major biomes.
- The climate is characterised by hot temperatures and high rainfall.
- A nutrient cycle shows how nutrients are balanced between the biomass, litter, and soil of that place.
- Rising moist air is cooled at altitude, resulting in condensation, clouds, and rainfall.

Ecosystems 245

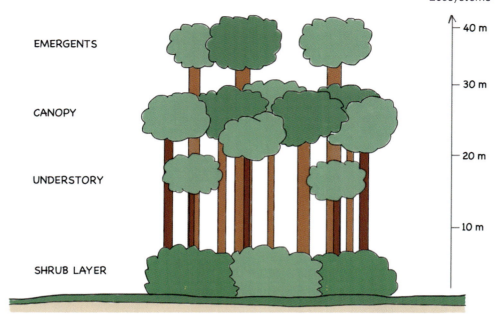

Figure 4.6.16 Layers of the rainforest.

The Explanation

Many students will have learnt about rainforests at primary school so may well have some familiarity with the different layers. Therefore, it is important to consider why it is worth reviewing the layers and getting students to draw and label the layers. If it is part of a wider "ecosystems" topic, then frame the explanation of this diagram around the role that the different layers have for both the nutrient and water cycles.

Start with the canopy layer. From here you can show how tropical rainforests are different from other forests by then adding the emergent layer and explaining why trees grow so tall. Then add the understory layer, explaining how the lack of sunlight leads to plants having to either adapt to get nutrients from elsewhere or to just wait until older trees fall and let the sunlight in. Then add the shrub layer and then discuss the conditions likely to be found on the forest floor. Some of the plants within the lower layers are epiphytes (they grow on other plants to take their nutrients and water).

246 *Ecosystems*

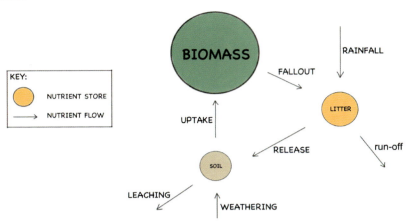

Figure 4.6.17 Rainforest nutrient circles.

Figure 4.6.17 shows the balance between three components of the nutrient cycle within a tropical rainforest. The biomass within a rainforest is greater than any other terrestrial biome (coral reefs have even more!), and this is due to the vegetation's ability to maximise the hot and humid conditions. These same conditions make decomposition on the forest floor so quick that nutrients don't stay within the litter for long. Similarly, the intense competition for nutrients from the huge biomass results in the nutrients not remaining in the soil for long before they are taken up by all the trees and plants.

The hot and humid characteristics of the tropical regions can best be shown with a climate graph. It is likely that you will be comparing the climates of different biomes, so try to keep the format (colour, style, labels) the same when you draw the different climate graphs.

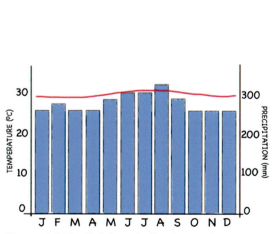

Figure 4.6.18 Rainforest climate graph.

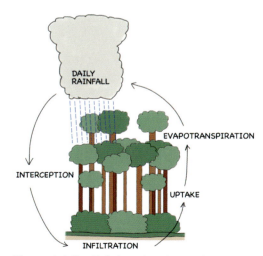

Figure 4.6.19 Rainforest water cycle.

Ecosystems 247

Rainfall Analogy

Students can sometimes get the two parts of the graph muddled and might read the line as the rainfall and vice versa.

Tell students to imagine each individual blue bar on the graph as an empty glass container, ready to fill up throughout the month with all the rain that falls.

Figure 4.6.19 can be drawn to help explain how the rainforest not only deals with the daily rainfall but also contributes to it. It is estimated that rainforests produce up to 75% of their rainfall from evaporation and transpiration.

The role that the trees play in protecting the soil from the heavy pounding of tropical storms can be discussed too. Without the slowing effect of the layers of vegetation, the soil would be quickly washed away.

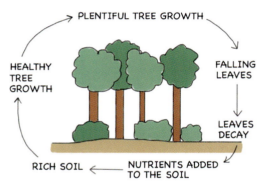 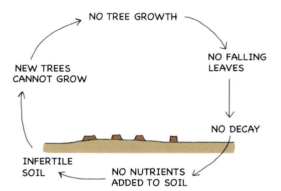

Figure 4.6.20 Deforestation.

A good follow-on from discussing the rainforest nutrient cycle is to consider what happens when the trees are cut down, and therefore the biomass removed from the equation. The lack of decomposing litter causes the soil to become quickly infertile.

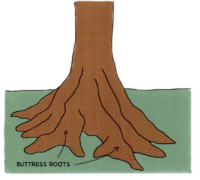

Figure 4.6.21 Buttress roots.

There are a number of different plant features that can be used to show how they have adapted to life in the rainforest. The buttress roots help keep the enormous trees from toppling over, especially as the relatively shallow soil prevents a deeper root system that would help support the trees.

Other drawable adaptations include drip-tip leaves, climbing lianas, and the competition to be the tallest trees. Similarly, animals have adapted to life in the rainforest by, for example, becoming adept climbers (e.g. monkeys) or being able to glide between trees (e.g. flying squirrels).

Buttress Roots Analogy

Buttress roots provide a wide base for tall trees to stop them from falling over.

Ask a volunteer to come up to the front and stand straight with their feet together. Suggest (gently!) what might happen if you were to push them. Now consider what would happen if their feet were spread apart on the floor.

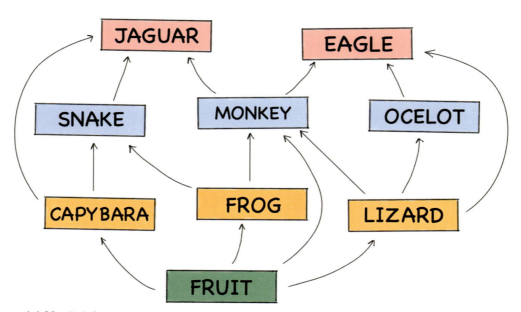

Figure 4.6.22 Rainforest food web.

As with other biomes, a food web can help students think about the rainforest as a flow of nutrients between some of the different components. The species shown on Figure 4.6.22 could just as easily be replaced by animals found through the students' own research.

Case Study

3.3103, 116.1865 Kayan Mentarang National Park, Malaysia (tropical rainforest)

Checking for Understanding

- What are the four layers of the rainforest?
- What is the climate like?
- Why does the soil contain fewer nutrients compared to the plants and trees?
- What happens to the soil when the trees are cut down?
- How have plants adapted to life in the rainforest?

4.6.8 Hot Deserts

Difficulty to draw: ●●○
Difficulty to explain: ●●○

What Students Should Already Know

- Hot deserts are one of the major biomes.
- The arid climate is characterised by hot temperatures and low rainfall.
- A nutrient cycle shows how nutrients are balanced between the biomass, litter, and soil of that place.

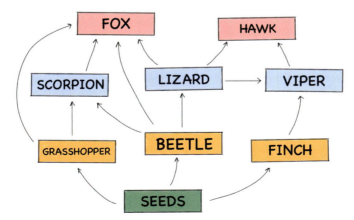

Figure 4.6.23 Desert food web.

250 *Ecosystems*

The Explanation

A food web is a good route "into" a biome with students. They will know several of the animals, and discussing what they eat and what life might be like can make the topic more relevant.

As with other food webs, start with one of the animals and tell its "story." Where is it getting its food from? Who does it need to watch out for? Using video clips of different desert animals is a good start. Allowing students to see the animal helps bring the food web to life. If you have particular video clips, then the food web you draw can be adapted to the featured animals.

This is unlikely to be the first food web the students will have been taught about, so the annotations could be more focused on some of the adaptations the plants and animals use to survive in the arid conditions. For example, the desert fox has thick fur on the soles of its paws to protect itself from the hot sand.

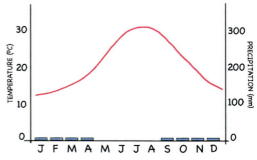

This climate graph for Tindouf in Algeria highlights just how difficult the conditions are for plants and animals to survive. Rainfall is very uncommon, and temperatures can soar.

It is worth noting that different deserts will experience different climates, and that typically, rainfall is very unpredictable. Deserts usually receive less than 250 mm of rain per year, but that average might include several years of no rainfall at all!

Figure 4.6.24 Desert climate graph.

The same Hadley cell diagram that explained the intense rainfall over the rainforests can be used to show the dry descending air common over most hot deserts.

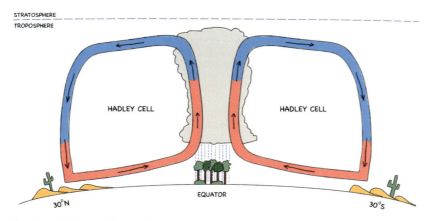

Figure 4.6.25 Hadley cells.

It is important to highlight that a desert's climate is not down to just one factor, such as latitude. Proximity to ocean currents and the presence of mountains can also play a role.

Ecosystems 251

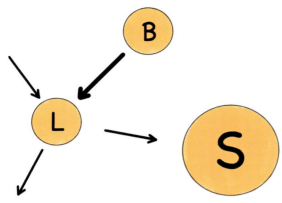

Figure 4.6.26 Desert nutrient circles.

The nutrient cycle in deserts will also vary from place to place. Figure 4.6.26 shows a desert where the soil has a relatively large proportion of nutrients. This is the case where deserts might have a naturally high mineral content. Most deserts have little plant life and next to no litter to speak of.

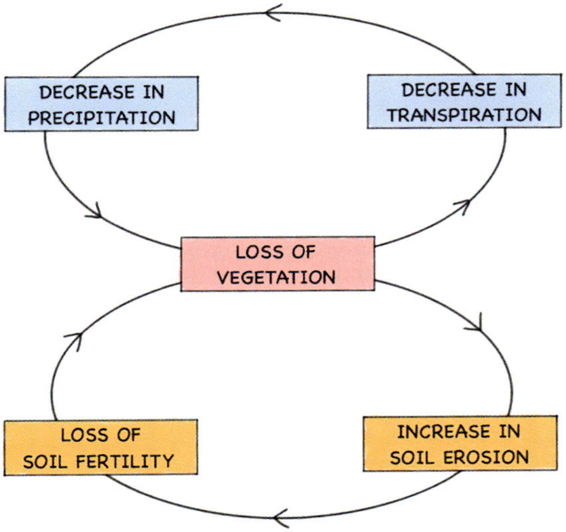

Figure 4.6.27 shows how a loss of vegetation, perhaps through deforestation, will lead to a further decrease in the amount of vegetation.

It is also a good way to discuss feedback loops. This is a positive feedback loop, in that it continues to cause more of the thing in the middle. Conversely, a negative feedback loop is one where the outcome is a reduction of the thing in the middle.

Figure 4.6.27 Desertification.

There are plenty of examples of how desert plants and animals have adapted to conditions in the desert. A cactus is a good one to use because it is one students are likely to be reasonably familiar with and able to imagine. They are also not too difficult to draw!

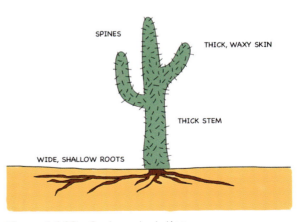

Figure 4.6.28 Cactus adaptation.

Checking for Understanding

- Describe the climate of a hot desert.
- What are *Hadley cells*?
- Why is there relatively little litter within the desert ecosystem?
- How does a loss of vegetation affect the desert?
- How are cacti adapted to life in the desert?

4.6.9 Tundra

Difficulty to draw: ● ● ●
Difficulty to explain: ● ● ●

What Students Should Already Know

- Tropical rainforests are one of the major biomes.
- The climate is characterised by cold temperatures and low rainfall.

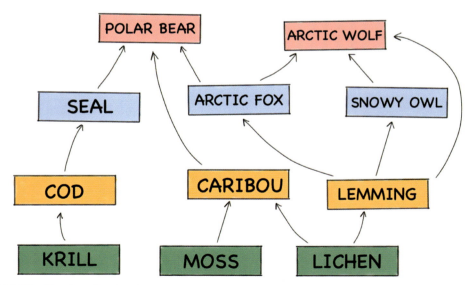

Figure 4.6.29 Tundra – food web.

The Explanation

It is a common misconception amongst students that *tundra* includes the polar ice caps, and they will often envisage the vast white expanses of Antarctica. It is important to tackle this, and using images and videos of tundra regions and species is a good way to start.

The polar bear is likely to come up as one that inhabits these regions, and it is true that polar bears do visit tundra when food sources are scarce. At the other end of the food web, the producers, such as moss and lichen, are able to survive the permafrost by having very shallow roots.

Figure 4.6.30 Tundra plants.

Figure 4.6.30 shows how typical tundra plants grow close to the ground. They are only supported by a shallow root system, which allows it to survive the frozen ground. The dense network of thick leaves also allows pockets of warmer air to collect within the plant, protected from the cold winds.

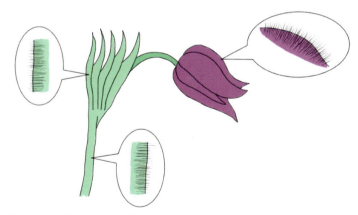

Figure 4.6.31 Pasque flower.

The pasque flower is common to many areas of tundra. Like other tundra plants, it grows relatively low to the ground to avoid the strong, cold winds. It is also covered in very fine, silky hairs. These help insulate the leaves and flowers from the very cold conditions.

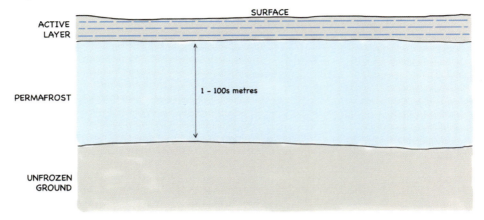

Figure 4.6.32   Permafrost.

One of the characteristics of tundra regions is the permafrost. Figure 4.6.32 is a useful way to explain the two main layers. Students may think that *permafrost* simply implies that all the ground is always frozen throughout the year. Whilst this may be true in polar regions, most tundra will have an active layer, a few metres deep, that does thaw for a couple of months a year. Though when it does thaw, the melted ice has nowhere to go, so the soil is usually waterlogged.

Checking for Understanding

- What are some of the species found in tundra ecosystems?
- How have some of them adapted to life there?
- Why are many plants low to the ground?
- What is *permafrost*?

4.6.10 Comparing Biomes

Difficulty to draw: ●●○
Difficulty to explain: ●●○

What Students Should Already Know

- Rainforests, deserts, and tundra are some of the major biomes.
- Each place is characterised by different climates.
- A nutrient cycle shows how nutrients are balanced between the biomass, litter, and soil of that place.

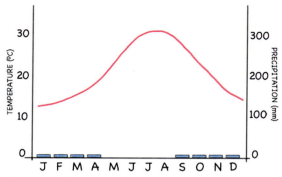
Figure 4.6.33 Desert climate graph.

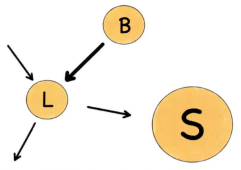
Figure 4.6.36 Desert nutrient circles.

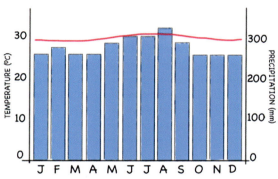
Figure 4.6.34 Rainforest climate graph.

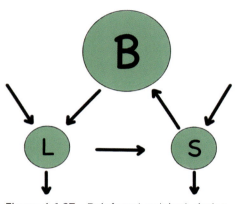
Figure 4.6.37 Rainforest nutrient circles.

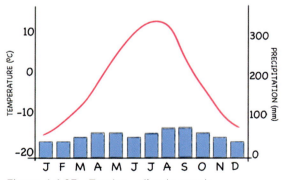
Figure 4.6.35 Tundra – climate graph.

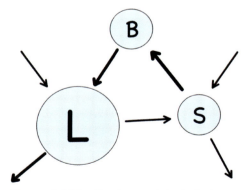
Figure 4.6.38 Tundra – nutrient circles.

1. Hot deserts are characterised by high temperatures and low rainfall.
2. Tropical rainforests have high rainfall and high temperatures throughout the year.
3. Tundra regions have low rainfall throughout the year and temperatures on either side of freezing.

256 *Ecosystems*

The Explanation

By this stage, you should have already looked at the three different biomes. The point of this section is to put the three climate graphs and nutrient cycles side by side to compare and contrast.

In the rainforest, where most nutrients are stored as biomass, the transfer of nutrients is fast. The warm conditions and plentiful supply of moisture allow for processes such as decomposition and weathering to readily occur. In the desert, most nutrients are stored in the soil (few plants exist, which also means there is little leaf litter). The processes are slow, as the lack of moisture makes weathering and other processes like leaching difficult. Interestingly, in many tundra regions, the largest store is the litter, as the decomposition of vegetation is slow due to the low temperatures.

4.7 Glaciation

4.7.1 The Glacier System Difficulty to draw: ●
Difficulty to explain: ● ●

What Students Should Already Know
- Snowfall will occur when temperatures are low enough.
- Snow and ice will melt when temperatures are high enough.
- Evaporation and snowfall are part of the hydrological cycle.

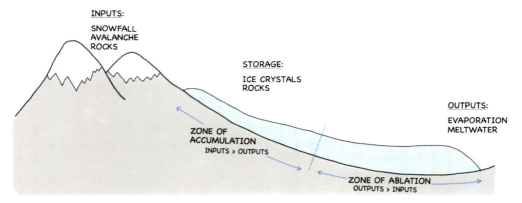

Figure 4.7.1 Glacier system.

1. Snow that doesn't melt in summer can start to form ice. A glacier usually takes 20-30 years to form.
2. A glacier will contain ice and rocks that it has picked up.
3. If there is more snow added at the top than melting at the bottom, a glacier will grow or advance.
4. If there is more ice melting than snow falling, then the glacier will retreat.

The Explanation

First, draw the mountains. Ensure the slope goes a considerable way down so that you can discuss how temperatures will change with height. The snow caps on top of the mountains help highlight the principal source of glacial ice. When drawing on the glacier, there is not a need to be too precise with shape, although they will often thicken towards the base of a slope.

Once drawn on, you can explain how the main input (snowfall) relates to the main output (meltwater). Keep this part simple: if snow > melting, then the glacier grows and advances. If melting > snow, then the glacier shrinks and retreats.

The main takeaway from this diagram for the students should be that glaciers are not simply massive stationary blocks of ice; they are affected by the local climate and are regularly moving, either shrinking or contracting, and it is this movement that can shape the landscape.

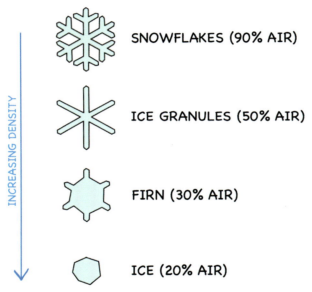

Figure 4.7.2 Glacial ice formation.

Drawing a perfectly symmetrical snowflake by hand is impractical. So when you draw this process, just concentrate on showing how the snowflakes steadily become more condensed and move from delicate to solid.

This is down to the repeated layering of more snowfall and the pressure these layers add to the snow. Air is squeezed out over time. The remaining trapped air is how climate scientists can study atmospheric conditions in previous years, particularly in Antarctica. So this process is relevant to our understanding of how we monitor the changing climate.

Types of Glaciers

There are four main types of glaciers:

Ice sheet: huge, continent-sized glaciers (e.g. Antarctica)
Valley glaciers: typical "river of ice" found within a valley
Corrie glaciers: smaller masses of ice that form in mountainous basins
Piedmont glaciers: when valley glaciers extend down from mountains and join together
In schools, we tend to focus on valley glaciers and corrie glaciers.

Case Studies

45.9901, 7.2997 Corbassiere Glacier, Switzerland (valley glacier)
48.8253, -121.6231 Lower Curtis Glacier, USA (corrie glacier)

Checking for Understanding

- What is the main input into a glacier?
- What is the main output from a glacier?
- How does glacier ice form from snow?

4.7.2 Glacial Erosion

Difficulty to draw: ●●
Difficulty to explain: ●●

What Students Should Already Know

- Glaciers are made of ice.
- They are always moving.
- Evaporation and snowfall are part of the hydrological cycle.

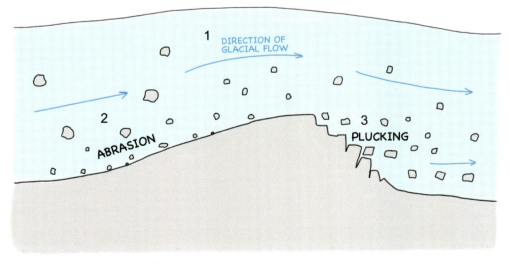

Figure 4.7.3 Abrasion and plucking.

260 *Glaciation*

1. As a glacier slowly flows over the ground, it erodes the land in two main ways.
2. Rocks and other debris carried within the ice scrape along the ground like sandpaper.
3. Ice freezes around protruding rock on the ground and pulls the rock away as the ice moves away.

The Explanation

Draw the ground first, and make sure that the bump that the ice flows over is asymmetrical. This is because plucking tends to occur on steeper slopes. It also happens more on already-weathered rock faces. Therefore, it is a good idea to make this steeper slope noticeably angular to highlight where weathering, especially freeze thaw, might have occurred. The pieces of rock that have been recently plucked are also drawn as squares to show how they fitted into the rock face.

Abrasion relies on debris within the glacier, so make sure that you include plenty of pieces of rock dotted about in the glacier. Gravity causes most of the debris to slowly make their way to the bottom of the glacier, so try to include more nearer to the ground.

You can also discuss attrition within the glacier, whereby rocks are ground down into a fine powder called rock flour. If you were to look at glacial meltwater, it has an almost-milky colour due to the presence of this powder.

Figure 4.7.4 Freeze thaw.

Reminding students about freeze thaw might be a good idea. It tends to occur at the back wall of a glacier, or along the base, where melting is more common. It is unlikely that glaciers can simply just "pluck" bits of rock from the ground, so it is likely that weathering makes the process possible.

Sandpaper Analogy

Ask students to consider the difference to their desks if you rubbed plain paper over it compared to rubbing sandpaper over the desk. This is a good way to think about glacial abrasion. You can extend the analogy further by thinking about what properties effective sandpaper has. A glacier that contains more eroded rocks and other debris will abrade the surface it flows over more effectively.

As a glacier flows over uneven ground, it can become stretched, particularly as it flows over a ridge. This leads to crevasses forming, which are deep cracks.

As the glacier reaches a shallower gradient, it can buckle up, forming ridges. These two features, and this diagram, may be a useful addition to students' knowledge of glacial features.

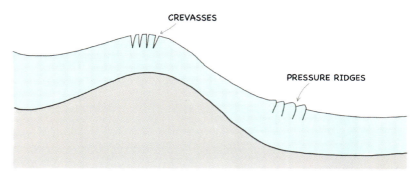

Figure 4.7.5 Crevasses and ridges.

Case Study

61.1426, -149.2713 Chugach State Park, Alaska, USA (crevasses)

Checking for Understanding
- What are the two main types of glacial erosion?
- What role does debris within a glacier play?
- How can freeze thaw help with plucking?
- What is a *crevasse*?

262 *Glaciation*

4.7.3 Glacial Transport

Difficulty to draw: ●○○
Difficulty to explain: ●●○

What Students Should Already Know
- Glaciers flow downhill by gravity.
- They carry along pieces of eroded rock.

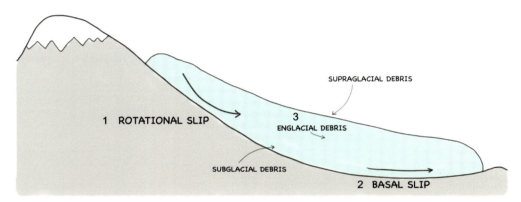

Figure 4.7.6 Glacial transport.

1. Where the slope is concave, ice compresses, which causes it to scour away the base.
2. The bottom of a glacier is often lubricated by meltwater. This, plus gravity, allows the glacier to "slide" along.
3. Debris can either be transported on the surface (supra-), within (en-), or beneath (sub-).

The Explanation

Draw the standard slope from mountain down to valley floor. The rotational slip part is best explained if you actually draw a concave slope. You can then show where the scouring occurs most, and therefore what creates the classic corrie or cirque shape.

Basal slip can be explained by meltwater being found at the base of the glacier. Those glaciers that experience summer temperature rise, and therefore more melting, will see more basal slip. Those glaciers that are suitably cold all year round will have less.

Most glaciers see more movement away from the valley sides and closer to the surface. Depending on local conditions, some glaciers may flow at tens of centimetres annually, whilst some may move tens of centimetres daily!

The debris a glacier carries can scrape along the ground. The huge forces involved leave scratch marks or striations on the ground. They are a helpful indicator of a glacier's direction and the force it was exerting as it moved over the rock face.

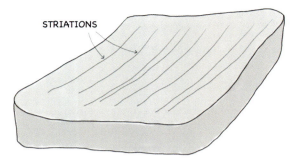

Figure 4.7.7 Striations.

4.7.4 Moraine

Difficulty to draw: ● ●
Difficulty to explain: ● ●

What Students Should Already Know
- Glaciers flow downhill by gravity.
- They carry along pieces of eroded rock.

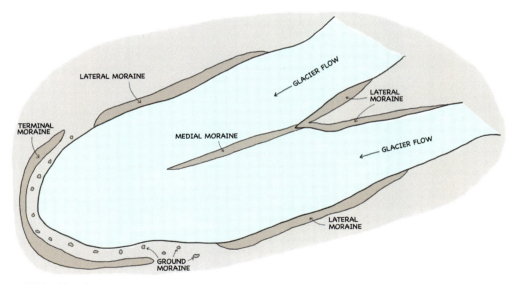

Figure 4.7.8 Moraine.

Lateral moraine forms when a glacier leaves debris on the side of the valley.
Terminal moraine marks the end of the glacier, where debris has been pushed ahead by the ice.

Ground moraine is made up of debris that collects underneath the glacier. Only visible after a glacier retreats.

Medial moraine forms when two glaciers meet and push their debris together.

The Explanation

This is a plan view of a glacier, although it works best to draw two glaciers meeting, so that you can include the medial moraine at their meeting. Draw the outline of the glacier first, and then the moraines can be added on top or alongside in another colour.

The debris that makes up the moraine, known properly as till, can range in size from fine rock flour up to large boulders. The terminal and lateral moraines are probably easiest to explain and for students to picture, but the ground moraine may be harder to understand. Figure 4.7.9 shows how terminal moraine forms but could also be adapted to show that till builds up throughout the glacier and will be deposited when melting occurs at the base.

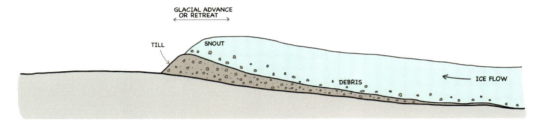

Figure 4.7.9   Terminal moraine.

The profile view of this diagram helps show the build-up of till (debris) that form the terminal moraine. A useful analogy is that of a bulldozer pushing along rubble. There is often deposition of debris at the snout of the glacier because more melting occurs here, usually due to the lower latitude of the lower end of the glacier.

> ### Tips and Tricks
>
> Why is a glacier blue? Because the red part of white light is absorbed by ice, whereas the blue light is scattered through the ice.

Case Studies

34.2711, 79.5449, Western Tibet (terminal moraine)
61.5486, -142.9045, Alaska, USA (lateral moraine)
60.7294, -138.8223, Alaska, USA (medial moraine)

Checking for Understanding
- What are the four types of moraines?
- What is till?
- Why are terminal moraines often found away from the snout of the glacier?

4.7.5 Corrie
Difficulty to draw: ●●
Difficulty to explain: ●●

What Students Should Already Know
- Glaciers flow downhill by gravity.
- They carry along pieces of eroded rock.

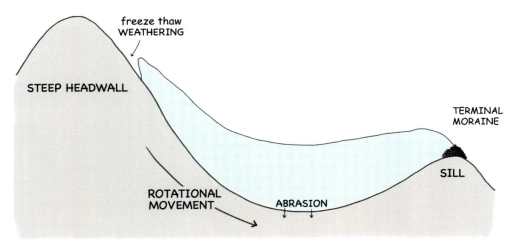

Figure 4.7.10 Corrie.

1. Headwall is weathered (freeze thaw), so rock debris falls onto the ice, to be used later for abrasion.
2. Ice moves downslope in a rotational movement. The downwards force abrades and deepens the corrie.
3. The rotational motion pushes ice upward, where a sill forms of loose rocks. This is also usually the location of the terminal moraine.

The Explanation

Start with a simple mountaintop and concave slope. Draw on the outline of the ice. Note the detached top. This is where freeze thaw occurs at the headwall, where the constantly moving glacier keeps detaching itself from the solid rock, forming a crevasse, known as a bergschrund, shown in Figure 4.7.11.

Add on the rotational movement, the downwards pressure that leads to abrasion along the base, before showing the upwards movement towards the raised sill. The pile of rocks at the end represents the terminal moraine.

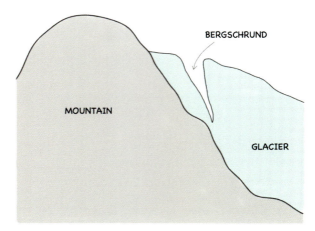

Figure 4.7.11 Bergschrund.

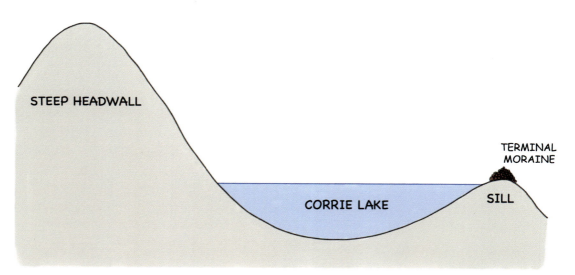

Figure 4.7.12 Corrie lake.

The corrie lake is shown using the same mountain outline, and hopefully the one is deep enough to show where the lake sits. To make the two diagrams even better, you could make the second one slightly deeper to represent more deepening from the glacier before it melted.

Glaciation 267

Etymology

Corries are also known as *cirques* or *cwms*. Corrie lakes are also called *tarns*.

- Corrie: Scottish Gaelic, meaning "pot or cauldron"
- Cirque: Latin, meaning "circus" (which were performed in bowl-shaped amphitheatres)
- Cwm: Welsh, meaning "valley"
- Tarn: Old Norse, meaning "a lake without tributaries"

Case Studies

47.7186, -123.3470, Mt Anderson, Washington, USA (corrie glacier)
42.9308, -0.4999, Lac d'Isabe, Pyrenees Mountains, France (corrie lake)

Checking for Understanding

- What is a *corrie*?
- Why does abrasion happen at the base?
- Where is the headward wall?
- Where is the sill?
- What is a *corrie lake*?

4.7.6 Arêtes and Pyramidal Peaks

Difficulty to draw: ● ● ●
Difficulty to explain: ● ● ●

What Students Should Already Know

- Corries are bowl-shaped depressions found on mountainsides that are carved out by glaciers.
- Abrasion is one of the ways that glaciers erode the land.

268 *Glaciation*

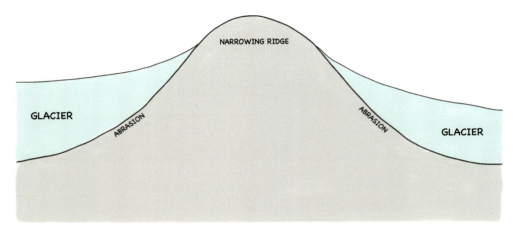

Figure 4.7.13   Arête 1.

1. Two back-to-back corries on either side of a mountain steadily erode away (abrasion) at the mountain from both sides.

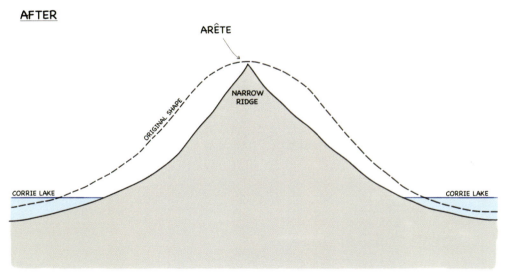

Figure 4.7.14   Arête 2.

2. Over time, the ridge between the two corries narrows until a narrow ridge is left between them.

The Explanation

The main arête diagrams showing before and after rely on students appreciating where on a mountain the two corries are sitting. Therefore, it might be worth starting with the sketch of a mountain, below, to remind students what a corrie looks like and how it is formed. Drawing anything 3D is not that simple, so it is worth practising the mountain to ensure you are confident of not needing to redraw mid-explanation!

Once you have drawn the three main lines of the mountain on, you can add the thinner lines/strokes to show the direction of the slope. The corrie lakes are difficult to put into perspective to keep them more oblong than circular. Don't add more on for now; rather, just use this incomplete diagram to provide the location and context for the arête.

Putting the mountain sketch to one side, draw the before and after main diagrams of the arête formation. This is a simple diagram. Focus on the narrowing ridge, and try to keep the size of the two diagrams similar.

Then you can go back to the mountain sketch and add on the arête label, as well as explaining the pyramidal peak.

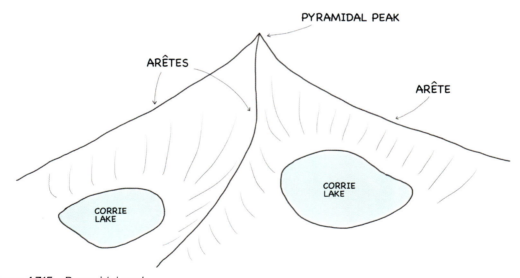

Figure 4.7.15 Pyramidal peak.

Case Studies

45.9764, 7.6582, The Matterhorn, Alps, Switzerland/Italy (pyramidal peak)
54.5254, -3.0060, Striding Edge, Helvellyn, UK (arête)

Checking for Understanding
- How does an arête form?
- What is a *pyramidal peak*?
- Why are they often found in the same location?

4.7.7 Glacial Troughs

Difficulty to draw: ●○○
Difficulty to explain: ●○○

What Students Should Already Know
- Glaciers form when the climate is cold enough and snowfall doesn't melt.
- They will often follow river valleys, which are usually V-shaped.
- Glaciers can erode and carve through the landscape.

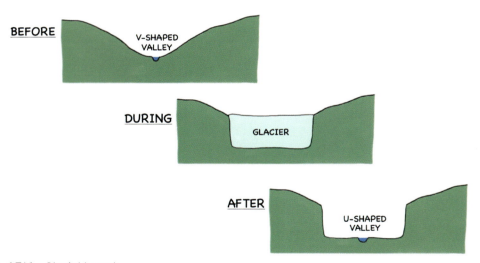

Figure 4.7.16 Glacial trough.

1. Before glaciation occurs, a river flows and creates a V-shaped valley.
2. The glacier will fill the valley and, over time, erode the base and sides.
3. Once the glacier has retreated, the river flows again, but this time through a U-shaped valley.

Glaciation 271

The Explanation

Three simple cross-section diagrams of a valley. The first could be supplemented with a simple sketch of how a river creates a V-shaped valley. It is also a potentially interesting discussion point to consider the different erosive speed and scale of rivers versus glaciers.

The explanation could also be done initially through one sketch where you draw the V-shaped valley, then rub it out to show how the glacier widens it. Finally, rub out the glacier, but leave the new U-shaped valley outline. This type of sketch-as-you-explain is a useful way to show your thinking. When you then draw the three stages, students should already have a good idea of what you are about to draw.

Case Study

48.6551, -113.8384, Glacier National Park, Montana, USA (U-shaped valley)

Checking for Understanding

- How does a glacial trough form?
- Why is it U-shaped?
- Why does a glacier create a different-shaped valley compared to a river?

4.7.8 Ribbon Lakes

Difficulty to draw: ● ● ●
Difficulty to explain: ● ●

What Students Should Already Know

- Glaciers create U-shaped valleys as they flow through river valleys.
- Abrasion is one of the ways that glaciers erode the land.
- Softer (less-resistant) rock erodes more quickly than harder (more-resistant) rock.

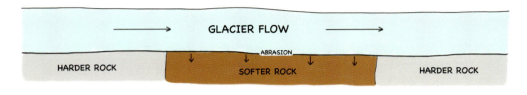

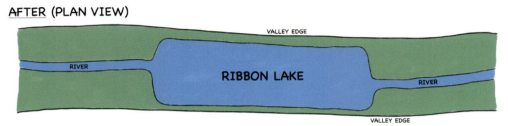

Figure 4.7.17 Ribbon lake.

1. As a glacier flows over the land, it will move over different bands of more- and less-resistant rock types.
2. Abrasion that occurs at the base of the glacier will act more quickly on the less-resistant rock, which carves out a deeper trough.
3. After the glacier retreats, then a river will return and fill the deeper trough. If there is no river, then rainwater could fill the trough.

The Explanation

First, draw the glacier flowing over the land. Draw on different bands of rock. The preferred terms should be *more-* and *less-resistant* rock, but *harder* and *softer* are also suitable. You can also use this diagram to remind students about how abrasion operates at the base of the glacier.

The second diagram is plan view so that you can show the relative size of the lake compared to the river. There are other ways that ribbon lakes can form, for example, if a terminal moraine blocks the whole valley, then a lake may form behind. It is worth noting that all these features are likely to change over time as rivers erode and weathering occurs.

Glaciation   273

Alternative Formation

Not all ribbon lakes are formed by glaciers eroding less-resistant rocks. Some are formed if a glacier's terminal moraine stretches across the whole valley. This acts as a natural dam to river water or rainwater. Some ribbon lakes will be a combination of the two, including Lake Washington, the case study listed below.

Case Study

47.6177, -122.2586, Lake Washington, Washington, USA (ribbon lake)

Checking for Understanding

- How does abrasion affect different types of rock?
- Why does the deeper trough fill up when the glacier has retreated?

4.7.9 Truncated Spurs

Difficulty to draw: ● ●
Difficulty to explain: ● ●

What Students Should Already Know

- Glaciers create U-shaped valleys as they flow through river valleys.
- River valleys often feature spurs, around which the river flows.
- Glaciers exert a greater erosive force than rivers.

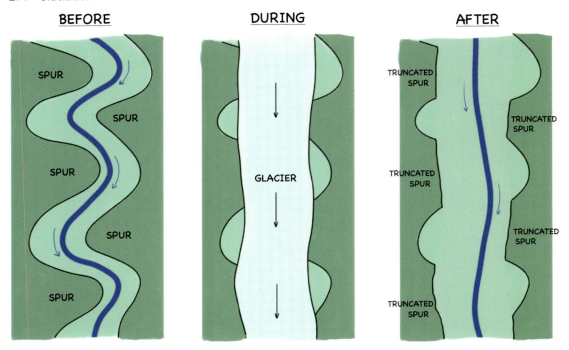

Figure 4.7.18   Truncated spur.

1. Before glaciation happens, a river flows around spurs of harder rock.
2. Glaciers will flow relatively straight and chop off the heads of the spurs.
3. After the glacier retreats, the river flows through a wider valley, with now-truncated spurs.

The Explanation

Students may need reminding about interlocking spurs and how they form when a river flows around different bands of more-resistant rock. This is worth highlighting because it demonstrates the greater erosive force of the glacier, which is able to break through the spurs.

The three diagrams are relatively simple to draw. Make sure you try to keep the spurs in the same place for each diagram, and that they are pronounced enough in your drawing to keep their locations visible in the final diagram.

You can also add that the river in the final diagram is known as a misfit, as it is too small to have created such a wide valley. Figure 4.7.19 shows a hanging valley, which forms when a tributary's valley has not been glacially eroded, so is left hanging above the main, U-shaped valley.

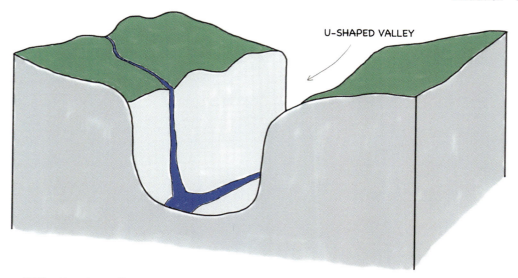

Figure 4.7.19   Hanging valley.

The explanation for the hanging valley is found on page 129. It is a difficult diagram to draw, but definitely a useful one to discuss, and is also a neat way to link different topics together.

Case Studies
54.6293, -3.0437, Blencathra, Lake District, UK (truncated spurs)
53.1298, -4.0329, Nant Ffrancon Valley, Snowdonia, UK (truncated spurs)

Checking for Understanding
- Why do rivers create interlocking spurs?
- What happens when a glacier reaches those spurs?
- What is a *truncated spur*?
- What is a *misfit river*?
- What is a *hanging valley*?

4.7.10 Roches Moutonnées

Difficulty to draw: ● ●
Difficulty to explain: ● ●

276 Glaciation

> **What Students Should Already Know**
> - Glaciers erode through abrasion and plucking.
> - They flow over land that may be made up of different rock types.
> - Some rocks are more easily eroded than others.

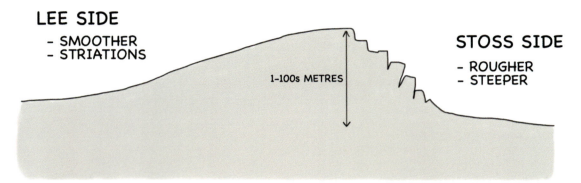

Figure 4.7.20 Roches moutonnées.

1. Glacier moves over a large chunk of resistant rock.
2. Abrasion occurs as the glacier flows over the rock.
3. The downstream side is left rougher and steeper due to plucking.

The Explanation

The diagram is almost identical to the earlier one showing abrasion and plucking. The key message is that the block of rock is more resistant and so stays in place, whilst the surrounding land is more easily eroded. Your explanation can either consist of two diagrams, showing the erosional processes first, followed by the resultant landform. Or it could be a combination of the two.

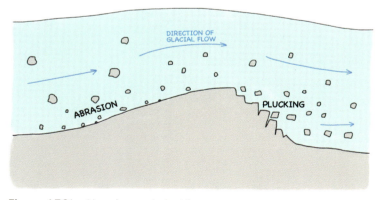

Figure 4.7.21 Abrasion and plucking.

Case Study

52.6938, -3.8959, Cadair Idris, Snowdonia, UK (roche moutonnée)

Checking for Understanding

- What are the two main types of glacial erosion?
- Why are some rocks slower to erode?
- Which is the lee side, and which is the stoss side?

4.7.11 Erratics

Difficulty to draw: ●
Difficulty to explain: ● ●

What Students Should Already Know

- Glaciers can erode and pick up rocks.
- They flow over land that may be made up of different rock types.
- When a glacier melts, it will deposit the rocks it was carrying.

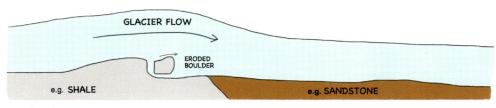

Figure 4.7.22 Erratics.

278 *Glaciation*

1. As a glacier flows, it can erode and carry (entrain) large boulders.
2. The boulders can be carried great distances and then deposited as the glacier melts and retreats.
3. Studying the rock type can show where the rock came from and can help show where a glacier flowed from.

The Explanation

The diagram and explanation are fairly straightforward. It is perhaps worth noting the scales involved. Erratics are usually boulders larger than 1m across. They can be transported hundreds of kilometres and are useful indicators that can show a glacier's movements.

> **Case Study**
>
> 41.8443, -69.9577, Doane Rock, Massachusetts, USA (erratic)

> **Checking for Understanding**
> - How can glaciers pick up large boulders?
> - Why will a glacier deposit rock debris?
> - How can erratics help geologists learn about former glaciers?

4.7.12 Drumlins

Difficulty to draw: ● ● ●
Difficulty to explain: ● ● ●

> **What Students Should Already Know**
> - Glaciers can erode and pick up debris known as till.
> - When a glacier melts, it will deposit the till it was carrying.

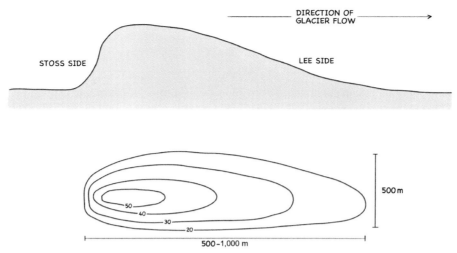

Figure 4.7.23 Drumlins.

The Explanation

There are two theories on the formation of drumlins, which is why the diagram chosen here just shows the landform rather than the processes that formed it. Once you have drawn the drumlin, given the scale and direction of flow, you can pose the question to students: how could this have been formed? You can add hints that one of the main theories is that drumlins are constructed (through deposition), and the other is that they are carved out (through erosion).

A common mistake from students is to confuse them with roche moutonnée, as they are a similar shape. However, drumlins are usually smoother and are often found in clusters, known as fields or swarms. The other point to note is that the more gently sloping, elongated side points in the direction the ice is flowing, which is the opposite to roche moutonnée.

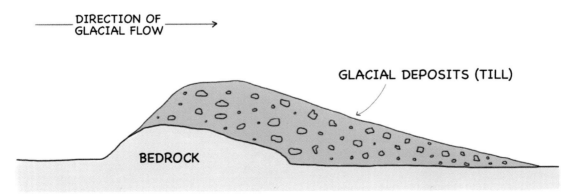

Figure 4.7.24 Drumlin formation.

280 *Glaciation*

This diagram shows one way that drumlins may form. As the ice flowed over the bump in the bedrock, glacial till was deposited on the sheltered side, protected by the bump. As the ice continued to flow, the bump grew larger, allowing more till to be deposited. The flowing ice also served to smooth the glacial till and shape it into the typical drumlin form.

Geologists can also analyse the position of individual pieces of till within the drumlin. This allows them to either confirm whether the drumlin was created in this way, through deposition, or perhaps another method, such as through erosion.

Dungeons and Drumlins

The lower ground between two drumlins is known as a dungeon. They are often cold and dark, because cold air can sink and sit between the drumlins.

Case Study

44.2370, -77.8410, Trent Hills, Ontario, Canada (drumlins)
71.3964, 129.0005, Tiksi, Sakha Republic, Russia (drumlins)

Checking for Understanding

- What shape and size are drumlins?
- Suggest one way that might have formed.
- What is a group of drumlins called?
- How can they help geologists learn about glaciers?

4.7.13 Crag and Tail

Difficulty to draw: ●● ●
Difficulty to explain: ● ● ●

What Students Should Already Know

- Glaciers flow over land that may be made up of different rock types.
- They will erode through abrasion and plucking.
- Erosion will be faster or slower, depending on the rock type.

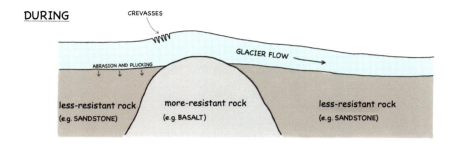

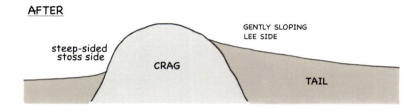

Figure 4.7.25 Crag and tail.

1. A glacier flows over land made of different rocks. Some are more easily eroded than others.
2. The rocky crag is left protruding as the ice erodes the rock either side.
3. The crag acts to shelter the lee side, which remains higher and forms the tail.

The Explanation

If students are confident in knowing that glaciers will erode different rocks at different rates, then this is relatively simple to explain. As with other diagrams, an initial explanatory diagram sketch showing the first of the preceding images can be modified with a rubber to show how the differential erosion will change the landscape. The tail side does not remain unaffected, so make sure you show the level dropping, albeit more gently.

Case Study

55.9479, -3.2004, Edinburgh Castle, UK (crag and tail)

Checking for Understanding

- Why do glaciers erode some types of rock faster than others?
- What is a *crag*?
- Why is the tail more gently sloping than the steeper stoss side?

282 *Glaciation*

4.7.14 Retreating Glacier

Difficulty to draw: ● ● ●
Difficulty to explain: ● ●

> **What Students Should Already Know**
> - Glaciers will melt if the climate warms.
> - Melting ice turns into meltwater streams.
> - Glaciers create moraines and other landforms.

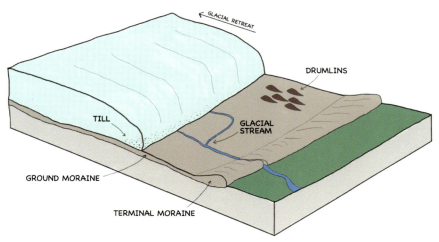

Figure 4.7.26   Retreating glacier.

The Explanation

This diagram is a useful way to "zoom out" and think about where some of the different landforms are found and how they will have been created. The diagram is definitely a difficult one to draw, as it requires various 3D components, and not many of them are simple straight lines!

To draw it, start with the flat block at the base to represent the bedrock. Explain that this is what the glacier flows over, and the bedrock's nature will help determine the landforms found once the glacier retreats. Then draw the glacier itself. The thinner lines just help show the sloping snout.

The terminal moraine should be raised, and this is probably the trickiest part to get right, especially as you will want to draw the glacial stream cutting through it. If students are going to draw this too, this is definitely one where you explain and draw it first to show how each part fits in. The drumlin swarm is one option, but you could also ask students to look back at their notes and add other landforms you have studied.

Glaciation 283

4.7.15 Isostatic Sea Level Change

Difficulty to draw: ●●
Difficulty to explain: ●●●

> **What Students Should Already Know**
> - Glaciers are very large masses of ice.
> - They sit on the land which is also part of the Earth's crust.

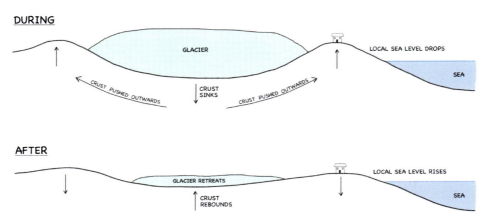

Figure 4.7.27 Isostatic change.

1. The weight of a glacier causes the crust to sink, as well as being pushed to the side.
2. This pushes up the surrounding land into a forebulge. If by the sea, the rising land also means that sea levels will drop.
3. When the glacier retreats, crust rebounds, the forebulge drops, and sea levels will rise.

The Explanation

This one is unusual in that the diagram is quite simple but the explanation can be difficult. It can be difficult because we are assuming that students are confident in knowing that the crust, which is usually taught as brittle and rocky, is elastic and can be squashed. Ideally, you should use the term *lithosphere*, but only if that is a term you and the students are comfortable with. Once you have established that the crust can be squashed and will also rebound, then the explanation becomes easier. Using marshmallows to show the "bouncing back" might be useful.

Another potential pitfall is the idea of how sea level change can be caused by the land moving, rather than the sea. Students will probably be fine with rising sea levels due to melting

284   *Glaciation*

ice, but it is worth spending time "zoomed in" on how sea levels can be affected by both the height of the sea and the land.

Also, make sure you highlight that the change in sea level is local rather than global. This distinction helps with the difference between isostatic and eustatic sea level change.

Marshmallow Analogy

Isostatic rebound happens when a glacier has retreated and the once-squashed crust is able to bounce back up again. Squashing a marshmallow, and then letting it fill out back to its original shape, can help show this idea.

Case Study

68.0984, -108.2917, Bathurst Inlet Beach, Canada (layered beach showing progressive changes to the beach as the rebounding underlying crust has pushed the land up higher compared to the sea)

Checking for Understanding
- How do glaciers cause the crust of the Earth to move up or down?
- What is *isostatic rebound*?

4.7.16 Eustatic Sea Level Change

Difficulty to draw: ● ● ○
Difficulty to explain: ● ● ○

What Students Should Already Know
- Water travels through the hydrological cycle.
- This includes evaporation, condensation, and precipitation.
- Glaciers are formed when snow doesn't melt.

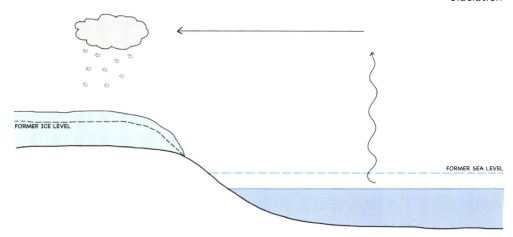

Figure 4.7.28 Eustatic change.

1. As part of the water cycle, seawater evaporates into the atmosphere.
2. If climatic conditions are cold enough, it will fall as snow rather than rain.
3. If it remains cold enough at ground level, the snow will stay and become glacial ice. The glacier steadily grows.
4. If more seawater is held as glacial ice, often for thousands of years, sea levels will drop.

The Explanation

Students will need to have an understanding of the hydrological cycle for you to explain eustatic sea level changes. Start by drawing the line of the land and the current sea level. Discuss how evaporation occurs, and draw on the cloud with the falling snow. The larger snowflakes help distinguish it from rainfall.

Then draw the glacier. The hydrological cycle just discussed relies on some of the snow melting and the water running back into the sea. Ask what happens if the weather remains so cold that there is no snowmelt.

Draw another line to show the glacier getting larger as the snow remains. Ask students what is going to happen to the sea levels if more and more of the water is becoming glacial ice. Then you can add on additional lines (dotted perhaps) to show how sea levels have dropped.

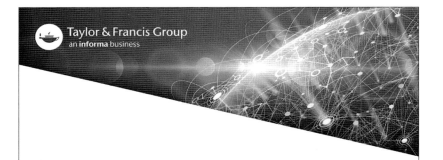